Secret Histories

Secret Histories

A New Era in Constance Fenimore Woolson Scholarship

EDITED BY
Kathleen Diffley,
Caroline Gebhard,
and Cheryl B. Torsney
Foreword by Anne Boyd Rioux

The University of Georgia Press
ATHENS

Most University of Georgia Press titles are
available from popular e-book vendors.

Printed digitally

Library of Congress Cataloging-in-Publication Data
Names: Diffley, Kathleen Elizabeth, 1950– editor. | Gebhard, Caroline, editor. |
Torsney, Cheryl B., editor. | Rioux, Anne Boyd, writer of foreword.
Title: Secret histories : a new era in Constance Fenimore Woolson scholarship / edited by
Kathleen Diffley, Caroline Gebhard, and Cheryl B. Torsney ; foreword by Anne Boyd Rioux.
Description: Athens : The University of Georgia Press, 2025. |
Includes bibliographical references and index.
Identifiers: LCCN 2024037631 | ISBN 9780820369839 (hardback) |
ISBN 9780820369846 (paperback) | ISBN 9780820369853 (epub) |
ISBN 9780820369860 (pdf)
Subjects: LCSH: Woolson, Constance Fenimore, 1840–1894—Criticism
and interpretation. | LCGFT: Literary criticism. | Essays.
Classification: LCC PS3363 .S43 2025 | DDC 813/.4—dc23/eng/20241024
LC record available at https://lccn.loc.gov/2024037631

CONTENTS

III. THROUGH AN INTERNATIONAL LENS

ILLUSTRATIONS

———————

A New Era for the Appreciation of Constance Fenimore Woolson as a "True Artist"

Anne Boyd Rioux

Today, what most readers know of Constance Fenimore Woolson—that is, *if* they know her—are the apocryphal stories of her having committed suicide out of unrequited love for her friend Henry James or his trying to drown her ballooning dresses in a Venetian lagoon after her death. Or they may think of her in light of the Master's reincarnation of her as a self-sacrificial heroine in his later fiction. But there is so much more to know and love about this exceptional woman and writer who, in her own day, was as highly regarded in many circles as James himself, if not more so.

At the height of her career, in the 1870s and 1880s, Woolson accomplished what many writers (including James) dreamed of, writing best-selling books while also impressing the critics, who often compared her work to that of James and George Eliot. Upon her death, she was hailed by *Harper's Monthly* editor Henry Mills Alden as "a true artist" whose writings possessed a "rare excellence, originality, and strength [that] were appreciated by the most fastidious critics."[1] Influential poet and critic Edmund Clarence Stedman called her "one of the leading women in the American literature of the century."[2] And for the *Atlantic Monthly*, Helen Gray Cone wrote of her that "[f]ew American writers of fiction have given evidence of such breadth, so full a sense of the possibilities of the varied and complex life of our wide land."[3]

Yet despite the nearly universal adulation she received, Woolson was soon forgotten, her reputation a victim of changing literary tastes and the exclusion of women writers from the literary canon taking shape at the turn of the twentieth century.[4] It didn't help that she had lost the support of the so-called dean of American letters, William Dean Howells, who criticized her portrayal of love outside of marriage in *East Angels* and domestic abuse in *Jupiter Lights*.

(Although he thought the latter unrealistic, we now know how realistic it was.) Some critics, such as Fred Lewis Pattee and Van Wyck Brooks, commended her writing in the decades to come, and two monographs appeared by scholars John Dwight Kern and Rayburn Moore, who judged Woolson to be an accomplished, albeit minor, author. However, she was largely forgotten until Leon Edel included her in his epic, five-volume biography of Henry James (1953–72). Regrettably, Edel had revived her memory only to ridicule her as a second-rate writer who had tried to ride the Master's coattails. In his eyes, she was nothing more than a "journey-woman of letters," whose writing was "magazineish," "minute," and "cluttered." "Posterity," he concluded, "would assign her a footnote in the regional fiction of America."[5]

Even more troubling, most subsequent feminist critics did not view Woolson as a worthy candidate for recovery because she did not participate in late nineteenth-century female literary communities or write consistently from a female point of view. In fact, her stories are much more complicated in their gender dynamics, often employing male narrators to undercut male perspectives of women. Another disadvantage for Woolson's reputation has been the fact that, despite her pioneering contribution to the field of American literary regionalism, she did not become identified with one region, as George Washington Cable did with Louisiana or Mary Austin did with the West. Woolson first wrote of the Great Lakes, which she knew from growing up in Cleveland, then the Reconstruction-era South, which she knew from her travels there with her invalid mother after 1873. Europe, particularly Italy and Switzerland, became the setting of her expatriate fiction after she moved across the Atlantic in late 1879.

Throughout, Woolson was always much more of a realist writer than a regionalist one, insisting that she wrote only from life. In fact, she made considerable contributions to the realist literary movement that remain largely unrecognized. For her, writing from life rather than the imagination entailed delving into her characters' hidden emotional lives, at a time when one's social façade had to be strictly maintained, particularly for women. While other realist writers remained obsessed with the surfaces of life or ventured into the mind where our perceptions of social reality are created, Woolson also brought her characters' sometimes volatile emotions to the surface, without ever writing sentimentally. She wanted her readers not only to see the world they knew reflected but also to feel the depth of her characters' lived experience. Her writing continues to succeed on that score, even in our more cynical age.

Yet throughout the twentieth century literary realism was generally a man's game, while regionalism was considered the proper province of female writers. Participating as it did in both literary movements, Woolson's work did not fit

the prevailing paradigm and was thus generally left out of the dominant narratives of nineteenth-century American literary history.

Perhaps most damaging to her reputation, though, has been how her friendship with James has continued to overshadow her own significance as a writer.
Her life ending in a probable suicide also eclipsed her earlier accomplishments,
pigeonholing her as a tragic victim of neglect at the hands of the male literary
world (and her friend James). This perception of Woolson as a victim also mi-
grated into the wider public consciousness through influential nonfiction works
about James as well as a spate of novels, most notably Colm Tóibín's Booker-
short-listed novel *The Master* (2004). In the midst of juicy literary gossip about
drowning dresses and burned letters, Woolson has remained for many simply a
footnote to the Master's life and work.

Nonetheless, Woolson's writing has endured, and her reputation today is
stronger than it has been since her death in 1894. The credit for this revival is
due to the Constance Fenimore Woolson Society, founded by a group of in-
trepid scholars in 1995 and still going strong, in spite of the many pressures felt
by scholars in today's volatile academic climate. The society's members have
produced multiple essay collections at key points in the revival of Woolson's
legacy, and the present one comes at a particularly exciting time. In the wake
of the publication of *The Complete Letters of Constance Fenimore Woolson*, edited
by Sharon Dean in 2012, and my biography, *Constance Fenimore Woolson: Portrait of a Lady Novelist*, as well as a new collection of Woolson's short fiction,
Miss Grief and Other Stories, in 2016, Woolson studies entered a new era of public recognition of her writing (something that can be said of only a few other recovered women writers, principally Zora Neale Hurston and Kate Chopin).

My goal in writing Woolson's biography was to bridge the gap between the
popular perception of Woolson—as James's confidant, muse, and even victim—and scholars' understanding of her as a complex, ambitious, and accomplished writer in her own right. Trying to piece together the various remnants
of a life Woolson hid from public view as much as possible was a sometimes
frustrating journey. She wanted her work, not herself, to be known. Yet even
though she made those closest to her (her sister, Clara Benedict, and Henry
James) destroy her letters to them, it was possible to find Woolson both in her
letters and in her published work. As she told her friend Francis Boott, "In my
fiction I never say anything which is not absolutely true (it is only in real life
that I resort to fiction)."[6] Indeed, it was in her fiction that she told the truth of
women's lives—and her own life.

In the wake of the publication of Woolson's biography and the collection of
her stories with the trade press W. W. Norton, a more comprehensive collec-

tion of her short fiction was published by the Library of America in 2020, inducting Woolson permanently into the American literary canon. These works have reintroduced general readers to her work through reviews in mainstream publications, including the *New Yorker*, the *New York Review of Books*, and the *Boston Globe*, even on the cover of the *New York Times Book Review*. Critics have been, without exception, very taken with Woolson's work. Vivian Gornick wrote a particularly beautiful tribute in the *Nation*: "The voice in these stories is as clear and fresh as the sound of a bell riding the early morning air in a place of natural wonder."[7] Amy Gentry in the *Chicago Tribune* declared, "Her short stories demonstrate irony, force and feeling that occasionally surpass the stories of Edith Wharton and Howells, rivaling 'the Master' himself even as they take aim directly at his privilege and presumptions."[8] And in the *Wall Street Journal* Cynthia Ozick wrote, "To read Woolson without prejudice, is to experience a mind untrammeled by pieties or programmatic restraints. She is at liberty to go wherever she likes," in spite of Edel's pejorative attempts to contain her as a minor regionalist. For Ozick, stories like "'Miss Grief'" and "The Street of the Hyacinth" should be read not as "stories of female grievance" in the context of the "Master" narrative that has long pigeonholed her, but, "in the realm of sublime craft," as "pre-eminent meditations on the elusive nature of art itself."[9]

With such appreciation and the assurance that the Library of America collection of Woolson's stories will never go out of print, I think we can say that Woolson has at last achieved a kind of literary persistence that should prompt not only a redrawing of the nineteenth-century American literary map but also a greater recognition of Woolson's particular value as a literary ancestor for today's writers.

This renewed appreciation comes at a time when the wider reading public is hungry for work by lesser-known writers, especially women. The *Paris Review* ran a series called "Feminize Your Canon," which featured Fanny Fern and Alice Dunbar-Nelson, among many other neglected women writers. And Parul Sehgal wrote in the *New York Times* about "the flurry of literary revivals, mostly of women writers." She wrote, "Everywhere, we see the full-throated ambition of these [women] writers, their industry. There is a wealth of options—of writers, lives and tactics. It suddenly feels paltry to describe this moment as a mere wave of literary revivals. It feels like the revelation of hidden ancestral lines."[10]

This reimagining of our literary ancestral tree with Woolson now firmly taking her place on the bough of late nineteenth-century American literature has important implications that, one hopes, will be felt within and beyond literature classrooms at all levels. To see Woolson migrate even further into creative writing and high school curricula would mean that her legacy would continue to grow. It is my own particular wish that young women will begin to recognize Woolson and other recovered American women writers as the foremothers of which they have long been deprived in our education system. More than that, if we take Ozick's lead, we can and should appreciate Woolson as the "true artist" she was once considered. Her work continues to bear close reading and continued rereading for its beauty, complexity, modernity, and ineffable transmutation of life into art.

NOTES

1. Henry Mills Alden, "Constance Fenimore Woolson," *Harper's Weekly*, February 3, 1894, 113.

2. Stedman, quoted in "Constance Fenimore Woolson," *New York Tribune*, January 28, 1894, 14.

3. Helen Gray Cone, "Woman in American Literature," *Century Illustrated*, October 1890, 927.

4. I discuss the critical response to Woolson's work and the decline of her reputation after her death in Anne Boyd Rioux, *Constance Fenimore Woolson: Portrait of a Lady Novelist* (New York: Norton, 2016).

5. Leon Edel, *Henry James: The Middle Years, 1882–1895* (Philadelphia: Lippincott, 1962), 203, 207. Yet in his letters to Clare Benedict in the Leon Edel Papers at McGill University, Edel praised Woolson's work highly and said he planned a subsequent biography of her.

6. Constance Fenimore Woolson to Francis Boott, February 7, [1890], Duveneck Family.

7. Vivian Gornick, "Ms. Grief," *Nation*, March 21, 2016, https://www.thenation.com /article/archive/ms-grief/.

8. Amy Gentry, "'Constance Fenimore Woolson' Gives 19th Century Novelist Second Look," *Chicago Tribune*, February 25, 2016, https://www.chicagotribune.com /entertainment/books/ct-prj-constance-fenimore-woolson-anne-boyd-rioux-20160225 -story.html.

9. Cynthia Ozick, "'Constance Fenimore Woolson: Collected Stories' Review: The Return of Miss Woolson," *Wall Street Journal*, July 17, 2020, https://www.wsj.com /articles/constance-fenimore-woolson-collected-stories-review-the-return-of-miss -woolson-11594997085.

10. Parul Sehgal, "What Is a Book Critic's Responsibility When a Work Is Rediscovered?," *New York Times*, January 25, 2019, https://www.nytimes.com/2019/01/25 /reader-center/sylvia-plath-story-discovered.html.

ACKNOWLEDGMENTS

The Constance Fenimore Woolson Society stirred to life in 1994, and in January 1995 we gathered for the first time at Rollins College in Winter Park, Florida. We met in Woolson House, a gift to the college from Woolson's niece, Clare Benedict. Our hope then was to revive interest in the author's fiction, nonfiction, and poetry. This third collection of essays evidences our latest success. Indeed, we assembled again at Woolson House for the twenty-fifth anniversary conference in April 2019, when the society first began to imagine this new volume.

The coeditors are grateful to many scholars, teachers, librarians, archivists, family, and friends, beginning with the Woolson family descendants, who have supported our efforts from the start. The inimitable Kate Reich, who opened the Rollins College archives and Woolson House to us, deserves special thanks; how we regret that she is no longer with us to celebrate this achievement. Similarly, we miss John Wharton Lowe, one of Woolson's devout champions, who passed away too soon. Institutionally, the Western Reserve Historical Society at Case Western Reserve University, which has also encouraged our recovery work, deserves our thanks many times over. We are further beholden to the University of Georgia Press and its two anonymous readers, whose reports sharpened every bit of this book. We appreciate their care.

Professor Lowe's contribution, "How 'The Oklawaha' Prefigures (and Indicts) Disney World," first appeared as the abbreviated "Not-So-Still Waters: Travelers to Florida and the Tropical Sublime" in the *Oxford Handbook of the U.S. South*, edited by Fred Hobson and Barbara Ladd (New York: Oxford University Press, 2016), 180–95. In addition, a version of Susan L. Roberson's

"'The Ancient City' and the Ethics of Sightseeing" will appear in her *Geographies of Travel: Images of America in the Long Nineteenth Century*, forthcoming in 2025 from Texas A&M University Press.

We are pleased to add that the University of Georgia Press has long supported scholarship on Woolson, beginning in 1989 with the publication of Cheryl B. Torsney's *Constance Fenimore Woolson: The Grief of Artistry* and continuing with several volumes that highlight Woolson's work, including Kathleen Diffley's *Where My Heart Is Turning Ever: Civil War Stories and Constitutional Reform 1861–1876* (1992); *Southern Local Color: Stories of Region, Race, and Gender*, edited by Barbara Ewell and Pamela Menke (2002); and *Literary Cultures of the Civil War*, edited by Timothy Sweet (2016). Our own book would never have been published without the dedication of Acquisitions Editor Bethany Snead—astute reader, able shepherd, and steadfast champion of our work.

The first-generation Woolson scholars who are owed our eternal gratitude include Sharon Dean, whose volume of Woolson's letters is the landmark endeavor that made this collection possible, and Victoria Brehm, scholar and webmaster extraordinaire. The most recent generation includes Jane Aman and Ashley Hemm, who have consulted on the cover and social media announcements of this volume. We owe a particular debt to Lisa Nais at the University of Salzburg and Sidonia Serafini at Georgia College & State University. They were doctoral students when this book first took shape, and they served adeptly when submissions were reviewed and revised. We thank all four of our junior colleagues for their intellectual generosity and continuing engagement. This volume is dedicated to our community of scholars, original and newly arrived, with deep gratitude for their inspiration and for their own venturesome successes, both independent and shared.

Secret Histories

What the Woolson Society Hath Wrought

Caroline Gebhard, Kathleen Diffley, and Cheryl B. Torsney

During 1887, Constance Fenimore Woolson (1840–94) was living in Bellosguardo, above Florence. Just before Henry James visited for several weeks that spring, his profile of Woolson appeared in *Harper's Weekly*, one of the most popular illustrated newsmagazines in the world. When James's "partial portrait" was published in February, Woolson's reputation was already well established as one of the country's greatest living writers, though not for predictable reasons. "She is interested in general in secret histories," James observed, "in the 'inner life' of the weak, the superfluous, the disappointed, the bereaved, the unmarried."[1] From those who refused prevailing gender norms to those who shrugged at the drawing rooms that James frequented and instead explored "rice-fields, dismal swamps, and other brackish inlets," her writing captures a startling postwar diversity.[2] By the late 1880s, Woolson was not only a productive writer but also a seasoned traveler who nonetheless settled down from time to time: among other places, in St. Augustine, Oxford, Florence, and Rome. Her novels, stories, poetry, and travel sketches likewise attended to figures from a larger canvas than James generally acknowledged: a young woman at the oars on the Cuyahoga River or an old man scavenging shipwrecks on Lake Michigan, a clutch of northern tourists in mysterious Florida or a wanderer from the Caribbean in the North Carolina mountains, the muezzins and harems of Cairo or the relocated expatriates in the villas of Florence, Rome, and Sorrento. With "a remarkable minuteness of observation and tenderness of feeling," as James put it, Woolson was among the first to pause along the Great Lakes or in the defeated South, one of the first to grasp what remained "so unrecorded, so unpainted and unsung" even across storied Europe and the Mediterranean.[3]

2   GEBHARD, DIFFLEY, AND TORSNEY

Born in New Hampshire on March 4, 1840, but brought up in Cleveland, Ohio, Woolson graduated at the top of her class from Madame Chegaray's Manhattan finishing school in 1858. During her twenties, she ardently supported the Union cause. Following her father's death in 1869, however, she traveled throughout the South for six years with her ailing mother. Her first travel sketches, poems, and stories were already appearing in national magazines beginning in 1870. Published under the pseudonym Anne March, her first book, *The Old Stone House* (1873), was written for children and won a prize; her first collection of fiction, *Castle Nowhere: Lake-Country Sketches* (1875), was published under her own name by Boston's James R. Osgood and Company. After her mother died in 1879, Woolson set sail for Europe. While living abroad she completed *Rodman the Keeper: Southern Sketches* (1880) and that same year began the serial publication of her first novel, *Anne* (1882), in *Harper's Monthly*. Her novella, *For the Major* (1883), and her second novel, *East Angels* (1886), were both serialized in the same literary monthly by the Harpers, who had acquired an exclusive claim on her work. Her third novel, *Jupiter Lights* (1889), and her last, *Horace Chase* (1894), also appeared serially in *Harper's Monthly* prior to publication. After her death on January 24, 1894, her publisher brought out *The Front Yard and Other Italian Stories* (1895), *Dorothy and Other Italian Stories* (1896), and a volume of her travel sketches, *Mentone, Cairo, and Corfu* (1896).[4]

Although Woolson has been variously described as a local colorist, a regionalist, a realist, and even a critic of realism as defined by male commentators, she has never fit easily into conventional categories of literary criticism.[5] Today, she remains unfamiliar to general readers as an important American writer in the way that her friend James, her granduncle James Fenimore Cooper, and her sometime supporter William Dean Howells have long been. While she was greatly admired and celebrated by the reading public in her own time, her literary reputation dimmed after her death for several reasons. First, a decisive fin-de-siècle shift in literary tastes favored a complete break with the genteel Victorian past that was out of step with the dawning American century and its imperial ambitions, often projected in white, masculinist terms.[6] Second, the twentieth-century professionalization of American literature as an academic discipline was dominated by men who generally thought of female authors as lesser writers; not surprisingly, they created a canon that admitted very few of their countrywomen. By midcentury, the rare selections were routinely dismissed as "minor." Typical are condescending judgments even from critics like Alexander Cowie, who devoted pages of *The Rise of the American Novel* to Woolson's work. Cowie styles her a "superior minor writer."[7] Yet Woolson has never been entirely consigned to literary oblivion. In almost every decade since her death, from the new century's shapers of the American canon to the present, critics have paid close attention to her writings.

Fred Lewis Pattee, one of the first professors to write an American literary history, credited her in 1915 with being "a strong force in the new Southern revival," a judgment that he confirmed almost twenty-five years later, arguing that she cannot be "dismissed" as one of "the local color school" because she "was a creative force in a dawning era."[8] During the 1920s, John Hervey found *For the Major* "one of the little masterpieces of American fiction" and called her "one of the finest novelists that America thus far has produced"; he nevertheless thought her work was destined to be read "by few people."[9] In the 1930s, Edward J. O'Brien judged her "difficult to classify" but labeled her a regionalist who "somehow commands our respect."[10] O'Brien's criticism ironically evokes Woolson's story "Miss Grief," about a man who admires the genius of a woman writer yet finds her writing as somehow flawed "like a case of jeweller's wares . . . with each ring unfinished, each bracelet too large or too small for its purpose."[11] Similarly, O'Brien finds Woolson's writings to be lacking despite her evident gifts: to him, she is a writer who might have "gone very far indeed" had she been "in a more settled environment."[12]

The 1930s also saw the publication of John Dwight Kern's dissertation, *Constance Fenimore Woolson: Literary Pioneer* (1934).[13] His was the first full-length study of her oeuvre, including her poetry, but he interprets her as primarily a pioneer of "Local Color" short fiction. In the 1940s and 1950s, Woolson's work, especially her short fiction, won praise from Lyon N. Richardson, Van Wyck Brooks, Arthur Hobson Quinn, Edward Wagenknecht, and Jay B. Hubbell, but it was not until the 1960s that another book-length study appeared.[14] Rayburn S. Moore's *Constance Fenimore Woolson* (1963) took issue with Leon Edel's claim that she pursued Henry James romantically, as well as Edel's denigrating assessment of her achievements as a writer. Moore pointed out that James himself had valued her work highly. Further, Moore argued that Woolson should be seen not only through the lens of local color but through her contributions to "the international theme" and "the novel of analysis" as well.[15] He also edited a volume of Woolson's work, *For the Major and Selected Short Stories* (1967), which appeared in paperback. This collection, along with reprints in several volumes by Garrett Press in 1969 and AMS Press in 1971, brought more of Woolson's pages to students of literature.[16]

While Moore did much to revive Woolson scholarship, it was only with the rise of feminism and feminist criticism during the 1970s and 1980s that Woolson's work drew sustained attention, enough to be read more innovatively. In the closing decades of the twentieth century, Sybil B. Weir, Sharon L. Dean, Joan Myers Weimer, and Cheryl B. Torsney deserve special credit for the recovery of Woolson as a serious writer.[17] Some feminist critics of that time, it should be noted, remained ambivalent about her literary accomplishments.[18] Still, her preoccupation with the subtle dynamics of gender and her skillful portraits of the woman artist, sometimes from a male perspective, intrigued feminist critics who were discovering for the first time that Woolson had been held in high regard during the nineteenth century. In Torsney's *The Grief of Artistry* (1989), the first book-length critical study in over twenty years, Woolson emerges as a woman committed above all to her art in a time when that brought grief. For Torsney, Woolson sought recognition as an artist but was hampered by social and cultural norms that urged women to suppress or disavow their ambitions. Torsney also edited *Critical Essays on Constance Fenimore Woolson* (1992), an important resource that brought together criticism of Woolson's work by her contemporaries and by twentieth-century critics, especially feminist reassessments.[19] At a key moment, Weimer's *Women Artists, Women Exiles* (1988), an anthology in the prestigious Rutgers University Press American Women Writers series, provided a critical introduction and a strong selection of stories that made Woolson accessible to readers within as well as outside the academy.[20] For Weimer, as for other feminist critics, Woolson's adventurous and independent life and courageous artistic choices made her art a worthy subject of study.

Although Woolson was never in danger of disappearing entirely from the literary scene, her place has only recently been secured among the ranks of the nation's most significant writers. Her inclusion in the Library of America has ensured that at least some of her work will never go out of print.[21] Indeed, in a review of this collection, Michael Gorra, esteemed critic for the *New York Review of Books*, wrote, "[E]ven after a generation of recovery her life remains better known than her work. The twenty-three stories collected in this volume should change that." He judged that "the pace and detail of the prose is exhilarating."[22] That is proof positive of a surging interest in Woolson owing most of all to the efforts of the Constance Fenimore Woolson Society for almost three decades.

Meeting at Rollins College in January 1995 to mark the centenary of Woolson's death, archivist Kate Reich and the group of Woolson scholars who helped organize the event—among others, Victoria Brehm, Sharon L. Dean, Caroline Gebhard, John Pearson, Cheryl B. Torsney, Carolyn Van Bergen, and Joan Myers Weimer[23]—decided to establish a literary society that would meet biennially to become a source of collaboration and criticism and, most importantly, to promote further scholarship on Woolson. Also on the program of that first gathering was Lyndall Gordon, who would go on to write an influential biography of Henry James that casts Woolson as one of the most important women in his life.[24] Before the new professional endeavor was even officially off the ground, however, Susan Koppelman, the meeting's keynoter and a prolific editor of collections of stories by recovered women writers, questioned the wisdom of creating yet another author society.

Believing that Woolson most certainly belonged in literary conversations, Koppelman was concerned in 1995 that such author societies would compete for recognition and scarce resources. What was needed, in her view, was a thorough revolution in the field of literary studies, which had always prioritized "Protestant cultured, apparently heterosexual, middle or upper-middle-class apparently white men."[25] Nevertheless, in the epilogue to the address she would later publish, Koppelman observed that one of the reasons for "the increasing valuation of Woolson's stock is the particularly auspicious combination of energy, enthusiasm, congeniality, and resources marshaled on her behalf by the members of the Constance Fenimore Woolson Society."[26]

In the twenty-first century, a large share of the critical scholarship on Woolson, not to mention new editions of her work and new lobbying for her inclusion in classroom anthologies, has been undertaken by members of the society. As the first president, Brehm organized the first official conference on Mackinac Island, Michigan, in October 1996 and edited a seminal collection, *Constance Fenimore Woolson's Nineteenth Century: Essays* (2001), which continued the feminist recovery of Woolson then underway. In addition to renewed focus on Woolson's exploration of place, this collection attended to Woolson's connections with other nineteenth-century women writers and looked at the "[l]esbian 'impossibilities'" in Woolson's work for the first time.[27] Most recently, Brehm has published *Constance Fenimore Woolson's Subversive Politics* (2023), which examines how Woolson uses "intertextual references, allegory, parody, and satire" to accomplish her political critiques.[28] Brehm also collaborated with Sharon L. Dean to produce *Constance Fenimore Woolson: Selected Stories and Travel Narratives* (2004).[29]

Another former president of the society, Dean had published *Constance Fenimore Woolson: Homeward Bound* (1995), a book-length study of Woolson's entire body of fiction that linked a new historicist perspective to a more personal feminist reading of Woolson's redefinitions of women's roles, particularly during an era marked by "new technologies, shifting demographics, and the increasing factionalism of different regional and social groups."[30] Dean, who then published *Constance Fenimore Woolson and Edith Wharton: Perspectives on Landscape and Art* (2002), is also responsible for a magisterial resource, *The Complete Letters of Constance Fenimore Woolson* (2012).[31] Not only does this painstaking and invaluable compendium offer a window into Woolson's relationships with her family and friends, but Dean's scholarship also provides a vantage point on the literary and cultural currents of Woolson's day because her correspondents included, besides James, the influential editor and writer William Dean Howells, southern poet Paul Hamilton Hayne, editor Edward Clarence Stedman, and John Hay, President Lincoln's private secretary in the White House.

A second collection of essays was edited by another society president, Kathleen Diffley, whose *Witness to Reconstruction: Constance Fenimore Woolson and the Postbellum South, 1873–1894* (2011) homes in on Woolson's "alternative and polyvocal account of Reconstruction."[32] As one of the first northern writers bearing witness to the nation's reincorporation of the defeated Confederacy, Woolson produced exceptionally insightful writing that has long been the foundation upon which her literary reputation has rested. *Witness to Reconstruction* brings out as never before the sheer variety and unusual complexity of the narratives that Woolson wove as she traveled through the South. Her aim, as Diffley observes, was to counter predictable postwar narratives, whether by "Southern apologists or Northern capitalists on the rise."[33]

Perhaps no Woolson Society member has done more than Anne Boyd Rioux to ensure that Woolson's place in American letters will never again be eclipsed. Rioux, who has served multiple terms as the society's president, first wrote about the scope of Woolson's literary ambitions in *Writing for Immortality* (2004).[34] In addition to editing *Miss Grief and Other Stories* (2016), she has written *Constance Fenimore Woolson: Portrait of a Lady Novelist* (2016).[35] Meticulously researched, this acclaimed biography has enabled the full dimensions of Woolson's life and art to emerge for the first time—for example, her revelation of Woolson's intimate friendship with American composer Francis Boott. Most recently, Rioux has edited the Library of America's *Constance Fenimore Woolson: Collected Stories* (2020) for the general reader.[36] And for many years she served as webmaster for the society's website, "Constance Fenimore Woolson: Pioneering American Writer (1840–1894)," available at https://constancefenimorewoolson.org.[37] The site offers a bibliography of her writings, online access to her works, links to archives that have preserved her letters and photographs, and information about the Woolson Society's past conferences. Moreover, scholarly books, book chapters, and articles published by (among others) Lynda Boren, Linda Grasso, Leonardo Buonomo, Kevin E. O'Donnell, Victoria Coulson, Carolyn Hall, Timothy Sweet, The-

odora Tsimpouki, Jacqueline Justice, and Jane M. Aman, the great majority
of them current or past members of the Woolson Society, attest to the artistic and cultural value of Woolson's writing.[38]

In a letter likely written in 1882, Woolson playfully chides her friend Henry
James about his inability to love his native land, especially places like Florida. For unless he could see them under the right conditions, Woolson told
him, she did not believe its beaches "could ever be more to you than so much
horizontal sand."[39] His answer to her was a grudging admiration for the way
she portrayed so exactly "every plant and flower, every vague odour and
sound, . . . every tint of the sky and murmur of the forest" as well as the accuracy of how the people spoke in such places.[40] Nevertheless, he challenged
her instead to write about Americans in Europe, which he claimed was "almost the sign and hallmark of American experience," perhaps in defense of
his own choice of subjects.[41] Woolson did go on to write about Americans
in Europe, but her characters and landscapes were never confined to Anglo-
American upper-class expatriates living abroad. Although James remains an
important interlocutor for critical conversations about Woolson's work, including their shared predilection for the "secret histories" and inner lives, the
essays in this volume mark a new era in Woolson scholarship because they
move beyond what James valued and instead cast into relief Woolson's extraordinary range. The first section, "A Writer's Experiments," demonstrates
that Woolson's formal play began during the 1870s but extended throughout her career, one reason for her wide nineteenth-century popularity and
the continuing enthusiasm of her readers. Edited by Caroline Gebhard, this
section reveals that Woolson pushed the boundaries of how women could be
represented in print by disrupting gender binaries and subtly underscoring
the female body and the erotic. Woolson also played with realism's bounds;
she was not afraid to create scenes bordering on the fantastic.

In "From Glimmerglass to Nowhere," Lisa West probes such fictional daring in the tale of a mysterious figure, "Old Fog," who lures ships plying the
Great Lakes to their doom. Rejecting the familiar clash of nature and civilization, Woolson revises the fiction of her famous relative James Fenimore Cooper, West argues, through envisioning natural, material, and social worlds as
interconnected and entangled, thereby anticipating twenty-first-century feminist materialisms. Her first collection's title story, "Castle Nowhere," recasts
male "civilizers" as wreckers and salvagers, while her radical eco-vision chal-

lenges ideas about the "wilderness" and blurs the lines between nature and culture.

In another feminist analysis, Cheryl B. Torsney explores how Woolson draws upon unexpected resources for a woman defining herself against gender binaries during an era of "separate spheres." In "Woolson's Cogito: Rowing as Epistemology," Torsney focuses on the intentional and rhythmic act of rowing, a thread running through Woolson's work from the early days of *Anne* (1882) through *East Angels* (1886) and *Jupiter Lights* (1889). Investigating her meditation upon the female body through rowing, usually associated with the masculine and the muscular, Torsney uncovers how Woolson arrived at her own cogito in both life and art: "I row, therefore I am."

Considering yet another form of experimentation, Kathleen Diffley's "*Anne* as Western-Border Mongrelosity" examines how her first novel, a female bildungsroman, explodes nineteenth-century literary genres like the regional sketch and the novel of manners to produce a panoramic American text. The sweep of this novel stretches from Michigan to Manhattan, from the Catskills to the Appalachians, from a frontier village to an elite resort, from a wartime hospital to a town facing murder on the Mason-Dixon Line. Woolson's Civil War novel, she proposes, realigns the country's postwar regions not across the now customary North-South divide but along a West-East axis. In the protagonist's final return to Mackinac, Woolson imagines a young woman endlessly postponing the marriage plot to become the hero of her own adventure.

In the same vein, Etta M. Madden's "Soaring Beyond Zoar: Woolson's Utopian Visions and Discourses" investigates a writer's inclination to go beyond the bounds of the conventional, always with women's needs in mind. Madden asserts that Woolson's attention to the Ohio German Separatist community Zoar—in "The Happy Valley" (1870), "Solomon" (1873), and "Wilhelmina" (1875)—nudges readers to imagine other worlds, where possibilities for social change or personal freedom exist. Juxtaposed with the turbulent forces of industrialization, capitalist individualism, and consumer desires is Zoar's pastoral world, where simplicity and community promise happiness. Yet Woolson reveals, as Madden points out, that neither outside nor inside alternative community is idyllic, thereby prompting readers to move toward still other alternatives.

Like the first essay of this section, the final one, "'Dear Mr. James . . . Do Not Leave It Merely Implied': *Jupiter Lights* as Response to Henry James's *The Bostonians*" by Kristin M. Comment, takes up the way Woolson reworks a famous male predecessor in her penultimate novel. Both novels, Comment claims, center on the same conflict: a battle between a northern woman and a southerner gentleman for possession of a young and innocent soul. Comment argues that both are also "queer" books: they disrupt binaries of gender and sexuality in their search for a viable solution to the problems of heterosexual marriage. Like all the contributors to this section, Comment acknowledges Woolson's artful boldness, her willingness to take her readers to strange places and to foreground female pain and strength.

The second section, "Postbellum Souths," returns to the defeated patchwork region that Woolson was among the first writers to portray in postwar literary magazines. Edited by Kathleen Diffley, this section builds on *Witness to Reconstruction* by mobilizing recent developments in theories of travel, collective memory, the Lost Cause, religious controversy, the race-bound South, regionalism, and southern studies that now include the Caribbean rim.

In "'The Ancient City' and the Ethics of Sightseeing," Susan L. Roberson scrutinizes Woolson's fictional party of northern tourists as they explore Florida's St. Augustine. Challenging easy assumptions about the South, history, race, and gender, Roberson explains that Woolson satirizes such visitors in an act of reverse ethnography that deploys and then complicates the tourist's gaze. By juxtaposing touristic misperceptions of history and place alongside corrective insider accounts, Roberson maintains that Woolson demonstrates an ethics of sightseeing that exposes the glib ignorance of northern travelers while also subtly modeling a truer appreciation of the semitropical South.

Like Roberson, Sidonia Serafini analyzes how Woolson complicates understandings of the region. In "'Sit Still and Remember': Woolson's Keepers and the Problem of the Archive," Serafini watches as Woolson probes what is at stake in creating and preserving historical records, calling into question the power dynamics always at play regarding an archive and its architect(s). Given today's public conversations and academic disputes about how southern history is commemorated, Serafini's timely exploration of Woolson's many "keepers," from a cemetery attendant to a family archivist and even the southern landscape itself, foregrounds an author interrogating the very act of chronicling.

How the past is remembered is also at issue in Caroline Gebhard's "The Confederate Widow of Myth and Artistry: 'In the Cotton Country.'" The double perspective provided by a northern narrator and a southern widow anticipates, Gebhard proposes, what would become staples of the southern myth of the Lost Cause: a young Confederate widow on the verge of starvation, Sherman's ruthless soldiers, and the loss of a noble generation of white men fighting for their country instead of slavery. Woolson is too much of an artist, Gebhard claims, to hide the widow's fierce attachment to white supremacy, which undercuts the myth even as this story reveals a troubling northern sympathy.

In "'This Vast, Many-Raced, Motley Country of Ours': Catholicism, Minorcans, and Difference in 'Sister St. Luke,'" Aaron J. Rovan asserts that Woolson manifests complexities that even the postbellum American South could not reduce to black-and-white binaries. Sister St. Luke's background as both a Catholic nun and an orphan of uncertain parentage blurs traditional racial demarcations of identity and opens a textual site to explore the meanings of difference decades before the modern articulation of such a concept.

Echoing Rovan's attention to ethnicity, Kathryn B. McKee's "Illustrating Race and Region in *For the Major*" plumbs ethnic and racial identities that trouble the narrative of uncomplicated southern whiteness. Seeing the region as bound up with the Caribbean, McKee argues that Woolson's South, despite its seeming isolation, is nonetheless connected with places far beyond the mountains of North Carolina, where the novella is set. Examining the wood engravings by Alfred Fredericks that accompanied Woolson's magazine installments, she demonstrates how these illustrations speak to the fiction's underlying anxieties about whiteness. Such anxieties are foregrounded for McKee in the figure of Julian Dupont, whose mysterious identity and ties to the West Indies create an uneasy presence that this mountain community remains unable to assimilate.

Karen Tracey then considers from another angle Woolson's penchant for peopling her fictions with heterogenous characters. In "'Assimilative Powers': Region, Nation, and Time in *East Angels*," Tracey points out that descendants from the Spanish settlers, displaced whites from the North and the South, the formerly enslaved, poor whites, Cuban immigrants, and northern travelers all inhabit Gracias-á-Dios, her fictional Florida town. While Woolson often reproduces the patronizing and racist assumptions of her time, as Tracey acknowledges, she also allows minority voices to be included in the story that an evolving nation tells of itself, thereby unsettling hierarchies of urban over rural, tourist over resident, whites over nonwhites, and the present over the past to create a vibrant representation of a multiethnic nation coalescing.

In "How 'The Oklawaha' Prefigures (and Indicts) Disney World," John Wharton Lowe comments upon tourism, history, racial and cultural difference, and the southern landscape in the postbellum South, preoccupations that dominate this section. Lowe highlights, however, the contrast between what he calls Woolson's "tropical sublime" and what replaced it: 1970s Disney World. Rather than the trip on the Oklawaha that Woolson penned to showcase Florida's history and unsettling beauty, Disney World produced its "Jungle Cruise" by trading in racist clichés and erasing the real damage to the river. Lowe underscores how Woolson's Florida resonates more than a hundred years later in the fraught need to honor the past and differing perspectives while preserving a natural world.

The third section, "Through an International Lens," explores Woolson's expatriate vignettes in fin-de-siècle Europe and North Africa as well as European misperceptions of the Gilded Age United States. Here and throughout the volume, travel sketches brush up against short fiction. Edited by Cheryl B. Torsney, this section confirms that Woolson rarely wrote in conventional ways. Here, she often reverses the usual tropes of Americans abroad.

In "Woolson's Italy and Cultural Difference in *Harper's Monthly*," Lisa Nais argues that instead of concentrating our gaze upon the exotic lives of Americans in Italy, the Italian setting of "A Pink Villa" becomes a vantage point from which her Americans gaze at the frontier in southern Florida. Nais further considers Woolson's interrogation of American nationalism by situating this tale within its initial publication context, an illustrated periodical that reflected the nation's imperialist views, especially in its travel sketches.

Similarly, Sharon Kennedy-Nolle in "Woolson's Veiled Cairo and the 'Shadowing' of Jim Crow" contends that Woolson offers a refreshing alternative to the rigid polarities that informed nineteenth-century American notions of race, gender, and space. She holds that Woolson's travelogue "Cairo in 1890" celebrates Egyptian women empowered by the complex fluidity of their household roles. Even more surprisingly, Kennedy-Nolle suggests that in describing the changing role of Egyptian female laborers as well as the vibrant sororal networks emerging from the harem tradition, Woolson reimagines postwar American labor and race relations beyond devalued women's work and segregated communities. Yet Kennedy-Nolle also points to the contradictions inherent in Woolson's position as a Western female tourist, both an agent of empire and a subordinate in colonial hierarchies.

As in previous sections, Katherine Barrett Swett considers how Woolson formulates her own take on a popular American work, in this case how she reshapes the figure of the "light weight" girl featured in Henry James's *Daisy Miller*. Swett explores how Woolson uses a Tuscan backdrop to expose the emotional damage created by patriarchal perceptions of the female body. In "Too Light to Fall: Female Bodies and Italian Precipices in 'Dorothy,'" she probes Woolson's portrayal of a woman's wasting death via anorexic suicide in a mysterious and powerful story that has wrongly been dismissed as sentimental. Moreover, she demonstrates that this late tale offers insight into the cultural and emotional causes of Woolson's own tragic final act.

The concluding essay of this section, Heather Hartley's "Letter from Vesuvius," takes the form of a personal epistle addressed to Woolson by a contem-

porary American writer based in Paris. Hartley pays homage to Woolson's rich
and variegated writing, her determination and resolve, and her travels and life
abroad in Italy. She also ponders the writer's intellectual and emotional relationship with Henry James. Hartley understands "wanderlust"; like Woolson,
she has lived and traveled in Europe for many years. This shared leitmotif enables a meditation on the addictive, visceral, unpredictable, and voracious aspects of the urge to go and live elsewhere but especially in Florence, Rome, and
Venice. Given the significance of Italy in Woolson's life, it is fitting that the af-
terword by Edoarda Grego, "Lost in Translation: From Woolson's *For the Major* to Grego's *Per il Maggiore*," traces the difficulties of translating Woolson's
portrait of the defeated South into Italian for a European audience, a transnational experiment in its own right.

The contributors to this volume delve into a range of thematic concerns that
preoccupied Woolson throughout her career, social complexities that still command attention. Among them are the representation of gender and the damage
done by patriarchal ideals; the representation of place, the ethics of tourism,
and the relation of humans to the natural world; the representation of the history of enslavement and Reconstruction; the quandaries posed by racial, ethnic, and cultural differences; the possibility of community despite the country's
fractured identity, both domestically and transnationally; and the possibilities that imaginative literature can offer in presenting unexpected angles from
which to comprehend these recurring concerns. Informed by a wide variety of
perspectives from feminist and queer theory to southern studies and decon-
struction, *Secret Histories: A New Era in Constance Fenimore Woolson Scholarship*
engages a mix of genres and topics—utopian discourse, visual art, genre analysis, ethics, archival practice, history, and autobiography—to bring a fresh understanding of how much this remarkable nineteenth-century writer has to say
to her newest readers.

NOTES

1. Henry James, "Miss Constance Fenimore Woolson," *Harper's Weekly*, February 12,
1887, 114; revised as "Miss Woolson" in his *Partial Portraits* (London: Macmillan, 1888),
181.

2. James, 114; *Partial Portraits*, 179.

3. James, 114; *Partial Portraits*, 180.

4. Many of her contemporaries as well as modern critics have assumed that Woolson
committed suicide, but Anne Boyd Rioux hesitates: "[B]ecause no one was in the room
with CFW and no description of the windows as they were then has survived, we can-

not definitively know if she fell or jumped deliberately." See *Constance Fenimore Woolson: Portrait of a Lady Novelist* (New York: Norton, 2016), 365–66, n.47.

5. See Donna M. Campbell, "American Realism and Gender," in *The Oxford Handbook of American Literary Realism*, ed. Keith Newlin (New York: Oxford University Press, 2019), 41–63. Campbell argues that women realists like Woolson registered in their fiction their "protest" against the "too restrictive" criteria for realism championed by Howells and James (60).

6. See Caroline Gebhard, "The Spinster in the House of American Criticism," *Tulsa Studies in Women's Literature* 10, no. 1 (Spring 1991): 79–91, and Judith Fetterley and Marjorie Pryse, *Writing out of Place: Regionalism, Women, and American Literary Culture* (Urbana: University of Illinois Press, 2003), 28, 42–55.

7. Alexander Cowie, *The Rise of the American Novel* (New York: American Book Co., 1951), 568, reprinted in Cheryl B. Torsney, ed., *Critical Essays on Constance Fenimore Woolson* (New York: G. K. Hall, 1992), 106–17.

8. Fred Lewis Pattee, *A History of American Literature since 1870* (New York: Century, 1915), 317–18, 317, and "Constance Fenimore Woolson and the South," *South Atlantic Quarterly* 38, no. 2 (April 1939): 130–41, 130. See also Cheryl B. Torsney, "Introduction," in Torsney, *Critical Essays*, 5–8.

9. John Hervey, "Sympathetic Art," *Saturday Review of Literature*, October 12, 1929, 268; reprinted in Torsney, *Critical Essays*, 90–91.

10. Edward J. O'Brien, *The Advance of the American Short Story* (New York: Dodd, Mead, 1931), 162–63; reprinted in Torsney, *Critical Essays*, 89.

11. Constance Fenimore Woolson, "'Miss Grief,'" *Lippincott's*, May 1880, 581.

12. O'Brien, *Advance of the American Short Story*, 163; reprinted in Torsney, *Critical Essays*, 89.

13. John Dwight Kern, *Constance Fenimore Woolson: Literary Pioneer* (Philadelphia: University of Pennsylvania Press, 1934).

14. See Torsney, *Critical Essays* for excerpts from all these critics except Van Wyck Brooks, who discusses Woolson's southern writings in *The Times of Melville and Whitman* (New York: E. P. Dutton, 1953), 351–60.

15. Rayburn S. Moore, *Constance Fenimore Woolson* (New York: Twayne, 1963), preface, 139.

16. Rayburn S. Moore, ed., *For the Major and Selected Short Stories* (Lanham, Md.: Rowman & Littlefield, 1967).

17. See Sybil B. Weir, "Southern Womanhood in the Novels of Constance Fenimore Woolson," *Mississippi Quarterly* 29, no. 4 (Fall 1976): 559–68; Sharon L. Dean, "Constance Fenimore Woolson and Henry James: The Literary Relationship," *Massachusetts Studies in English* 7, no. 3 (1980):1–9; Joan Myers Weimer, "Women Artists as Exiles in the Fiction of Constance Fenimore Woolson," *Legacy* 3, no. 2 (Fall 1986): 3–15; and Cheryl B. Torsney, "'Miss Grief' by Constance Fenimore Woolson," *Legacy* 4, no. 1 (Spring 1987): 11–25.

18. See, for example, Ann Douglas [Wood], "The Literature of Impoverishment: The Women Local Colorists in America, 1865–1914," *Women's Studies* 1, no. 1 (1972–

73): 3–45, and Anne E. Rowe, *The Enchanted Country: Northern Writers in the South, 1865–1910* (Baton Rouge: Louisiana State University Press, 1978), 58–65.

19. Cheryl B. Torsney, *Constance Fenimore Woolson: The Grief of Artistry* (Athens: University of Georgia Press, 1989); Torsney, *Critical Essays.*

20. Joan Myers Weimer, ed., *Women Artists, Women Exiles: "Miss Grief" and Other Stories by Constance Fenimore Woolson* (New Brunswick, N.J.: Rutgers University Press, 1988).

21. It should be noted that the Library of America edition contains only her short stories; none of her novels or poems are included in this volume.

22. Michael Gorra, "Constance Fenimore Woolson: Collected Stories," *New York Review of Books,* July 23, 2020, 16–17.

23. Brehm, Dean, Gebhard, Pearson, Torsney, and Van Bergen-Rylander have all served as president or co-president of the Constance Fenimore Woolson Society.

24. Lyndall Gordon, *A Private Life of Henry James: Two Women and His Art* (New York: Norton, 1999).

25. Susan Koppelman, "The Politics and Ethics of Literary Revival: A Test Case— Shall We, Ought We, Can We Make of Constance Fenimore Woolson a Kate Chopin?," *Journal of American Culture* 22, no. 3 (Fall 1999): 1.

26. Koppelman, 7.

27. See Kristen M. Comment, "The Lesbian 'Impossibilities' of Miss Grief's 'Armor,'" in *Constance Fenimore Woolson's Nineteenth Century: Essays,* ed. Victoria Brehm (Detroit, Mich.: Wayne State University Press, 2001), 207–23.

28. Victoria Brehm, *Constance Fenimore Woolson's Subversive Politics* (Washington, D.C.: Lexington Books, 2023), 2.

29. Victoria Brehm and Sharon L. Dean, eds., *Constance Fenimore Woolson: Selected Stories and Travel Narratives* (Knoxville: University of Tennessee Press, 2004).

30. Sharon L. Dean, *Constance Fenimore Woolson: Homeward Bound* (Knoxville: University of Tennessee Press, 1995), xv.

31. Sharon L. Dean, *Constance Fenimore Woolson and Edith Wharton: Perspectives on Landscape and Art* (Knoxville: University of Tennessee Press, 2002); and Sharon L. Dean, ed., *The Complete Letters of Constance Fenimore Woolson* (Gainesville: University Press of Florida, 2012).

32. Kathleen Diffley, "'People Who Remember': The American South and Woolson's Postbellum Sojourns," in *Witness to Reconstruction: Constance Fenimore Woolson and the Postbellum South, 1873–1894,* ed. Kathleen Diffley (Jackson: University Press of Mississippi, 2011), 5.

33. Diffley, 4.

34. See Anne E. Boyd [Rioux], *Writing for Immortality: Women and the Emergence of High Literary Culture in America* (Baltimore: Johns Hopkins University Press, 2004).

35. Rioux, *Constance Fenimore Woolson: Portrait*; Anne Boyd Rioux, ed., *Miss Grief and Other Stories* (New York: Norton, 2016).

36. Anne Boyd Rioux, ed., *Constance Fenimore Woolson: Collected Stories* (New York: Library of America, 2020).

37. Victoria Brehm has now taken over the duties of managing the society's website.

38. See, for example, Lynda S. Boren, "'Dear Constance,' 'Dear Henry': The Wool-son/James Affair—Fact, Fiction, or Fine Art?," *Amerikastudien / American Studies* 27, no. 4 (1982): 457–66; Linda Grasso, "'Thwarted Life, Mighty Hunger, Unfinished Work': The Legacy of Nineteenth-Century Women Writing in America," *American Transcendental Quarterly* 8, no. 2 (June 1994): 97–118; Leonardo Buonomo, "The Other Face of History in Constance Fenimore Woolson's Southern Stories," *Canadian Review of American Studies / Revue Canadienne d'Etudes Américaines* 28, no. 3 (1998): 15–29; Kevin E. O'Donnell and Helen Hollingsworth, eds., *Seekers and Scenery: Travel Writing from Southern Appalachia, 1840–1900* (Knoxville: University of Tennessee Press, 2004), 131–72; Victoria Coulson, "Teacups and Love Letters: Constance Fenimore Woolson and Henry James," *Henry James Review* 26, no. 1 (Winter 2005): 82–98; Carolyn Hall, "An Elaborate Pretense for the Major: Making Up the Face of the Postbellum Nation," *Legacy* 22, no. 2 (2005): 144–57; Timothy Sweet, "'You Talk Like a Book': Constance Fenimore Woolson's Civil War Poetry and the Regionalization of Speech," *J19* 5, no. 1 (Spring 2017): 129–50; Theodora Tsimpouki, "Agency in Complicity: The Aesthetics of Trauma in Constance Fenimore Woolson's 'Miss Grief,'" in *Literature and Psychology: Writing Trauma and the Self*, ed. Önder Çakirtus (Newcastle upon Tyne: Cambridge Scholars, 2019), 154–74; Jacqueline Justice, "Landscapes of Resistance: Polar Allusion and the Northern Frontier in the Fiction of Constance Fenimore Woolson," *ESQ* 66, no. 3 (2020): 409–44; and Jane M. Aman, "Gothic Spaces and the Nation in Constance Fenimore Woolson's Tales of the Great Lakes and Reconstruction," in *American Women's Regionalist Fiction: Mapping the Gothic*, ed. Monika Elbert and Rita Bode (London: Palgrave Macmillan, 2021), 253–68.

39. Letter of Constance Fenimore Woolson to Henry James, February 12, [1882], in Dean, *Complete Letters*, 184.

40. James, "Miss Constance Fenimore Woolson," 114; *Partial Portraits*, 180.

41. James, "Miss Constance Fenimore Woolson," 114. The section that contained this challenge was omitted when he revised his article for *Partial Portraits* (1888). Lyndall Gordon comments that Woolson was important to James for many reasons, but in particular because "she remained incurably American"; moreover, he envied her knowledge of post–Civil War Florida and the South, something his own brothers had known but he had missed, something that came to represent literary material he could never access but that she had (164).

I

A Writer's Experiments

From Glimmerglass to Nowhere

Lisa West

From the point, the canoe took its way toward the shoal, where
the remains of the castle were still visible, a picturesque ruin. The
storms had long since unroofed the house, and decay had eaten into
the logs. All the fastenings were untouched, but the seasons rioted
in the place, as if in mockery at the attempt to exclude them. The
palisades were rotting, as were the piles, and it was evident that a
few more recurrences of winter, a few more gales and tempests,
would sweep all into the lake, and blot the building from the face of
that magnificent solitude.

—JAMES FENIMORE COOPER, *The Deerslayer*, 1841

The castle was left alone; the flowers bloomed on through the
summer, and the rooms held the old furniture bravely through the
long winter. But gradually the walls fell in, and the water entered.
The fogs still steal across the lake, and wave their gray draperies up
into the northern curve; but the sedge-gate is gone, and the castle
is indeed Nowhere.

—CONSTANCE FENIMORE WOOLSON, "Castle Nowhere," 1875

The fates of the floating huts or "castles" in *The Deerslayer* and "Castle Nowhere" are hauntingly similar and yet so different in their literary expression.
In the first epigraph, James Fenimore Cooper describes a picturesque ruin,
whereas in Constance Fenimore Woolson's tale, the castle disappears into "Nowhere." In Cooper's description, objects lose their boundaries, rotting, decaying, or becoming unroofed, whereas in Woolson's description, flowers, furniture, the sedge-gate are still discrete. In Cooper's, there are human witnesses
through which the scene is focalized, whereas in Woolson's there is no human
witness, and things—water, rooms, fogs—are given agency apart from human
perception. These passages show the degree to which Woolson aligns the plot

of her novella with the novel of her famous granduncle precisely to undercut his insistence on viewing nature through human eyes. By representing objects disappearing into "Nowhere" rather than disintegrating, Woolson experiments with articulating connections between the human and nonhuman that not only reject Cooper's human-centric vision but also anticipate twenty-first-century ideas of how a focus on "matter" reframes an understanding of the human body as only one of many other bodies coexisting and comingling in a "more-than-human world."[1]

These current philosophies or theoretical approaches stress how "matter" is dynamic and multiple; conceptualize bodies—both human and nonhuman—as having an inclination to attach or reattach to other bodies, consistently forming new "assemblages" or combinations; and posit human agency as limited, working *within* networks of human and nonhuman bodies rather than working *upon* a nature that is separate from the human.[2] After brief plot overviews, this argument unfolds in three stages, beginning with Woolson's initial dismantling of Cooper's world, then taking up her materialist aesthetics and ethics of recombination, and ending with a discussion of how Woolson's characters are often less recognizable as representations of humanity than as chemical catalysts or elemental forces.

The Deerslayer and "Castle Nowhere"

Cooper set *The Deerslayer* on the shores of Lake Otsego, a place that he associated with his childhood and family homestead. The plot follows a series of conflicts with Native Americans, revolving around the kidnapping of Chingachgook's fiancée and the efforts he, Natty Bumppo / Hawkeye / the Deerslayer, and others make to restore her. In these adventures, they meet Tom Hutter, a reclusive man living off the land who we later learn is associated with past crimes of piracy. Hutter has a floating "hut" or "ark" that he can maneuver through the tall grasses in the marshy inlets and borders of the lake, and which becomes essential to the hiding, escaping, and ambushing ubiquitous to the plot. Hutter lives on his floating home with two daughters, one of whom (Judith) falls in love with the Deerslayer and the other of whom (Hetty) is portrayed as simpleminded, yet a moral compass. In the end, Chingachgook's beloved is restored, Deerslayer rejects Judith's advances, and the novel concludes with the epigraph cited, as the central characters return to the setting of their adventures and meditate on how the landscape reveals or hides signs of their experiences. While nature displays a "face of that magnificent solitude," it also is a legible text, retaining traces of human action.[3]

The Deerslayer is both the last written of the so-called Leatherstocking Tales and the first in chronological order, a prequel more than a sequel of the 1823 *The Pioneers*, which likewise is set along the shores of Otsego, or the "Glimmerglass," as it is more romantically called. At the end of the novel, the readers too have a sense of memories impressed on a landscape; they too remember the setting from the prior novel and negotiate interpreting past, present, and future cues from the landscape along with the characters. Thus, readers evaluate the final scene of *The Deerslayer* as a palimpsest of various other lakeshore scenes from both novels.[4] Readers are rewarded for thinking of the landscape as a text that humans both inscribe and interpret.

Woolson was the grandniece of James Fenimore Cooper; her mother's mother, Ann Cooper Pomeroy, was James Fenimore Cooper's sister. The Woolson family spent time in Cooperstown, on the shores of Lake Otsego, both before moving to Cleveland and during many summers afterward. Woolson set "Castle Nowhere" in the Great Lakes region, which was to her a more familiar and intimate nature retreat. Mackinac Island, with its indigenous legends, distinctive natural landmarks, and distance from urban life, arguably was her literary muse as much as Lake Otsego was her relative's.[5] Rather than draw on her childhood memories, however, she sets "Castle Nowhere" off the grid, on the "shore bordering the head of Lake Michigan" that was "a hundred miles of nothing," empty space on maps even after it had been explored by white trappers.[6] Thus, she chose to set this tale in a place devoid of memories—or, to be more precise, a place that resisted the possibility of memory or textual representation.[7]

In "Castle Nowhere," Jarvis Waring, an educated young white man, leaves East Coast society for a sojourn in the remote regions of the Great Lakes. Assuming he is far from any human presence, he is surprised when joined by the older Amos Fog, who had spied his camp and claims to be a local inhabitant. Fog steals from Waring when he departs under cover of night, and Waring, furious, follows him onto the perilous lake, eventually happening upon Fog's floating habitation, where he lives with his adopted daughter Silver and servant Orange. As befits his name, Fog is a wrecker who—"'Only four times'" he insists (27)—lured ships to the treacherous shoals around the lake's northern curves to provide for his daughter since he could not get food, clothing, shelter sufficiently from the "land" itself. Silver is not portrayed as innately "feebleminded" as is *The Deerslayer*'s Hetty; instead, she is described as someone so removed from social influence that she does not know Christianity. Although we are to believe she lives in "nature," she does not grasp even the concept of death.

During the unfolding of the plot, Fog, Silver, and Waring all temporarily leave the floating castle. Each is injured on the departure, with injury caused or compounded by exposure to the brutal winter wind and cold. Each is returned to the castle by another character to be healed and to establish complex bonds of obligation, resentment, and loyalty. Silver from the start shows a magnetic but not overtly sexual attraction for Waring, but he resists her until near the end of the tale, when he agrees to marry her and sets the stage for the final abandonment of the floating castle.

The most obvious changes between the novel and the novella are that Woolson reduces Cooper's work from about five hundred pages to roughly fifty, and she does not use Indigenous people as a device. Instead, the conflicts that drive her plot are located among this small group of "strangers" and their interactions with the "matter" of the landscape, particularly fog, waves, cold, rain, ice, and lightning. Yet there are numerous similar motifs. Woolson too features a floating "castle" that is impossible to find in the lake; a recluse with a mysterious past of crime, Amos Fog, whose name connects him to the landscape as Tom Hutter's name links him to his "hut"; a daughter, Silver, who combines the "child of nature" aspect of Hetty with the attraction of Judith; and a young white man, Jarvis Waring, who brings these elements together. From the opening, Woolson dismantles the trope of the heroic white man alone in the wilderness and Cooper's sharp dichotomy of civilization and nature.

Woolson: The White Man Wandering in Nature Finds Mahogany Chairs and a Girl Eating Sugar

In "Castle Nowhere," the reader is introduced to the young white man as naïvely and unproductively self-reflexive, glorying in the "entangling of himself in the webs of the wilderness" (3) merely by refusing to look at his pocket compass. "'I wish I was a tree,'" he muses to himself. "'See that young pine, how lustily it grows, feeling its life to the very tip of each green needle!'" (2). Waring continues with a parody of the Emersonian view that man is a god in ruins: "'[W]hat a miserable, half-way thing is man, who should be a demigod, and is—a creature for the very trees to pity!'" (2).

The critique of Waring's reverence for solitude is not limited to his almost comical transcendental views of the wild. Woolson suggests that while people think they are entangled in the wilderness, they never leave civilization fully behind. Waring brings with him more than matches, dogs, and firearms; he brings his experiences, including what he has read. When not actively debating with the "Spirit of Discontent," as the narrator calls his querulous inner voice, "he was repeating bits of verses and humming fragments of songs that

kept time with his footsteps, or rather they were repeating and humming themselves along through his brain" (4). It is worth stressing the bodily nature of
this quote, from the physical sensation of humming to the way the verses seem
to have their own agency. A Shakespearean sonnet, "When to the Sessions
of Sweet Summer Thought," repeats in his brain (not mind), vibrates his lips,
keeps time with his footsteps, follows the rhythm of the lake's waves, and even
seems to conjure oars on the water. He is reciting to himself when a mysterious
stranger—Amos Fog—emerges from the foggy lake in a small craft to join him
at his campsite. There is no boundary between "civilization" and "wilderness,"
no border between rhyming couplets and waves because what a person reads,
remembers, or imagines is always part of their body as well as their mind.

When Fog returns to his mysterious abode under cover of night, he steals
Waring's book of sonnets, a miniature of a Titian painting, and a stash of white
sugar cubes. These particular items are significant: they stand for "civilization,"
which is what Fog steals, rather than the means to live in the wilderness, such
as food and firearms. It is significant that Jarvis wants these back: he builds a
simple dugout, which "took some days," to recover them (10). As he moves further into the lake and unknown regions, he loses not only his sense of direction but also his sense of agency. He comes across the floating habitation of
Fog through forces (wind, current, watercraft) not under his control. Here the
reader and Waring are introduced to Silver. Unlike Cooper's Hetty, Silver can
never be seen as a "child of nature" because from the start she is connected to
art objects and culture. When Waring first sees her, she is reading his book of
Shakespearean sonnets and sucking on his white sugar cubes; like the sonnets
written into a book, she is the material presence of art and imagination.

The first sight of her reads like an ekphrastic description of a painting, perhaps titled *Girl with Sugar*: "But the west shone out radiant, a rude little bal-
cony overhanging the water, and in it a girl in a mahogany chair, nibbling something and reading" (12). The narrator continues, "Her hair, of the very light
fleecy gold seldom seen after babyhood, hung over her shoulders unconfined
by comb or ribbon, falling around her like a veil and glittering in the horizontal
sunbeams; her face, throat, and hands were white as the petals of a white camelia, her features infantile, her cast-down eyes invisible under the full-orbed lids"
(12–13). Her very description even sounds like a painting, and the references to
nature—mahogany, fleece, camelia—reflect nature used in the service of art:
furniture, clothing, decoration.[8] Furthermore, her presence takes the place of
the Titian miniature; a book, sugar cubes, and the image are stolen from him,
and he encounters the book, the sugar, and this painterly image of a young girl
caught up in what civilization has to offer.

Silver continues to reveal herself as the center of collections—of silks from pilfered steamer trunks, gulls that return to her side after their daily flights, mahogany chairs, a "chandelier adorned with lustres" from a steamer cabin (14), and more. Her hothouse on the floating castle is in many ways a parody of Edenic description in its abundance and variety: "flowers growing every-where,—on the floor, up the walls, across the ceiling, in pots, in boxes, in baskets, on shelves, in cups, in shells, climbing, crowding each other, swinging, hanging, winding around everything,—a riot of beauty with perfumes for a language" (15). The flowers are no longer "natural" in this profusion; they are removed from an ecological niche and living instead in cups, pots, and other domestic objects, reduced to ornamentation rather than part of a natural cycle. Silver seems to attract these items, just as she seemed somehow to attract Waring to the castle itself. Her explanation that Fog gathers them could be interpreted as another source of her attraction; he gathers them for her.

In the climax of this first encounter, Waring enters a "long narrow room" (14) that is described more like a curiosity cabinet than a pleasing blending of harmonious elements: "The walls and ceiling were planked, and the workmanship of the whole rude and clumsy; but a gay carpet covered the floor, a chandelier adorned with lustres hung from a hook in the ceiling, large gilded vases and a mirror in a tarnished gilt frame adorned a shelf over the hearth, mahogany chairs stood in ranks against the wall under the little windows, and a long narrow table ran down the centre of the apartment from end to end" (14). This catalog lists decorative objects, the glitter of things glaring in contrast with the rough workmanship of the space. "It all seemed strangely familiar; of what did it remind him? His eyes fell upon the table-legs; they were riveted to the floor. Then it came to him at once,—the long, narrow cabin of a lake steamer" (14–15). And yet this floating vessel has no point of departure and no destination, which further disorients Waring in space, time, and purpose. To draw upon concepts from Yi-Fu Tuan, Waring initially thought he was in vast, "undifferentiated space" in the wilderness, but he finds he is in neither "space" nor "place," for the floating vessel is clearly demarcated by human presence yet is disorienting and unable to satisfy basic human needs.[9]

An Aesthetics and Ethics of Recombination and Assemblage

Woolson's purpose is not to clutter wild, remote areas with manmade objects. Rather, she is interested in showing how humans, nonhuman entities, and other objects comingle in whatever space they find themselves, complicating human-centered assumptions about fate, agency, and intent. Perhaps the most telling contrast between Tom Hutter's and Fog's assortment of objects can be found in a comparison of the figures of the trunk and the wreck. In *The Deerslayer*, Hutter's locked trunk seems to hold the secrets of his sins and of the origin of his presumed daughters. When the central characters open the trunk to see if they can find objects of value with which to ransom Hutter from the Mingoes, they find clothes, a sword, a chess set, pistols, and letters. The letters and items indeed tell a story of Judith's and Hetty's mother. As if relating an eighteenth-century novel plot, the objects, in connection with the letters, reveal how a dashing British officer seduced her, fathered her children, then abandoned her. The objects and writings prove not only that Hutter is not the girls' biological father but also that he is wanted for a state crime.

Fog's castle as a source of artifacts is never so contained. Instead of being crowded into a trunk, its objects are continually dispersed when the narrator traces them from their original places through the water, wind, and fog (via steamer or canoe) to the castle. Unlike pistols and letters, they have no story to tell of individual lives. In contrast to the items in Hutter's trunk, they are, if not meaningless, at least not laden with personal value. Fog gathers these found objects and repurposes them for his benefit and the comfort of Silver.

The idea of the wrecker becomes more sinister as Jarvis catches Fog setting a lure to destroy a schooner during a storm, a disaster that will allow him to collect items such as those within the castle's dining room. Yet the wreck itself is described impersonally, so unlike the overdetermined description of Hutter's trunk's contents. Readers parse the narrator's detached description intermingling various objects: the flash of Fog's lantern, the reef, the rocks, the waves, the vessel. In one moment, they come together for the crash, and then they separate; as Fog anticipates, "by daylight the things will be coming ashore" (25) while the bodies are "more likely to drift out to sea" (27). What had been an organic collective—the ship—is broken down into constituent parts, so it becomes pieces of matter rather than organism or system.

This concept of wrecking becomes the moral heart of the tale. Waring accuses Fog of being a murderer and watches in horror as the schooner fails: "'Can anything be done for the men on board?'" (24). The answer clearly is no. Fog rationalizes his role by arguing that he was not the sole cause of their harm; among other factors, the storm, the rocks, and the captain of the ship played a role. Fog also insists that if Waring leaves him to die after shooting him in the back as a wrecker of men, he too would be a murderer, responsible not only for Fog's death but also for the deaths of Silver and Orange, who have no way to leave their lake-bound home. While the reader is not expected to accept Fog's justifications, he does have a point. He articulates a dramatic way to rethink the romantic, Cooperesque ideal of humans definitively shaping or at least managing the landscape. Fog reminds readers that humans don't control, master, or even fully understand things outside themselves, nor does intention alone provide the means to get desired results. Instead, people are participants in a broader network of forces that have consequences rippling across human and nonhuman bodies.

"But what could he do?" (23), the narrator asks, specifically from Waring's point of view in the first moment he sees the struggling schooner. Fog and Waring repeat versions of this question throughout the story, both directly and indirectly, and in both past and future tenses. While Fog is clearly wrong in setting a false light to mislead a ship, how to judge his gathering beached supplies is not so clear. The moral ambivalence is a consequence of recognizing that we cannot draw a clear line between what we do (intentionally or not) and what the nonhuman world does. How can we judge intention and action in a world where humans do not determine entanglement or where they cannot simply pull out a pocket compass to reorient themselves? Waring in these moments recognizes his complicity in the workings of this human-object-nature network, asking, as he picks up the pieces, "'Am I, too, a wrecker?'" (29).

It is at this moment when the white-man-reciting-sonnets-in-the-wilderness recognizes he is part of a larger entanglement, one that he is ambivalent about at best.

Silver and Catalytic Power

Silver herself, like the "things" that drift to shore, is a "found object" of sorts. When Fog finally reveals his history, he explains, "That day I found by the wayside a little child, scarcely more than a baby; it had wandered out of the poorhouse, where its mother had died the week before, a stranger passing through the village" (49). She is a double both for her mother and for the sin Fog recalls, seeing in her life an exchange for the life he took. Although less elegant by far than the repurposed chandelier, she too is a replacement object that is intended to bring light to Fog. He explains how raising her could expiate his sin: "I would take this forlorn little creature and bring her up as my own child, tenderly, carefully,—a life for a life" (49). It would be too simple to consider that Silver, a girl/aestheticized object, is an exchange item between male characters, fulfilling first Fog's fantasies, then, Pygmalion-like, Waring's. In Woolson's wilderness, Silver has her own power.

Like her namesake metal, Silver is not magnetic but has catalytic capabilities and the capacity to form bonds. This power is unrecognizable to Waring largely because she seems less fully human to him, or at least less adult. While Silver is "ardent," Margot Livesey notes, her being "has no sexual dimension."[10] When she chases him upon his first attempted departure, following his unseen path through channels in the lake, her pursuit is described as a way of knowing that is more instinctual than human: "'[S]omething told me you had gone that way,'" she explains (37), and the narrator continues, "That was all: no reasoning, no excuse, no embarrassment; the flight of the little seabird straight to its mate" (37). Her attachment to Waring is different in intensity from her attachment to flowers, gulls, chairs, or sugar, but perhaps not in kind. She suggests to the reader a way humans can grow attached that blurs the line between human and nonhuman bodies and that minimizes the role of reason or intent or conscious desire.

Her power is marked not by intention or command but through a kind of influence on others. Silver is the cause of both men's actions at many times in the story: Fog wrecks (and therefore kills) for her; Waring decides not to kill Fog when he realizes that his murder would lead to Silver's death. Waring returns to the castle when she follows him and falls ill. She drives much of the decision making of others, and it is not just a form of justification or excuse making but something more complex. The narrative links her power to that of the landscape, the kind of inexorable power that is variable (like wind, snow crust, ice, and fog) but irresistible when at its strongest. Through Silver, Woolson suggests that the human will is not as strong a force as Cooper and his contemporaries believed; human intention is only one factor in a series of events that involve different bodies, both human and nonhuman.

Orange too wields a kind of power as Woolson asks the reader to think about boundaries between human and nonhuman bodies. Formerly an enslaved person, Orange reminds readers that humans have been systemically treated as objects. Like the mahogany chairs and her namesake fruit, Orange has been relocated through global colonialism from southern climes to the Great Lakes. In the process of becoming enslaved, she "'lost her voice'" (17) and "'seems to have forgotten how to form words'" (17), in Silver's explanation to Waring, but even so Silver believes that Orange understands all, and she hums African dirges and melodies, a corollary to Waring's humming of Shakespearean sonnets. While most of the "things" in the novella are impersonal, stripped of human connection as they are repurposed, she has a red ribbon that has personal connotations since it had belonged to her master. She places that around Waring's neck, and the gesture can be interpreted as a kind of noose that pulls him into the network of the floating castle and the association of her past. Orange cannot speak her wishes, but her presence in the novella is prophetic: like Sil-

ver, she suggests a broader way of thinking about what it means to acknowledge existence in a network that crosses human and nonhuman bodies, material
objects, and things like wishes, commands, or wills. Although her treasured red
ribbon carries personal connotations, they will potentially reinscribe her as an
object rather than construct her as a simple owner of the ribbon.

The most significant moment of Silver's power occurs when Waring realizes
he can no longer resist her attraction. Having left the floating castle a second
time, Waring is injured by falling on the ice and slowly freezing in the intensity
of the winter night with its snow pellets, wind, ice, intense cold, and exposure.
Whereas in the opening scene of the story he spoke of how he wished he were a
tree, or a bear, and in the wrecking scene he mentally acknowledges he is entangled with a world of objects, now he *experiences* what that means as a bodily reality. He confesses to Fog, who finds him, that he was "crawling backwards and
forwards all day to keep myself alive" (43), on all fours, freezing, and confessing
that "it is too strong for me" (44), referring to the attraction or power of Silver,
not the depth of the cold. Since it is at this moment when he recognizes Silver's
power, it is as if she is combined with the ice, wind, snow, and cold that made
him experience his human body in such a different way. Instead of asking once
again "What can I do?," his solution is focused more on his body than his mind.
He seems to accept the limitation of concepts like intention and to understand
that he is materially part of nature, not apart from it.

It is worth returning to the idea of Silver as a being so innocent, so un-
exposed to human conventions, that she does not comprehend death. Such a
claim is unrealistic in nature per se and even in her flower bower, where not
knowing sex or death seems to make her the ultimate artificial being. But in
this tale, "death" does not happen. Bodies, like objects, recirculate. Dead bodies stay in the lake, becoming linked in a material though indirect way to the
forces that drive flotsam to the shore. Were Waring to freeze, his body would
become part of the land, ice, or water. In Woolson's lake, nonhuman bodies are
also transformed. Steamer furniture is used in a dining room or as plant hold-
ers; provisions barreled for sailors are consumed by Silver and Fog. This is an
ecosystem of sorts, one that is non-teleological and refuses to suggest that human will is more powerful than the agency of the nonhuman. In Silver's world,
there is no death as we typically think of it, for all kinds of matter can be transformed, changed, or reconfigured. This is a radical way of rethinking how networks that cross the human and nonhuman might look as they challenge not
only notions of imperial human will but also concepts of life, death, fate, and
purpose.

With these ideas about assemblages, wrecking, and the power of attachment in mind, the challenge in the epigraph from "Castle Nowhere" resonates. If place is space marked by human memory, association, or meaning, Castle Nowhere is indeed no place. Woolson's insistence on revisiting motifs from *The Deerslayer* adds to this disorientation. Her literary allusions function, in a broad sense, like the steamer cabin within the floating castle or Fog's deadly lure: they feel familiar and safe but are, at best, jarringly repurposed and, at worst, misleading. It is not just that Waring—and Woolson's readers—must rethink the glamour of a wilderness sojourn and how it promises to free us from the constraints of being human (i.e., to be a bear! Or a tree!). "Castle Nowhere" makes us recognize that some of the attributes we most associate with the category of human—the capacity to nurture relationships, the adherence to and confidence in a moral code, the acknowledgment of death—are themselves not contained within a human or social realm. Instead, they rely upon the limitations of our capacity to see ourselves as entangled in a world where we are only part of a larger pattern of material change.

NOTES

I am grateful to the Drake University Center for Teaching and Research in the Humanities for their support in developing this project.

1. Stacy Alaimo, *Bodily Natures: Science, Environment, and the Material Self* (Bloomington: Indiana University Press, 2010), 2. For more on the "materialist turn" in environmental humanities and social sciences, see Alaimo, esp. 6–17, and Jane Bennett, *Vibrant Matter: A Political Ecology of Things* (Durham, N.C.: Duke University Press, 2010), xv–xix. For feminist materialism and literature, see, for example, Dewey W. Hall and Jillmarie Murphy, eds., *Gendered Ecologies: New Materialist Interpretations of Women Writers in the Long Nineteenth Century* (Clemson, S.C.: Clemson University Press, 2020).

2. My approach here is deeply informed by the work of Stacy Alaimo and Jane Bennett, and these theoretical approaches go back to those of early philosophers such as Bento de Spinoza and more recent social science theorists such as Bruno Latour, Gilles Deleuze, and Félix Guattari. See, for example, Alaimo, *Bodily Natures* and Bennett, *Vibrant Matter*.

3. James Fenimore Cooper, *The Deerslayer* (New York: Penguin, 1996), 546.

4. For discussion of the Leatherstocking Tales and representation of nature, see, for example, H. Daniel Peck, *A World by Itself: The Pastoral Moment in Cooper's Fiction* (New Haven, Conn.: Yale University Press, 1977); Donald Ringe, *The Pictorial Mode: Space and Time in the Art of Bryant, Irving, and Cooper* (Lexington: University of Kentucky Press, 1971); and Matthew Wynn Sivils, *American Environmental Fiction, 1782–1847* (Burlington, Vt.: Ashgate, 2014), chaps. 4–5.

5. Biographer Anne Boyd Rioux considers Woolson's first two signed publications "tributes to her two favorite places, both still hidden away from the bustle of the mod-

ern world," and writes how Woolson's interest in these places links the power of memory with the detail of realistic observation. Anne Boyd Rioux, *Constance Fenimore Woolson: Portrait of a Lady Novelist* (New York: Norton, 2016), 63, 63–64.

6. Constance Fenimore Woolson, *Castle Nowhere: Lake-Country Sketches* (Ann Arbor: University of Michigan Press, 2004), 1; hereafter cited parenthetically.

7. Several scholars discuss isolation or remoteness as features of "Castle Nowhere." See Victoria Brehm, "Island Fortresses: The Landscape of the Imagination in the Great Lakes Fiction of Constance Fenimore Woolson," *American Literary Realism* 22, no. 3 (1990): 51–66, and Jacqueline Justice, "Landscape of Resistance: Polar Allusion and the Northern Frontier in the Fiction of Constance Fenimore Woolson," *ESQ* 66, no. 3 (2020): 409–44.

8. Later in the text, Waring refers to her as a "pretty piece of wax-work" (41), and other connections to flowers—her "violet" eyes and how she is "pallid as a snow-drop"—not only are conventional but use flowers as figures of speech rather than living things in a real world.

9. Yi-Fu Tuan, *Space and Place: The Perspective of Experience* (Minneapolis: University of Minnesota Press, 1977), 6. Tuan explains space as vast, undifferentiated, and characterized by movement (12), which is apt for Waring's sense of his purpose and location. Place, on the other hand, is identified as a locus of "felt value, where biological needs, such as those for food, water, rest, and procreation, are satisfied" (4). We can add security and shelter to this list of needs. The floating castle's steamer cabin is not a "place" because it is displaced and repurposed, which detracts from the notion of felt value or security.

10. Margot Livesey, "Introduction," in Woolson, *Castle Nowhere*, ix.

Woolson's Cogito

ROWING AS EPISTEMOLOGY

Cheryl B. Torsney

No matter how much the local landscape changed from region to region, continent to continent, water foregrounded Constance Fenimore Woolson's sense of self. She grew up in Cleveland, Ohio, on the banks of Lake Erie and the Cuyahoga River. During her summers, she experienced Otsego Lake in Cooperstown, New York, and Lake Michigan on Mackinac Island. Her travels with her mother led her to write about the Oklawaha, the Ashley and Cooper, the St. Johns, and the Atlantic Ocean. During her adult international peregrinations, she experienced the River Avon, Lake Leman, the waters at Baden-Baden, the Mediterranean Sea, the Tiber River, the Nile, and the canals and lagoons of Venice.

A quintessential child of the Western Reserve, Woolson was taught that her command of water conferred power. For her, rowing was instrumental in identity formation. This physical engagement requires strength, a quick ability to redirect with either hand, and an understanding of nature, both when it is calm and when storms cloud the horizon. It is also rhythmic, musical, and poetic.[1] Her cogito might have been "I row, therefore I am," or, even better, "I row, therefore I can." Rowing provides, in fact, a through line in Woolson's life, letters, poetry, and fiction, serving as a metaphor for writing as well as a strategy for approaching problems, sorting out solutions, and persevering through pain.

The domestic Angel of the House responsible for either being tied to her home and children or preparing for the opportunity was not the only role model for girls of Woolson's era. As an upper-middle-class girl in a growing industrial city, Woolson grew up rowing. A natural outgrowth of Catharine Beecher's promotion of physical education and outdoor leisure activity in her

1820s curricula for girls' schools, rowing came to the Cuyahoga River around 1855 with the advent of several rowing clubs for women and girls. The earliest women's colleges, including Mount Holyoke, alma mater of Woolson's beloved teacher Linda Thayer Guilford, promoted sports for women. Praised for how it "hardened the muscles, strengthened the back, and increased the breathing power of the lungs,"[2] rowing required a female to sport boots, a shorter skirt, hat, and gloves, an appearance that was anathema to the image of the True Woman. By the mid-nineteenth century women competed in rowing competitions, and Ida Lewis, a lighthouse keeper just a few years younger than Woolson, was celebrated, including in *Harper's Weekly*, for her rowing expertise and lifesaving courage.[3]

Woolson's letters confirm her interest in rowing, frequently mentioning the activity in ways that position it as a site for friendship, healthy self-confidence, and at-homeness. In a letter to childhood friend Arabella Carter (later Washburn) circa 1864–65, Woolson writes, "I would challenge you to a row to the Island [Mackinac] this very minute. I presume you would not go, as I fancy we are more particular about our hands than we used to be! If you would not row, you might sit in the stern of my boat—see how good-natured I am."[4] She chides her new friend, Charleston poet and critic Paul Hamilton Hayne, on January 16, 1876, "A person who writes such letters as you can, and with such ease, ought to excuse the friend who cannot do anything of the kind. Come now,—can you skate? Can you walk? Can you row twenty miles in a boat? I can. . . . I have long thought that a good strong dose of self conceit was the best medicine for the creative mind" (61–62). Later that year, Woolson describes her location in Cooperstown, New York, "Otsego Lake is lovely; I have a little row-boat, and can now substitute a row for the long afternoon walks I generally take. Ferns grow here, and some rare varieties of orchids" (71). She discusses the depression, which casts a pall over her entire life, saying, "Tomorrow I am going to row ten miles,—up to the Dugway and back again. There is a small Unknown River up there which I wish to explore for ferns. I should like to take you as a passenger. I never allow any one to row save myself" (75). She rows daily "five or six miles always" (77). By way of introducing herself to Daniel C. Eaton, the famed Yale botany professor, an expert in ferns (another of her passions, which she finds hiking in the woods), she writes, "I am very fond of rowing, and when there [Lake Otsego] I row on the Lake every day" (80).

In the last decade of her life, Woolson wrote to her former school mistress, Linda Guilford, "I am now going out for a long walk, I have been rowing, during the autumn, on the Avon; Shakespeare's Avon. Such a pretty little river, winding among the soft green English fields. Flora Payne and I used to row on the meandering Cayuhoga [sic]. I am afraid we cannot row there now" (555). In her tone we hear a star pupil still currying the favor of the instructor whom she worships. We can imagine Woolson saying, "See? As you taught me, I'm still walking and rowing. I still care about these things you taught me: about exercise and living in nature." She knows that her beloved teacher is likewise appalled that she cannot currently row on the Cuyahoga River, which had caught fire for the first time in 1868 (555n2).

Woolson's poetry also engages rowing. "The Florida Beach," for example, is set at a beach campfire, near "[o]ur boat [which] is drawn far up the strand."[5] The poem presents a rhythmic meditation on sea creatures, beach vegetation, and destiny. The rhythm of rowing, implied by the boat drawn up on the beach, serves as a model for poetic meter. This link between poetry and rowing has not been lost on both literary critics and proficient rowers. For example, Professor H. B. Cotterill, a contemporary of Woolson, writes, "The rhythm of music, and also of verse, is doubtless derived from the rhythm of movement, such as that of marching, dancing, and rowing, in which the chief characteristic is a well-marked beat or stroke recurring after a certain interval."[6] More recently, rhythm has been discussed "as an almost mystical achievement . . . it's often described as the reason you lost a race or had a bad outing." This rowing rhythm, where one feels relaxed, "your oars going in and out of the water on time," also works to describe the habit of successful writing where "you feel relaxed and you move through the transition from power phase to recovery phase without hesitation."[7] Woolson yearned for rowing rhythm, both on the water and where she made her home. It was precisely that rhythm, which she understood so well, that would bring her happiness.

Beyond her letters and poems, rowing appears throughout Woolson's fiction, from her earliest stories to her last novels as a physical, emotional, and moral strategy for identity formation, meditation, and escape. It is her version of Descartes's "Cogito, ergo sum." Rather than "I think, therefore I am," for Woolson it is "I row, therefore I am." During summers spent in the bosom of her beloved Cooper aunts, Woolson often rowed on Otsego Lake. One of her earliest published stories, "A Day of Mystery," is set in a fictional Cooperstown, where the narrator, Janet, and her sister, Eva, on the spur of the moment decide to take a later train for their annual visit to Aunt Penelope "in search of adventure." Janet and Eva rent a rowboat, the Lorelai: "The Lorelai proved worthy of her name, skimming the water lightly under the impulse of our oars, for Eva and I were accomplished oarsmen, and rowed with a long sweep and light, feathery stroke, very different from the short, deep jerks of most young lady-mariners."[8] Janet and Eva, of course, are trained "oarsmen" as opposed to "lady-mariners": they might well have learned the skill at school.

Like the siren after whom their rowboat is named, they are of the water, endowed with power, and in ultimate control. As Béatrice Laurent points out, "[W]ater became gendered at the same time as women were perceived as the natural possessors of, and made to adopt, fluid qualities such as adaptability, or intuitiveness."[9] Despite this gendering of women echoing the tenets of True Womanhood, water is a powerful force, atmospheric as well as environmental, responsible for giving life as well as wreaking havoc and causing death. The story reads like a mystery. The girls row a bit, experience the beauties of nature in summer—descriptions of flowers and such are elaborate—or witness and/or imagine an event on shore, and invent a narrative to explain it. Water is the setting for the narrative and rowing a metaphor for the skillful creation of a story: "long sweep and light, feathery stroke" as opposed to "short, deep jerks." They row out onto the lake "until a point concealed the station-house and severed our connection with reality."[10] The female oarsmen, not "lady-mariners," are in control. They follow "the curves of the beach," revel in nature, take off their shoes and stockings to "let the sun-tempered water ripple over [their] feet," visit a cemetery, observe a picnic complete with Cliquot champagne, move into the realm of myth, discover a long-lost signet ring possibly belonging to a British aristocrat during the American Revolution, among other things, and escape a potential villain.

The story is often classically inflected, featuring Pan and Bacchus. It also alludes to Lorelai, the seductress of German myth associated with the Rhine River. The thread along which these narratives are strung is the rowing expedition—the creation of narrative itself—which causes the girls to be "heated with . . . vigorous exercise."[11] The twenty-first-century reader cannot help but recognize the sexual subtext here: women in a boat named for the mythical seductress and water spirit, exerting "feathery strokes" (as opposed to "short, deep jerks") until they are "heated with our vigorous exercise."[12]

A boy cousin home from college appears for the first time at the very end of the story, explaining Janet's and Eva's adventures in Wonderland in a straightforward "Postscriptum: Eva's Narrative." He undermines the women's command of their rowboat adventure narrative by providing quotidian explanations for each fascinating episode of their adventure. He believes that "prosaic reality was all that was left for us, and that the increase of knowledge had banished romance, which was another name for ignorance." Janet labels him, however, "a rude utilitarian, a living Gradgrind" (292). He dismisses their story by explaining, for example, that the Lorelai was named by "a sentimental chap"

Figure 1. Alfred Fredericks, "'Loose your hold, or I will strike.'" Woolson,
"Lily and Diamond," *Appletons' Journal*, November 2, 1872, 477. Wood engraving.
Courtesy of the HathiTrust.

"after some German song."[13] One by one, he pulls the curtain back on the
events the women have witnessed, turning the tale of adventure into simple reportage. Even his college, absurdly named Learnington, suggests a lack of imagination so valued by Janet and Eva. The women row and make meaning. The
male cousin strips the narrative of magic even as he misses the mythical meaning of Lorelai.

Another of Woolson's earliest stories, "Lily and Diamond," features two
women, one light and one dark, wrangling over two men, one rich and one
poor.[14] Again, a rowboat, the physical representation of the action of rowing,
becomes a setting for struggle. The accompanying illustration (figure 1) depicts
Dakota Weston and Eleanor Rarne lakeside, with the blonde "Kota" standing in a rowboat, an oar raised above her head to challenge the darker young
widow, whose hands are on the rowboat's bow.

Both here and elsewhere in Woolson's fiction rowing requires muscular-
ity and physicality that provide women with methods for coping with a world
that may seem to undervalue their strength. The blonde beauty rows out to
rescue a poor lawyer: "[T]he lake was like a dark mirror, and out in the west
a mass of black clouds, and a white line on the water, showed the incoming
squall."[15] Although she had been presumed to be a mere flirty young woman

prospecting for a rich husband, her rowing technique suggests solid values and both metaphoric and physical strength, both of which contribute to her beauty: "Dakota bent to her oars. She rowed well, with a long stroke and practised dip, and the muscles on her rounded arms, and her vigorous physique, did good service. She was a skilled oarswoman."[16] Although the reader immediately takes a dislike to her for her love of diamonds and her desire to find a wealthy husband, she shows her true colors when she launches the skiff to rescue John Vinton. Like the reader, Vinton confesses that he had believed her to be seeking someone rich to marry. Kota responds, "How dared you weigh love against money? How could you so mistake me? Didn't you know that, if I loved you, I would rather have your love than all the rest of the world?"[17] Her muscular mastery of the oars, especially in the face of danger, signals to the reader and to Vinton that Kota is, in fact, a serious and accomplished woman, like the writer of the story in which she appears.

In the climax of Woolson's first novel, *Anne* (1882), the heroine borrows a rowboat and pursues the real murderer of her friend, Helen Heathcote, thus getting her lover, Captain Heathcote, released from a murder charge. Rowing for her is a completely natural activity, part of her past as a meditative strategy that allows time and perspective to sort out the riddle of her friend's murder. Day after day she rows to entrap the real murderer and "to calm her excited fancies."[18] Upon validating her suspicion that a local fisherman is the real murderer, she "rowed round the curve out of sight, trying not to betray her tremulous haste and fear. All the way home she rowed with the strength of a giantess, not knowing how she was exerting herself."[19] One of Charles Stanley Reinhart's twenty-eight illustrations for the first edition of *Anne* in 1882 depicts the climactic moment (figure 2) when the two women in the skiff that Anne rows spot the murderer fishing.[20]

Boats and canoes also figure importantly in the various subplots of intrigue in *East Angels* (1886), set in Florida. Lanse Harold pilots one; Everett Winthrop rows and paddles; and when Lanse disappears in the swamp, heroine Margaret urges Winthrop to take a boat to search in the Monnlungs swamp for her husband, who visits the swamp daily: "'I have followed in the larger boat with one of the men to row.'"[21] Since she is the only one who knows the way and is not afraid of the swamp at night, she takes complete control over the rescue operation. Alligators, which Woolson understood inhabited the local waters, are a concern. Margaret confesses that she wishes she could go herself but that "'I cannot paddle well.'"[22] Throughout the operation, she bravely navigates: "Her nervousness had disappeared; either she had been able to repress it, or it had faded in the presence of the responsibility

Figure 2. Charles S. Reinhart, "The second boat, which was farther up the lake, contained
a man." Woolson, *Anne* (New York: Harper & Brothers, 1882), facing p. 514.
Wood engraving. Courtesy of the HathiTrust.

she had assumed in undertaking to act as guide through that strange water-
land of the Monnlungs, whose winding channels she had heretofore seen
only in the light of day."[23] As she and Everett grow discouraged, Everett suc-
cumbs to the air of the swamp. Margaret, however, wets her lace scarf, wraps
it around his head, and so assists in his recovery. When she volunteers to
paddle, Winthrop pushes her hands away saying, "'Women never know.'"[24]
When they are out of the swamp, Winthrop complains, tells Margaret that
she does not understand how hard it was for him, and then, in a moment of
perfect irony, calls her childish.

Woolson, an expert rower, is clearly Margaret's champion, and many have
argued that this woman without an oar is a Woolson stand-in. The reader
likes Winthrop less for patronizing Margaret, who may or may not know
how to row but who is more familiar than anyone else in the narrative with
the quality of boats—she knows "the best"[25]—and the directions in and out
of the swamp. I would argue that Margaret's acquiescence to not rowing—
her refusal to demonstrate herself as capable—further supports Katherine
Swett's assertion that the novel is "a detailed psychological exploration of
the silencing of Corinne,"[26] the archetypal female artist created by Mme.

Germaine de Staël in the early nineteenth century whose gender-defying talent and ambition are revisited by Woolson in "At the Château of Corinne" (1887).

As *Jupiter Lights* (1889) begins, Cicely Abercrombie Morrison, the newly widowed yet recently remarried mother of young Jack, is embroiled in a struggle with her dead husband's sister, Eve, over the guardianship of Cicely's son, Jack. Chapter 5 opens with Eve's incredulous response to an unheard question: "'Out rowing? If you are doing it to entertain me. . . .'"[27] The reader learns that Cicely has likely asked whether Eve would like to go out rowing, one of their few shared pastimes: "The voyages in the row-boat had been many; they had helped to fill the days, and the sisters-in-law had had not much else with which to fill them. . . . They had floated many times through the salt marshes between the rattling reeds. . . . Sometimes they went inland up the river, rowing slowly against the current; sometimes, when it was calm, they went out to sea."[28] Eve, of necessity, learns to row, enabling her, Cicely, and baby Jack to escape from the murderous Ferdinand. "'Row hard; tire yourself'" is the sage advice Cicely offers Eve as a strategy to calm her.[29] Here, rowing is a lifesaving skill in more ways than one: it serves not only as a focusing mechanism but also as a safety vehicle. It provides experience transporting oneself bravely into unfamiliar spaces, both physical and metaphysical; practicing perseverance in moving against the current; and also establishing and maintaining balance, peace, and calm. Woolson's use of rowing testifies to her unrelenting belief in her own power to persevere. Her repeated return to this experience confirms her belief that rowing hard not only exercises one's muscles but also conquers obstacles posed by gendered social expectations.

In Woolson's letters, poetry, and fiction, then, rowing is an encompassing metaphor, or, better yet, an epistemology, a way of knowing, deeply connected with eros, adventure, struggle, meditation and wellness, achievement, entertainment, and safety. It is also daring, muscular, masculine—qualities that undermine nineteenth-century notions of appropriate female behavior described in Barbara Welter's canonical "The Cult of True Womanhood."[30] Women who rowed, like Woolson, must have run afoul of the ideology of domesticity and its overvaluing of piety, purity, and submission. Indeed, times were changing: forces in the nineteenth century would press for women's suffrage and other ways to liberate women from the norms shackling their participation in the public sphere. Still, women like Woolson, born in the 1840s, understood that to row they had to be strong, flexible managers of their own paths through life and death if for nothing other than their own sanity.

As Woolson aged, rowing was highlighted as an enduring feature of her life.

When her girlhood friend Flora Payne Whitney died in February 1893, just a year before her own death, Woolson wrote to share memories with her widower: "I prized also the afternoons when we went out rowing together in a little boat I then had" (502). The month before she died in Venice, she told her nephew Samuel Mather that she had "learned to row gondolier fashion, as that is a good way to get exercise here" (535), highlighting that even as she struggled with increasing deafness and depression, rowing was her solace.

Woolson was born on March 5, 1840, under the sign of Pisces, a water sign and the last of the zodiac's constellations. Its symbol is two fish swimming in opposite directions. While astrology is not science and we have no evidence that Woolson followed its increasing popularity, which began during the last quarter of the nineteenth century in England, it is nonetheless interesting to speculate on the relationship between her sign and her life.[31] Those born under the sign of Pisces are characterized as sensitive, sympathetic, creative, and spiritual. It is said that the fish swimming in opposite directions suggest the push and pull between reality and fantasy. Rowing, with its reach and pull backward in order to move forward, would be the perfect meditative exercise, especially for a Pisces, to craft an identity and to engage with the world.

As one who embodied the sensitivity and imagination popular astrology attributed to those born in March, Woolson was deeply concerned about her health. And for good reason. Three of her older sisters had died of scarlet fever when her parents lived in New Hampshire before moving to Cleveland. Two others died as young adults. Her family was plagued by depression. Evidence suggests that both she and her brother, Charley, suffered from it as their father had. Charles Jarvis Woolson's depression was exacerbated by financial reversals caused, in part, by embezzlement perpetrated by his business partner. Constance also grew deaf as she grew older, isolating her further from the world. Her writing helped to keep her sane, but so did exercise, specifically rowing. There was no rest cure for her.

When her health began to fail in Venice, she was rowed on the canals by her adored gondolier, Angelo Fusato, John Addington Symonds's lover. Anne Boyd Rioux's biography, *Constance Fenimore Woolson: Portrait of a Lady Novelist*, describes all the health challenges of Woolson's last days and argues that Woolson thought about taking her own life.[32] She was short of funds, had experienced a recent bout of influenza, was increasingly deaf and depressed as well as lonely, had not gotten much relief from prescribed morphine, and was probably suffering from cholecystitis or gallbladder inflammation, as Rioux documents.[33]

Much has been written about Woolson's fall from her third-story window at the Casa Semitecolo. Scholars now believe her defenestration was intentional, not accidental, given the height of the windowsill. I believe that falling from the window was planned but that landing on the pavement was undoubtedly a grave error: she was aiming for the canal. For a child of the Cuyahoga devoted to rowing, abandoning her Pisces-born body to water, the site of so many of her positive and powerful connections in life—to rivers and lakes on several continents and to her beloved form of exercise and her most original statement of self—would have been blissfully akin to "rowing in Eden," to borrow Emily Dickinson's language.

Woolson was an athlete well over a hundred years before the 1972 passage of Title IX, which allowed women to participate in organized athletics in schools. She recognized the mental health properties of walking in the woods and rowing on water well in advance of the current focus on wellness that has been underscored by the COVID-19 pandemic. She moved abroad permanently, as have several contributors to this volume. Many of us read Woolson because we recognize her in ourselves. Our cogito may be "I read Woolson, therefore I am." As readers continue to discover her writing or rediscover in Woolson a mentally and physically strong role model, they increasingly recognize her as our contemporary.

NOTES

1. Jonna K. Vuoskoski and Dee Reynolds, "Music, Rowing, and the Aesthetics of Rhythm," *Senses and Society* 14, no. 1 (March 2019): 1–14.

2. Patricia A. Vertinsky, "Stereotypes of Aging Women and Exercise: A Historical Perspective," *Journal of Aging and Physical Activity* 5, no. 3 (July 1995): 223–37, cited in Andréa Riesch Toepell, Ann Marie Guilmette, and Stephanie Brooks, "Women in Masters Rowing: Exploring Healthy Aging," *Women's Health and Urban Life* 3, no. 1 (2004): 74–95, https://tspace.library.utoronto.ca/retrieve/2334/Womens_Health_Women_in_masters_rowing.pdf.

3. Leone Skomal, *Lighthouse Keeper's Daughter: The Remarkable True Story of American Heroine Ida Lewis* (Lanham, Md.: Rowman & Littlefield, 2010).

4. Sharon L. Dean, ed., *The Complete Letters of Constance Fenimore Woolson* (Gainesville: University Press of Florida, 2012), 3; hereafter cited parenthetically.

5. Constance Fenimore Woolson, "The Florida Beach," *Galaxy*, October 1874, 482–83.

6. H. B. Cotterill, *Milton's Lycidas* (London: Blackie and Son, 1902).

7. "Rhythm in Rowing," *Faster Masters Rowing* (2024), Creative Agency Secrets Limited, https://fastermastersrowing.com/rhythm-in-rowing/.

8. Constance Fenimore Woolson, "A Day of Mystery," *Appletons' Journal*, September 9, 1871, 290.

9. Béatrice Laurent, *Water and Women in the Victorian Imagination* (New York: Peter Lang, 2021), 1.

10. Woolson, "Day of Mystery," 290.

11. Woolson, 291.

12. Woolson, 291.

13. Woolson, 292.

14. Constance Fenimore Woolson, "Lily and Diamond," *Appletons' Journal*, November 2, 1872, 477–83.

15. Woolson, 481.

16. Woolson, 481.

17. Woolson, 482.

18. Constance Fenimore Woolson, *Anne* (New York: Harper & Brothers, 1882), 518.

19. Woolson, 519.

20. Woolson, 515.

21. Constance Fenimore Woolson, *East Angels* (New York: Harper & Brothers, 1886), 463.

22. Woolson, 465.

23. Woolson, 466.

24. Woolson, 478.

25. Woolson, 464.

26. Katherine Swett, "Corinne Silenced: Improper Places in the Narrative Form of Constance Fenimore Woolson's *East Angels*," in *Constance Fenimore Woolson's Nineteenth Century: Essays*, ed. Victoria Brehm (Detroit, Mich.: Wayne State University Press, 2001), 163.

27. Constance Fenimore Woolson, *Jupiter Lights* (New York: Harper & Brothers, 1889), 42.

28. Woolson, 44–45.

29. Woolson, 297.

30. Barbara Welter, "The Cult of True Womanhood: 1820–1860," *American Quarterly* 18, no. 2, pt. 1 (Summer 1966): 151–74.

31. See Library of Congress, "Zodiac Craze: Topics in Chronicling America" (n.d.), https://guides.loc.gov/chronicling-america-zodiac-craze/introduction.

32. Anne Boyd Rioux, *Constance Fenimore Woolson: Portrait of a Lady Novelist* (New York: Norton, 2016), 308.

33. Rioux, 300–301.

Anne as Western-Border Mongrelosity

Kathleen Diffley

Woolson's first major novel is a story of the Civil War, one whose episodic structure ought to suggest a nation coming apart at the seams. Serialized in *Harper's Monthly* beginning in December 1880 and published by Harper & Brothers shortly after installments ended in May 1882, the bildungsroman falls informally into several sections, a series of place-bound social portraits that also assume the shape of fictional experiments. The novel opens on antebellum Mackinac when the frontier island was backwater poor, caught between the decline of Michigan's fur trade and the postwar tourist boom yet to come. As Anne Douglas grows older, that island sketch turns into a study of manners at a well-heeled Manhattan school for girls and later a country resort. The novel's second half chronicles the war's outbreak, and fictional events are initially punctuated by the war's early clashes—at Bull Run during the summer of 1861, at Fort Donelson and Shiloh church during the spring of 1862, near Richmond for the seven days of fighting during June and July. In what becomes a tale of national adventure, Anne volunteers to nurse the wounded in mountainous western Virginia before she collides in the fourth section with murder in a Pennsylvania hamlet, where her declaration of love upends a scandalous trial. For almost all reviewers during the 1880s, the local details of these sections and the book's geographical scope are insistent. As the *Atlantic Monthly* put it, Woolson composed this early book "somewhat as one might paint a panorama," most often a series of separate sketches.[1] In that sense, the novel's sharply divided sections should epitomize a nation sharply divided by sectional war.

But *Anne* only nods in passing to the South. The mountains of western Virginia had become by 1863 the mountains of West Virginia and thus a northern state, which was constitutionally committed to emancipating the enslaved well in advance of the novel's first installment. The mysterious murder is set on the Maryland-Pennsylvania border and therefore on the Mason-Dixon Line, but nothing is made of later battles at Antietam and Gettysburg; instead, the fourth section invites a greater sense of borderland, particularly on the edge of Maryland as a wartime border state. Significantly, the novel's arc does not run from north to south, as wartime sectionalism would require, but from west to east and back again, with several arresting consequences. As consecutive social-cum-fictional experiments, *Anne* becomes a series of grafts, East spliced to West, upheaval to reckoning, Civil War to Reconstruction. In addition, its geographical sprawl is repeatedly tied to effective national networks beginning with rail lines, postal routes, and newspaper circulation, networks that Woolson makes so organic they almost throb. Against their keen sense of connectedness, the novel nonetheless foregrounds islands in the stream, most noticeably in shuttling between Mackinac and Manhattan. Yet *Anne* is finally intent not on contrasting Eden and the modern but on examining inclusion and exclusion as competing reconstructive models, whose converging dramas deliver Woolson's heroine to a fictional climax and a national choice.

Organizing a female bildungsroman so that the outbreak of civil crisis is anticipated in an episodic structure was a considerable risk, especially for a young novelist who had built her reputation through shorter fiction. Indeed, the *Outing* saw Woolson's plot as "somewhat complicated,—composed of several parts, each of which might have been the foundation of a novel," as well as a tribute to place.[2] The *Californian* worried that the whole never coalesces, that *Anne* leaves "an impression of ability not yet fully under control" amid perpetually shifting perspectives.[3] *Lippincott's* also complained about the "disjointed" result with "so many incidents that the impression left upon the mind is rather fragmentary," particularly when formal coherence was "confused" by endless proliferation.[4] Certainly the novel's dramatis personae burgeons. At Mackinac, for instance, the Catholic priest Père Michaux collects the arrowheads, pottery shards, and fossil fragments that together tell the story of Mackinac's past as a welcome "relief" from the present,[5] while the Protestant parson stumbles through one domestic servant after another like Mistress McGlathery, a widow with wobbly health but strong opinions. At the New York resort, the socially indolent are joined by an itinerant reverend who knows rare orchids in the wild and by a country miss who sets her bonnet for an urban dandy. Even in the small depots through which *Anne* then passes, Woolson makes a byway spectacle of the train boy, the peanut vendor, the brakeman, the baggage porter, the "pallid" telegraph operator, and the melancholic conductor paring an apple

(302). While her novel's internal logic favors both a nation's risk and a storyteller's invention, readers as spectators can easily feel bombarded.

For that reason, the *Atlantic Monthly*'s nod to a painted "panorama" is intriguing, hinting as it does at a contemporary entertainment that would convert this book's seeming faults into this period's familiar practices. A newly minted term in 1792, "panorama" derived from the Greek for "all seeing," initially a vast prospect that Angela Miller describes as "a 360 degree painting taken from an elevated vantage point and allowing a visual survey that extended from the fore- or middleground to the distant horizon."[6] With a scenic plentitude that captivated the eye, outsized panoramic canvases bound together grew in popularity across the nineteenth century, ultimately in mesmerizing displays that were well attended by the curious of all classes. In Britain and on the Continent, as Stephan Oettermann has documented, the earliest panoramas were urban views, landscape vistas, and battle scenes that required customized exhibition spaces such as London's Leicester Square rotunda in 1794, two linked rotundas in Paris on the Boulevard Montmartre in 1800, and New York's Broadway rotunda in 1804. There, a multipaneled canvas could be mounted to create the "perfect illusion" in an immersive circular display.[7] As Wendy Bellion has demonstrated, the new art form took a peculiarly American hold when Charles Willson Peale stepped onto the balustrade of the Maryland State House dome in 1788 and sketched eight separate views of Annapolis, a sequence that could be reassembled in a circular print. "That year," Bellion writes, "marked the successful culmination of months of campaigning by Federalist writers urging Americans to imagine their new republic in the shape of a circle and to 'extend its sphere' of representation by adopting the federal Constitution."[8] While Peale's print never materialized, the American hunger for panoramic displays soon did.

Especially successful in the United States were moving panoramas that unrolled from one outsized cylinder to another in a darkened public hall, thereby trading costly rotundas for itinerant exhibits that were readily portable, easy to install, and comparatively inexpensive by the 1840s. Set to music and featuring Miller's "peripatetic showman" as narrator, moving panoramas of the Hudson, the Ohio, and especially the Mississippi of John Banvard's "three-mile" extravaganza (1846–63) translated artistic panels and episodic scenes into the prepared narrative of a new nation on the move.[9] "Frame by frame," Susan Tenneriello declares, "the scenic text, like the creation of the panorama itself, convey[ed] a never-ending campaign to fashion the diverse character of the people and the prosperity of the land into the perpetual motion of nationhood."[10] Ubiquitous by midcentury, the moving panorama offers an unusual apparatus for reading

Figure 3. Pavel Yakolevich Pyasetsky, demonstrating his panorama of the Trans-Caspian Railway at a public lecture in Saint Petersburg. *Niva* (Field), March 1895, 68. Wood engraving. Courtesy of https://runivers.ru/contact/.

Woolson's *Anne*, less as a direct writerly influence than as an available readerly lens. With its carefully sketched places, ever-shifting perspectives, multiplying figures in a consolidating nation, and boundless sweep immersing spectators as the canvas spooled, the moving panorama capitalized on "several parts" and "so many incidents" to become less "disjointed" than audience-tested, an invitation to see distant places that would appeal as far away as Russia (figure 3) and as far forward as the "Universal Exposition" or World's Fair staged by Paris in 1900.[11] Mapping the midcentury United States through a distinctly female education, Woolson's bildungsroman then transforms the appeal of the panorama into peopled places, two-way traffic, a new social politics, and a measured reexamination of local "color" in a darker hue, a reexamination that pays less attention to disunion than to connection and national growth.

Western-Border Mongrelosity

Mackinac Island was historically a trading center where goods, cultures, religions, and peoples mingled. Although Anne's family has been fractured by the death of her mother years before, Dr. William Douglas soon resigned his position as army surgeon at the island's fort and married a beautiful French Indian woman. When the novel begins, Anne's half family has long been managed by Miss Lois, a New Englander who objects to the rash behaviors of the frontier and the "Western-border mongrelosities" this novel will champion (27). For Woolson, Mackinac is a place of racial mixing, of inclusive multiplicity in the blood tied to the island's social mélange of old fur company families, army wives, German soldiers, Scotch clerks, French fiddlers, Irish servants, and the "guttural" Chippewa (32). Harper editor Henry Mills Alden found these exotic pages "novel and fascinating," and James Herbert Morse praised their "fresh material, got at first hand," while the *Century Illustrated* commented on the "curious mixed society" Woolson limns.[12] With the careful eye and skillful hand of a panorama artist, she deploys a method strikingly similar to the techniques that Curtis Dahl has seen Twain absorb from the moving panoramas of his boyhood, a method that was "accurate, explanatory, and anecdotal."[13] Rather than tightly thematic, as Dahl has shown, a succession of local pictures had an alternate logic: "Rich variety was a merit; digression was a virtue" when place superseded "escapades."[14] It is therefore worth examining the moving picture in Woolson's opening paragraph.

It is Christmas Eve in the island's small chapel, whose walls Anne has decorated with evergreens for the winter holidays. Lifting garland after garland, she has woven a "thread-like green lace-work" (3), but she must now find a place for an ill-conceived wreath made by Miss Lois. On this frigid December evening, her father (now a double widower) sits at the chapel's organ, while Anne is perched high on a ladder. When darkness comes suddenly, they will leave for home and the festivities of Anne's half family, three clamorous boys and her half sister Tita, who is thirteen to Anne's sixteen. In the last rays of the sun setting through the chapel's west windows, as the fort's bugle sounds to the east, Anne places the wreath above the altar and thereby anchors so many garland chains.

Winter boughs and chapel walls, the setting sun and the fort's bugle combine to lend the novel's first scene both regional appeal and national stature. Anne herself is described as "a young Diana" built "big" (2–3), and she is tasked in the novel with delivering western sanctuary to an ailing nation. That she needs the intellectual engagement the East provides is underlined by Woolson's chapter epigraphs, which come from Longfellow, Emerson, Hawthorne, and Thoreau as well as Chaucer and Shakespeare, Wordsworth and Scott, Carlyle and Tennyson, to suggest a literary scene that reaches epigraphically still further east to Turgenev and Saadi, a Persian poet and storyteller of the twelfth and thirteenth centuries. Anne must negotiate that expansive intellectual territory through grafting, a cultural fusion that has already begun at Mackinac when

her Saxon name is converted through the affectionate patois of her French Indian half brothers into "Annet." Both western place and eastern aspiration are
thus figured in her name, as though a "peripatetic showman" had captured the
panorama's expansiveness in a single revealing episode. And yet the island is
also home to an "upper circle" (34), a "crowd of Indians" (37), and between
them a "motley assemblage" (36) as well as the calculating theatricality of Tita
and her plan to elope with Anne's childhood sweetheart. If Mackinac is finally
an Eden already unraveling, New York will be a Dutch enclave already on the
wrong side of history, a place in which the "motley assemblage" was beginning
to stretch its commercial sinews.

Of Arms and the Women

The Manhattan boarding school where Anne arrives at seventeen is a place in
which her intellectual ambitions expand alongside an idiosyncratic cast. As the
Independent put it, "Miss Woolson's metropolitans are neither copies nor commonplace."[15] The Italian singing master who is "fat, rosy, and smiling" (152),
the German music master with the "little gold rings in his ears" (155), the in-
structors in drawing and dancing as well as the "old and soiled" teacher of Italian (152) guarantee Anne's formal education in return for a winter's tuition paid
grudgingly by her Grandaunt Vanhorne. At the school of Mme. Moreau, the
"solid old customs" of Dutch New York are also invoked, even on New Year's
Day, as "a barrier, sir—a barrier against modern innovation!" (167). The more
intricate social lessons that are equally essential Anne soon learns upriver at
Caryl's, a secluded tourist resort where schoolgirl and grandaunt travel for
summer lounging, verandah romancing, garden strolling, and occasional ven-
turing into a Catskill countryside made famous by James Fenimore Cooper. Instead of providing well-maintained corridors overseen by an elite staff, which
Dona Brown attributes to the Catskill Mountain House and the resplendent
hotels that followed its grand opening in 1824, Caryl's has been a "stage inn"
or "'tarvern'" on the old post road (192). When the railroads replaced post rid-
ers, Caryl's found itself on a road to nowhere beside a ruined bridge, Woolson's
covert hint at a declining Dutch culture despite its continuing Knickerbocker
clout. As Brown puts it, "[T]he word 'inn' implied uses deeply embedded in
tradition, while the word 'hotel' implied a new sort of market transaction."[16] In
next to no time, however, Anne's party of leisured picnickers stumbles into real
danger, as an unanticipated moving picture unrolls.
    While dancing fetchingly on the rim of an abandoned quarry, the group's
young women see the country miss eyeing her dandy slip over the edge, barely

catching herself on the stump of a cedar sapling. With the men some sixty feet below but on the run, Anne reaches down to grab the girl's wrist as the interrupted dancers form a chain of arms. Handmade and hurried, the female chain helps rescue the terrified Miss Morle from a quarry world, which is suddenly unpicturesque. Brief as this perilous moment proves to be, the picture of joined arms lingers and could stand in for the hinterland appeal of the Catskills, figured in the rootedness of the trees to which the girls cling, the engaging charm of their dance to the harp of a wandering musician, and the morning's lure of a rare orchid so far from the avenues of Manhattan. For the visitors, the girlish chain bespeaks the long arm of Manhattan's prospering trade and the widening appeal of Cooper country, where Hudson River painters had for decades been codifying an American wilderness for city patrons.

Yet just as importantly in Woolson's novel, the panorama's expansionist agenda includes the sure grip of the ambitious Miss Morle. Woolson's moving picture resurrects the Catskill quarry, its commercial channels, and the network of rail connections that enable traffic up and down the Hudson and beyond, two-way traffic that links Caryl's to a much wider world and proves steady enough to rescue an imperiled rural economy. Advancing a cooperative model, which joins the scope of the global to the smack of the local, Woolson's novel tempers the Hudson River School's "wilderness" with Catskill industry, the necessary labor of peanut vendors and baggage porters and melancholic conductors, as well as the arms of girls (later women) who know how to use trees and chains, half houses and railroad schedules, inns and waterway outings for purposes of their own.

In *Anne*, the most pastoral scenes are often touched by industry's imprint on the mountains. Woolson alludes, for instance, to the tanneries that became a major industrial enterprise in the Catskills after 1816, thanks to the broad stretches of hemlock that could be stripped for the tannin in which uncured hides from the Caribbean, South America, and California had to soak, a process to which the once clear streams of the mountains also contributed. But where painted tree stumps could insinuate wilderness dismay at imperial intrusion, Woolson gives Anne's beau Heathcote a summer hat with a "Brazilian" lining, a hat he uses to screen a tearful Anne from wandering piazza eyes. Here in passing, tanned South American leather is put to use rather than disdained, much like the mountain roads that tanneries built and tourists inherited. Woolson references global networks of supply and demand—for example, by setting her moving picture in the bluestone quarry that a dying industry left behind. Her Catskill scenes also include a host of enterprising laborers: the sawmiller and his family, the itinerant harpist with his Italian boy and monkey, the stationmaster Hosy Plim and his wife's cousin Mirandy, who works at Caryl's. As historian William Cronon observes, "It was not just that wealthy tourists, artists, and intellectuals spent so much time and money in the Catskills; it was that local residents found their own economic opportunities shaped by these urban visitors and also influenced by the demands of nearby urban markets."[17] Put another way, the long arm of a metropolitan entrepôt like Manhattan meets in *Anne* the strong grip of the precarious Miss Morle and all her Morleville kin.

In the novel's perpetual economic negotiations, it is significant that several national networks remain open and effective, beginning with the expanding reach of rail lines. When Tita elopes with Anne's island sweetheart, for instance, they board a mail train, a reminder that railroads were laying new tracks before the Civil War. Indeed, Wolfgang Schivelbusch has emphasized "the American notion of steam power as the force that joined the parts of the country into a living nation."[18] Woolson's attention to the country's elaborate array of lines is perhaps most acute in this section when she describes the annual trek west of a commuting New Jersey teacher, who is both very deft and very French in devising economies. "The remainder of the continent was an unknown wilderness in her mind," Woolson writes, "but these lines of rails, over which she was obliged to purchase her way year after year, she understood thoroughly" (300). A stricken Anne learns that same genius well enough to elude Heathcote on a small branch line out of Stringhampton Junction, a testament to the country's growing rail network, to the possibility that the tangle of trunk lines and their branches could be mapped, and to this novel's structural certainty that the railroads were a nationalizing agent, a panoramic path, and an escape route west for a girl whose insouciant young man has become engaged to her best friend. As Anne and Heathcote both travel up and down the Hudson, which Whitman called an "unrivall'd panorama,"[19] Woolson's first readers were likely to notice the trains that always run on time. But where Anne's education is nurtured across widening markets and a growing transportation web, so too was the rise of sectional unrest.

The Lightning Flash of War, the Thunderbolt of Emancipation

In one of the most neglected segments of Woolson's novel, Anne responds to the klaxon of Civil War by volunteering in "Weston" at the local Aid Society, which soon accepts her offer to relocate as a temporary nurse. During the late summer of 1861, her wartime contributions in the field are brief enough to require just four chapters but long enough to see Anne through several reassignments: first to a regimental hospital in the western Virginia hills, then to a barn called Hospital Number Two closer to the war's early fighting, on to "a sorter hospital" at Peterson's Mill far up in the mountains (366), and finally to a farmhouse across a mountain spur, a spot so isolated that it is less regional than remote. Separated from everything except the war's relentless skirmishing, the new nurse learns of a feverish Captain Heathcote and the novel takes a turn.

The fate of Anne and her wayward lover may owe less to these peculiar circumstances, however, than to three soon forgotten characters: a dead Union soldier in a mountain ravine and the Black couple, July and Diana, who bury him. The moving picture of their few moments graveside is short lived, and yet the key to the novel's improbable developments, its peculiar structure, and its metaphoric reconstruction of a postwar nation arguably lies in the mountain recesses that saw the Civil War's earliest guerrilla attacks. No wonder the dead man is described as "an isolated soldier taken off by a bullet from behind a tree" (382). After Anne discovers him and leaves to share the news, July and Diana return, he and two others to lower the body into a leaf-lined grave, she on her knees to offer what he calls "'a powerfu' prayer'" (390). In Woolson's hands, the Black couple approximate the pre- and post-emancipation contrast that regularly appeared in wartime periodicals. The result, Alice Fahs argues in *The Imagined Civil War*, was "a doubled consciousness of African Americans as both slave and free, rooted both in the past and in the future."[20] Where July is large and high-spirited, Diana is lean and short on words, though she is often heard "chanting" Baptist hymns as she hangs out hospital laundry (373). *Anne* effectively recasts past and future as his stereotype and her idiosyncrasy. She is a figure of industry, a reminder of the more than two thousand Black laundresses whose wartime labor Jane Schultz has detailed in *Women at the Front*.[21] Because she and July "balance" one another in Woolson's diptych (373), it takes both of them to bury the Michigan soldier, a shared responsibility that recalls both Black families on the road and Black regiments on the battlefield once emancipation was proclaimed.

It is also instructive that Anne's fitful romance makes unforeseen headway on the evening of these graveside rituals. Spurred by Heathcote's hasty lie that he is unwed, Anne privately admits her love in "an outburst of happiness" (388), the language of an emancipated heart. From their past obligations to others, she and Heathcote are seemingly "released" (389), the New York "idler" (388) made momentarily strong by the embrace of the "vivid" West (391) as a panoramic future shimmers. From a burgeoning cast to their shifting perspectives and then to finding commonalities among diverse characters as Woolson's postwar nation mends, her novel is consistent with "the romantic, picturesque tradition" that Robert Carothers and John Marsh see governing panoramic display as well as the scenes of whale harvesting in Herman Melville's *Moby-Dick* (1851).[22] More than that, Fahs has noted the "new white freedoms" that "black emancipation" produced.[23] In *Anne*, the example set by July and Diana in the shaded ravine releases a series of white self-emancipations, starting with Anne's full-hearted declaration and Heathcote's reluctant confession that he has actually married Helen Roosbroeck Lorrington.

As the prospects of Woolson's principals fall apart once again, it is striking that yet another national network she invokes does not. The U.S. postal system had been serving the republic since its early days as the long arm of federal intervention. "No other branch of the central government," observed Richard John, "penetrated so deeply into the hinterland or played such a conspicuous role in shaping the pattern of everyday life."[24] In Woolson's novel, letters appear ahead of time and replies come early, even across the Mackinac ice. Anne arrives in Manhattan after being handed from lake boat to rail car by one Catholic priest after another, thanks to Père Michaux's large circle of correspondents. Farther west, Anne's final letter to her eloping island sweetheart repeatedly misses him to end up at the Dead Letter Office, but its folded pages are then returned to her. In the "defiles" of western Virginia (371), boxes from northern aid societies routinely reach scattered mountain hospitals. Even the dead Michigan soldier has pocketed a letter from his mother with her full name and distant village address, the very information a nurse needs to share sad news. In apparently disparate scenes, much like those of moving panoramas, *Anne* confirms the entertaining genre's guarantee: that no matter how protracted the process and how numerous its details, destinations will always be reached. But in Woolson's novel, the grafting begun in the Michigan West will beckon again only after Heathcote is arrested for murdering his wife.

Trial by Newspaper

In the book's last major sequences, rural Pennsylvania becomes the scene of Helen's nighttime murder and the theft of her jewels. Blame falls upon her husband as newspaper reporters converge on tiny Timloesville, their big-city muscle recalling the nationalizing networks of train and post that suture Woolson's sprawling novel. Seamlessly in their turn, the New York dailies provide the telegraphic summaries that keep Anne informed about Heathcote's trial, just as the railroad delivers a helpful Miss Lois from Mackinac and the post brings a willing Père Michaux in record time. But correctly discerning guilt in Pennsylvania amounts instead to tracking the tug of the local, thanks to three unusual developments. In the first of these, Anne abandons interviewing every visitor to Timloesville as a careful investigator might to work instead through instinct and a rented skiff. Even more unexpectedly, the local murderer she exposes is feral, brutish, and Catholic, nothing like the cosmopolitan Heathcote who is just passing through. Most unpredictably, Père Michaux rescues the misshapen criminal through the personal care and moral responsibility fostered by the fishers of men. In this fourth section, Woolson's reliance on the kindness of strangers taps more than efficient networks to draw together a county and a country shaken by violence.

Already, the footloose Anne has discovered significant information from newspaper reports: her aging and moneyed grandaunt has died in Switzerland (361–62), Captain Heathcote has returned to the front (435), and he has been killed in the fighting (435–36), though that erroneous report comes from the regiment's mistaken casualty list (438). With the sensational murder of Helen Heathcote, the power of the press becomes so pronounced that its peculiar language leaks into Woolson's text: newspaper extracts displace the narrator to reconstruct events at the Timloe Hotel in the public sphere (440–46). Where Melville or Twain might have employed narrative rupture to satirize the public's intrusive need to know, Woolson admits that Anne is not adept at examining evidentiary welter, that she relies instead on the summaries reporters provide (452). Having become via extract the Olympian voice of Woolson's narrative as well as yet another far-flung network, newspapers are consistently cited as authority rather than disruption. Resourcefully, they will cover Anne's testimony on the stand, her exculpatory letters from Helen, and her courtroom confession of love that the Literary World called "an original and powerful stroke."[25] So it is surprising when a divided jury leads to a new trial and newspaper tactics no longer work. Playing reporter, for example, an agile Miss Lois pursues one innocent wanderer after another, even a patent medicine man who turns out to be a cross-dressing single mother. Undone by "mental faculties" alone (508), like a network of synapses that do not quite fire, Miss Lois misreads the locals because she misses the neighborly touch of hand to earth in the Virginia ravine, of arm to arm at the Catskill quarry, and of fingers to wreath in the Mackinac chapel that Woolson casts as metamorphic, while another moving picture materializes.

Anne's quiet alternative when newspaper practices fail is to put her hand to the oar of her rented skiff and reconnoiter upriver. Following a dragonfly, the "filmy" embodiment of a local ecology (509), she is drawn against the current into an upriver past, which is first green, then stranded, then narrow, then derelict, especially after she discovers a "gaudy" picture of the Blessed Virgin in an upriver shanty (510). Away from rail lines, the main road, and finally the last farms, Anne gives into a "vague terror" (510) before encountering the shanty dweller, a fisherman who regularly brings his catch to market. Putting a face to the gravity of local attachments beyond the panoramic Hudson, *Anne* offers up the disquieting mug of Sandy Croom, with its "small eyes," "massive jaw," and yellow "fangs" (517). In Pennsylvania, Croom becomes the image of autochthonous horror, what the New York *Zeus* will later call "deficient," "cunning," and "grotesque" (529). Scarcely the figure of urban nostalgia, Croom stands in for a world of economic blight and rural shortfall while anticipating the shifting functions of late-century panoramas and their radical appeal. Writing about Stephen Crane's "The Open Boat" (1897), Michael Devine has considered "the extent to which the new panoramic experience was inflected across the arts, how . . . the original encyclopedic form became a backdrop to something else entirely in the age of the attraction: a wish to give oneself over to the moving machine, and, by extension, the lived, material environment."[26] Adrift in a naturalistic scene, where Croom's shanty does not suggest a picturesque cottage, Anne in her "terror" reveals what makes this section so haunting, so akin to Devine's "tumbling world" that is "confrontational, transformative, kinetic, bodily."[27] Woolson's derelict Pennsylvania concludes the skiff panorama as an edgy spectacle in which readers are suddenly immersed.

The river that carries Anne back along a de-evolutionary track also carries Croom and his fish downstream to market day, to the village, and to the Timloe Hotel. In this regard, river traffic differs significantly from a system of roads and the cultural paradigm that Chris Ewers has described in "Roads as Regions, Networks and Flows." Historically, Ewers points out, roads have radiated from urban centers like London as "lines of power emanating outwards" when capital investment grows. "The core-periphery model," Ewers argues, "tends to construct a more or less homogenous set of spaces, eliding the many differences within each region."[28] Unlike roads, rivers customarily run the other way, not out but in, from headwaters to port. Since metropolitan demand is partly responsible for the resulting trade, rivers (and moving panoramas) enable a call-and-response paradigm that should be one of mutual benefit. Yet despite what ecological historian David Stradling has called a "long collaboration" between urban outreach and local grip,[29] regional differences are not so quickly effaced, particularly at the Timloe Hotel on the night of the murder. Curious and greedy, Croom climbs the outside staircase and peeps through the window's wooden blind just when the light catches the sleeping Helen's diamonds. Crafty enough to steal and brutish enough to murder, he is still Catholic enough to fear Helen's ghost and to bury the gems. The *Zeus* would call him "a superstitious, almost craven, believer" (531). On his hands and knees inside the hotel window, he embodies the bourgeois horror of shanty beast crawling toward the baubles of the rich, a dragonfly with a sting.

Conclusion

At length, Woolson's narrative couples the *Zeus* extracts with a reprinted letter to Anne from Père Michaux, who tells a different story of mutual vulnerability and moral reckoning, a story of two fishermen and what boats on the river can engender. In Père Michaux's account, there is further villainy: Croom envies the priest's fishing tackle and attacks him from behind. But the old man returns the next day with a kind word and a bruised arm that he asks his attacker to dress. "You people who live in the woods," says the priest, "have better balms than those made in towns; and besides, I would rather ask *your* help than apply to a physician, who might ask questions" (528). By baring his arm, he demonstrates his trust, and an addled Croom responds with liniment. That development, from wound to liniment, approximates where Highland roads lead Ewers in assessing Walter Scott's *Waverley* (1814), whose traveling Englishman "carries a constant border within him," a "fluid space" that binds "romance" to "the quotidian," Scotland to England, even the Highlands to the Lowlands.[30] For Woolson, Père Michaux effectively binds Mackinac to the Mason-Dixon Line, inclusive resolution to divisive upheaval. What Ewers calls "fluid space" might in *Anne* be called the logic of a moving panorama where all the world's a flow, and Woolson's novel concludes in Mackinac's "water parish" (535) as Anne and Heathcote are married.

For some of Woolson's first critics, their happy ending was itself a western-border mongrelosity, both social improbability and fictive mésalliance. But their wedding also marks the beginning of a national family newly reconstituted in a western chapel. The quiet achievement of Woolson's novel is to discover where fluid mutuality has already begun, where coherent reconstructive possibilities have already started to emerge as a national liniment. From this perspective, Anne's postwar marriage is enabled by a New York education and a new white freedom sparked in western Virginia by Diana's emancipation. Not at all the harsh wartime lessons that remake Heathcote's "carelessness" into "stern reticence" and "measured self-control" (495), Anne's education replaces naïveté with discernment, hardship with empathy, a hand on a heart with a hand on an oar. In the moving panorama that begins and ends on Mackinac, a western island is spliced into a reconstructing nation spooling out of wartime upheaval through the lightning flash of reckoning, the thunderbolt of choice.

NOTES

1. "Recent American Fiction," *Atlantic Monthly*, July 1882, 111.

2. "Beauty in the Household, 'Anne,'" *Outing*, October 1882, 79.

3. "Anne. By Constance Fenimore Woolson," *Californian*, September 1882, 287.

4. "Four American Novels," *Lippincott's*, August 1882, 215.

5. Constance Fenimore Woolson, *Anne* (New York: Harper & Brothers, 1882), 73; hereafter cited parenthetically.

6. Angela Miller, "The Panorama, the Cinema, and the Emergence of the Spectacular," *Wide Angle* 18, no. 2 (April 1996): 35.

7. Stephan Oettermann, *The Panorama: History of a Mass Medium*, trans. Deborah Lucas Schneider (New York: Zone Books, 1997), 49.

8. Wendy Bellion, "'Extend the Sphere': Charles Willson Peale's Panorama of Annapolis," *Art Bulletin* 86, no. 3 (September 2004): 529.

9. Miller, "Panorama," 39; [John Banvard], *Description of Banvard's Panorama of the Mississippi River, Painted on Three Miles of Canvas: Exhibiting a View of Country 1200 Miles in Length, Extending from the Mouth of the Missouri River to the City of New Orleans; Being by Far the Largest Picture Ever Executed by Man* (Boston: John Putnam, 1847). As Oettermann has noted, the advertisements for river panoramas in particular made "outrageous exaggeration" a priority (*Panorama*, 325).

10. Susan Tenneriello, *Spectacle Culture and American Identity, 1815–1940* (New York: Palgrave Macmillan, 2013), 15. Although Tenneriello focuses here on *The Frieze of American History* in the U.S. Capitol rotunda, she uses her opening paragraph to anticipate the "immersive sensibilities" (1) her first chapter discusses.

11. As Erkki Huhtamo has reported, Pavel Yakolevich Pyasetsky (1843–1921) made multiple watercolor sketches on-site beginning in the 1870s for "small" panoramas of differing lengths in several rolls. The most famous of these, likewise 48.5 centimeters high, was *The Great Siberian Route: The Trans-Siberian Railway Panorama*, which won the jury's Grand Prix at the Exposition Universelle de Paris 1900. See Huhtamo, *Illusions in Motion: Media Archaeology of the Moving Panorama and Related Spectacles* (Cambridge, Mass.: MIT Press, 2013), 46, 310–11, 376–77. In the United States, Kevin J. Avery points out, "small" was not big enough: "In length, moving panoramas typically reached a thousand or more feet and stood eight to twelve feet high." Most scenes were painted in distemper, which Avery describes as "the transient, water-based medium of the theatrical scene-painter." See "Movies for Manifest Destiny: The Moving Panorama Phenomenon in America," in *The Grand Moving Panorama of Pilgrim's Progress* (Montclair, N.J.: Montclair Art Museum, 1999), 1.

12. Henry Mills Alden, "Introductory Sketch," in *Anne*, Biographical ed. (New York: Harper & Brothers, 1899), iv; James Herbert Morse, "The Native Element in American Fiction, since the War," *Century Illustrated*, July 1883, 369; "Miss Woolson's 'Anne,'" *Century Illustrated*, August 1882, 635.

13. Curtis Dahl, "Mark Twain and the Moving Panorama," *American Quarterly* 13, no. 1 (Spring 1961): 25. Dahl also points out that St. Louis was "a world center of panorama-making" from 1840 to 1850 (21).

14. Dahl, 31, 32.

15. "Literature: Miss Woolson's 'Anne. A Novel,'" *Independent*, September 7, 1882, 11.

16. Dona Brown, *Inventing New England: Regional Tourism in the Nineteenth Century* (Washington, D.C.: Smithsonian Books, 1997), 26.

17. William Cronon, "Foreword: In a City's Mountain Shadow," in David Stradling, *Making Mountains: New York City and the Catskills* (Seattle: University of Washington Press, 2007), xi.

18. Wolfgang Schivelbusch, *The Railway Journey: The Industrialization of Time and Space in the Nineteenth Century* (1979; repr., Berkeley: University of California Press, 2014), 107.

19. Quoted in Charles Zarobila, "Walt Whitman and the Panorama," *Walt Whitman Review* 25, no. 2 (June 1979): 57. Zarobila notes that Whitman lived in Manhattan during the antebellum "heyday" of panorama exhibitions (52), which left their mark on his poetry: "What else but panoramic are those interminably long lines?" (51).

20. Alice Fahs, *The Imagined Civil War: Popular Literature of the North and South, 1861–1865* (Chapel Hill: University of North Carolina Press, 2001), 169.

21. Jane E. Schultz, *Women at the Front: Hospital Workers in Civil War America* (Chapel Hill: University of North Carolina Press, 2004), 19–39.

22. Robert L. Carothers and John L. Marsh, "The Whale and the Panorama," *Nineteenth-Century Fiction* 26, no. 3 (December 1971): 325. Carothers and Marsh describe the similarities between Melville's "seedbed" scenes and those of the Benjamin Russell–Caleb Purrington panorama, *A Whaling Voyage Round the World*, which was completed in 1848 and first exhibited in Boston during 1849.

23. Fahs, *Imagined Civil War*, 154.

24. Richard R. John, *Spreading the News: The American Postal System from Franklin to Morse* (Cambridge, Mass.: Harvard University Press, 1995), 4.

25. "Anne," *Literary World*, July 15, 1882, 227.

26. Michael Devine, "The Whole Thing (and Other Things): From Panorama to Attraction in Stephen Crane's 'The Open Boat,' Ashcan Painting, and Early Cinema," in *Sensationalism and the Genealogy of Modernism: A Global Nineteenth-Century Perspective*, ed. Alberto Gabriele (New York: Palgrave Macmillan, 2017), 230.

27. Devine, 236.

28. Chris Ewers, "Roads as Regions, Networks and Flows: *Waverley* and the 'Periphery' of Romance," *Journal for Eighteenth-Century Studies* 37, no. 1 (March 2014): 105.

29. Stradling, *Making Mountains*, 242.

30. Ewers, "Roads as Regions," 109.

Soaring Beyond Zoar

WOOLSON'S UTOPIAN VISIONS AND DISCOURSES

Etta M. Madden

In 1881 Constance Fenimore Woolson wrote to her friend, author and editor Henry Mills Alden, from her lodgings near Rome's Spanish Steps: "[T]his loggia is a little square room, with windows towards all points of the compass, and an arbor outside, made of lemon-trees, plants in pots, and climbing vines. The walls are hung with pretty hangings, and it is prettily furnished. Here among the roofs and campaniles, and under the deep blue sky of Rome, I can sit and write in perfect solitude when tired of my little parlor below. It all seems so wonderful and strange,—the being here at all!" Her comments conjure up a utopian space—both "wonderful and strange," a perfect and good place that is elsewhere, removed from mind-numbing routines or trouble-filled dystopian life. Yet even here Woolson takes herself away from this seemingly utopian Roman loggia as she continues the passage: "I think of Ohio and the Zoar farm where I used to spend so much time; of Mackinac and the peculiar color of Lake Huron; and of Florida, and the pine-barrens. And, all the while, I am in 'Rome'!"[1]

This passage suggests how Woolson's visits to Zoar stimulated her creativity, enabling her to soar as a writer, as she connects this perfect Roman retreat with the place that first drew her to write. That is, long before her arrival in Rome, Woolson's writings on life in and around the presumed utopian but flawed German Separatist community Zoar embodied a kind of imaginative time-space travel that engaged readers early in her career. Readers of "The Happy Valley" (1870), "Solomon" (1873), and "Wilhelmina" (1875)—not bothered by her mixture of romance and realism in these works—bolstered her confidence and pushed her into a nomadic life that has been described as essential to her position as a successful female author.[2] Most significantly, though, this reading of Zoar as a type of utopian otherworld in Woolson's life and works is of a piece with the island imagery, travel and imaginative processes, which Brehm noted years ago in Woolson's Great Lakes fiction. Drawing from studies of utopian literature—specifically, Jennifer A. Wagner-Lawlor's attention to the "nomadic" and Tom Moylan's emphasis on movement between two cultures—I highlight here Woolson's similar attraction to leave the mundane to travel and explore new cultures in both her life and her writing.[3] Readers move back and forth between disappointing, dystopian social contexts and imagined alternative, utopian settings. The gloomy mundane includes increasing industrialism, consumer desires and capitalist individualism, and ongoing limitation of women's roles. The alternatives emphasize pastoral proximity to nature, simplicity of production and goods, and dedication to community—all of which seem to promise happiness. As nineteenth-century Shaker communities were to Catharine Maria Sedgwick and Nathaniel Hawthorne and the Harmony Society was to Rebecca Harding Davis, Zoar as an alternative "utopian community" prompted Woolson to spin stories.[4] Yet Woolson's stories finally reveal that neither outside nor inside of alternative communities is ideal.

Instead, each work demonstrates that the potential for social change lies within the dialectical process, as readers move with Woolson's narrators between the two worlds. These oppositional imaginative worlds leave an opening that may prompt readers to move toward yet other possibilities, an impact both Moylan and Wagner-Lawlor discuss in their analyses of utopian literary discourses.[5] Beyond either Zoar or its larger context in the Reconstruction-era United States, other options for social action can emerge as Woolson's stories refuse closure. Considering the Zoar writings in this light enables us to see their role for Woolson as an artist whose imagination ventures beyond the familiar. As such, they illuminate her position among nineteenth-century authors who wrote realistically of social problems—especially for women who appeared trapped within or outside of marriage. Without the rosiness of romances, the Zoar works suggest that Woolson nudged critical readers to imagine other worlds, where possibilities for social change might loosen those entrapments.

These tales and sketches have been discussed previously for their themes of travel, marriage, and the isolated artist's life, which remained with Woolson throughout her career. As Anne Boyd Rioux has written, "[T]he Zoar settlement in Ohio"—not a utopian community but "an enclave of German separatists in the Tuscawaras Valley"—was one of Woolson's "favorite spots" to visit.[6] Zoar historian Kathleen Fernandez notes Woolson's sometimes "romanticized" depictions of the society, pointing out a few inaccuracies: the society had access to newspapers; and many men, living within the generally pacifist community, enlisted in the Civil War due to internal commitments rather than external pressure. She concludes, however, that "the stories . . . serve as an eye-witness account of someone who really cared about Zoar and its people and help to show Zoar as it appeared."[7] Literary rather than merely historical analysis illuminates other subtleties. As Carolyn VanBergen has explained, "Wilhelmina" and "Solomon" "defy conventions of the period through their refusal to indulge in nostalgia, [and] their refusal to be simple."[8] In fact, "Zoar is not a Happy Valley where one can escape into an imagined past, but it is, in fact, a microcosm where all of the stresses of the larger world are only magnified."[9]

Both the "refusal to be simple" and "the larger world" and its problems being imagined by a supposed "other world" are long-standing aspects of utopian literature that go back at least to Thomas More, who coined the term whose etymology signifies the "good place" that is, in fact, "no place" with his *Utopia* (1516). More recently, Moylan invented the phrase "critical utopias" to classify fiction that highlights the "continuing presence of difference and imperfection within [what might be called a] utopian society."[10] In these works, "the conflict between the originary world and the utopian" as well as the ongoing "difference and imperfection" in both are laid bare as characters move back and forth between the two settings. The critical utopias foreground a "human subject in action, now no longer an isolated individual . . . stuck in one social system but rather . . . the human collective in . . . time[s] and place[s] of deep historical change."[11] Within Woolson's Zoar writings, I assert, the narrators are active agents within the era of post–Civil War social changes, but readers—past and present—also become part of the larger circle of humanity, asked to consider their own positions within moments of social transformation.

To begin this reading, consider first how "The Happy Valley," "Wilhelmina," and "Solomon" call attention to themselves as narratives—a point Moylan makes about the "self-reflexivity" of critical utopias.[12] Woolson employs such reflexivity through her first-person traveling narrators, who speak to us as they reflect on experiences in this supposed utopian otherworld. In "The Happy Valley" we question whether women laboring to produce such abundance of the hearth within seemingly heartless marriages have chosen a better lifestyle than what women outside Zoar endure. In "Wilhelmina" a loveless marriage within the community strikes a contrast to either marriage or spinsterhood outside Zoar. And in "Solomon" a male artist's dreams of depicting beauty all but die, thwarted by the grueling day labor required of him in a coal mine, although he lives nearby but not within the supposedly idyllic Zoar community. In each case Woolson's narrators draw readers back to the known world of post–Civil War industrialism after having presented Zoar as a strange world that causes wonder, a sense of dislocation or estrangement, and sometimes "disorientation."[13] Readers may consider these narrators to be Woolson's alter ego or, in the case of "The Happy Valley," where the narrator remains unnamed, to be Woolson herself. But most important is that the narrators capture this self-reflexivity, with movements into and out of the supposed utopias and shifting views of life within and outside.

Readers become like the narrators, "traveler[s] in a foreign culture" who are "observing and gradually absorbing information, making patterns, discovering ways to see and understand the larger picture in its own right."[14] Woolson's narrators, whose judgments are not necessarily clear, put the burden on readers to wrestle through the estrangement of travel to consider how, to borrow Moylan's words, to "act decisively" in order "to . . . reestablish justice and well-being" within their contemporary contexts.[15] The unsettling disruptions brought about by Woolson's narrators' and readers' movements between supposed perfect places and imperfect places push for further contemplation of possible new world futures.

The Question of Happiness in "The Happy Valley"

In "The Happy Valley," beginning with the narrator's "leaving behind" the "misty lake" and "the sleeping town" of northern Ohio, readers travel on this "pilgrimage" along "the windings of a sparkling river" and across "an old red-covered bridge."[16] Throughout the narrative, such pastoral details obliquely remind readers that the narrator has left behind the booming industrialism of mid-nineteenth-century Ohio. These signs of natural beauty and older human constructions contrast with the newer engineering feats conquering nature: the railroad on Mount Washington, "the suspension bridge spanning . . . Niagara," and the transatlantic telegraph cable, which open the sketch (282). The sketch closes not with a return, however, but with attention to this self-reflexive framing, as the narrator addresses and questions the "Happy little Valley" (285). The sensuous pastoral details of what might otherwise be seen as simple and rustic farm life draw readers into this setting, which contrasts so markedly from tales of horrific urban and industrial life, such as Harding Davis's *Life in the Iron Mills* (1861). Typical of sketches, Woolson's work oozes with thick description rather than enticing readers with intrigues of plot. As Fernandez notes, the sketch "gives wonderfully detailed descriptions of everyday life in Zoar": "the milk pails, to the 'bretzels [pretzels], queen of cakes,'" to "a church service and its music."[17] Yet the narrator's distance and estrangement from community members emerge most through her emphasis on their German language, faith practices, and, notably, arranged marriages, which deny passion and sensuality. The narrator embeds a German song, translated to reveal an emphasis on contentment "come what may," and without "wealth" (284). A young Trustee "take[s] a wife" as the pastor wishes and then turns "back to his account-books without a word to his bride, who returned to her spinning as phlegmatically as she had come" (284–85). In these moments the narrator ruptures what at first seems sensuously ideal, raising questions about the Zoarites' happiness.

References to religious simplicity, for example, may remind educated readers of *Harper's Monthly*, where the work first appeared, of debates about Biblical authority and sectarian schisms, brought forward by the German higher criticism of sacred scripture. Yet here, in this haven, the debates appear non-existent. Similarly, comments about romantic love conflict with the outside world's ideals that marriage should be based upon heartfelt passion; here, instead, a pervasive work ethic prevails. As Sharon Dean has written, "[T]he Zoarite system . . . disconnected marriage and human relations in general from sexuality."[18] While the communal life provides an economic safety net, less isolation, and perhaps more emotional support for married and unmarried women alike, this moment with the Trustee underscores a similarity between Zoar and the outside culture—that men, in women's eyes, often focused on economic success more than domestic bliss and that women, looking for passion and romance, might always be disappointed. And the pastoral bounty of home-cooked foods—a type of sensual materialism—appears on the table only due to largely female labor, akin to the situation of the outside world. Before we see "a spotless table-cloth and shining blue crockery" on which appear "hot coffee, pitchers of rich cream, little rolls of fresh butter, Dutch cheese, apple butter, bretzels, and cold meat" (285), we have witnessed a row of "ruddy milkmaids . . . balancing . . . heavy tubs upon their heads" (283). In all three instances the sketch slips into readers' sights elements of community that seem blissful yet demand an eyewink to potential problems: lack of critical thought, lack of passion in relationships, and labor—especially female labor—essential to luxurious bounty.

As the sketch moves toward its conclusion, then, this estranged point of view—reinforcing "us" and "them"—has raised questions about the place of happiness in either "world." While the narrator praises these people of faith as "pictures of perfect contentment," in part because "ignorant of the value of money" yet "living in the simplest manner" as "a rich community," in other ways readers should question the cost of what appears to be "the happy valley." When the narrator comments in the final lines, "our ways are not as thy ways," and asks, "but who can say that thou hast not chosen the better part?"

(285), Woolson puts the question not only to the community but to thoughtful readers. By withholding an answer, and by allowing the narrator to stay within the community, Woolson provides the kind of opening Wagner-Lawlor emphasizes. She asks readers to consider what other possibilities might exist.

The Utopian Dialectic in "Wilhelmina"

This refusal to provide an answer appears more poignantly in "Wilhelmina" and "Solomon." On the surface, these tales also make points about women and marriage, as they consider romantic love imagined within the context of communal confinement and societal strictures. "Wilhelmina," Rioux explains, is based on Woolson's jilting and tells "the story of a young woman who patiently waits for her fiancé to return from the war only to find out that he has grown away from her and wishes to marry another."[19] But the tale does more than comment on marriage, as it upends the simple binaries of utopia inside and dystopia outside Zoar, and vice versa.

In "Wilhelmina" as in "The Happy Valley," the narrative point of view of a visiting narrator opens with the question of marriage to the title character, known as "Mina," who explains she has been waiting three years for her beloved Gustav to return from the Civil War. The narrator imagines that "Mina" sees her as "the superior being . . . from the outside world."[20] Upon learning that Gustav's regiment is soon returning, the narrator asks whether she would like to accompany her to the city, presumably to fulfill their utopian dreams through marriage. Mina's response is, "No; I's better here" and "I am contented" (74). Echoing "The Happy Valley" sketch, the narrator responds with an "ignorance is bliss" phrase: "So were they taught from childhood," so "they knew no better," before asking, "after all, is there anything better to know?" (74). The unanswered rhetorical question lingers. However, in contrast to "The Happy Valley" sketch, the question does not cap the story but remains an undercurrent throughout, raising doubts about the limits of knowledge and the limits of happiness in both worlds.

The blurred boundaries between the two worlds and the misunderstandings about them emerge, for example, in the references to newspapers and enlistment in the Civil War, as Fernandez observes. Counter to what the tale suggests, "newspapers, the modern Tree of Knowledge, were *not* forbidden" (70, emphasis added). And the enlistment of pacifist Zoarites in the Civil War was not due to external legal pressures. Rather, "enlistees left voluntarily and exemptions were purchased for others."[21] The men who enlisted may have been motivated by internal patriotism as much as a desire to escape community.

Such misrepresentations in Woolson's writing caused at least one contemporary local reader to respond in the *Tuscarawas Advocate*, just three weeks after "Wilhelmina" first appeared there. The respondent wrote, "[Woolson] would try and make the world believe that . . . the whole Society was as ignorant as the Fejee [*sic*] Islanders."[22] The response reveals that the boundaries between the two worlds—outside Zoar and within—were more permeable than the first sketch and "Wilhelmina" present them.

That is, if readers idealize the community at first for their pacificism during the Civil War and their protection of women by providing for them regardless of their marital status, those ideals have been crushed by the tale's end. Likewise, if the outside world seems ideal to the narrator, by providing access to knowledge and to passionate romance, those utopian dreams are deluded as well. Readers see, for example, that the narrator believes she can save Mina, just as perhaps white Christian missionaries in the South Pacific believe they can save Fiji islanders who may not want their help. The narrator's movements and self-righteous idealism may prompt readers to consider whether the possibility of some new middle ground between the two worlds exists. Mina's death—and supposed happiness in the afterlife—brings this question to a head with the narrator and a final scene.

Before that scene, however, readers learn that Mina's father wants her to marry an older, widowed baker rather than the younger Gustav, exposed to the world during the war. Also, when the soldiers return jubilant to a "rejoicing" community, Gustav slights Mina (83). As he leaves the community to marry a Cincinnati woman, Mina, who has not spoken for three days, throws herself before him, and cries out, before collapsing "as if dead." She soon becomes "thin and shrunken" with "a strange dark pallor, and her lips were drawn in as if from pain . . . the brown shadows beneath [her eyes] extended down into the cheeks" (87). The sad scene is reminiscent of a jilted Miriam, who collapses in death at the end of Hawthorne's "The Shaker Bridal," except that Mina's collapse does not conclude the story.

Also important, readers see *the narrator's* failed utopian visions. As the narrator explains, "[A]ll *my castles* fell to the ground. *My* plan for taking Mina home with me, accustoming her gradually to other clothes and ways, teaching her enough of the world to enable her to hold her place without pain, *my* hope that *my* husband might find a situation for Gustav . . . , in short, all *the idyll I had woven*, was destroyed" (86, emphasis added). The narrator has been employing Mina and Gustav to her own utopian end—to weave her own idyllic kingdoms of romantic love in marriage. The couple provide imaginative stepping stones that allowed her to revisit her own past, with its failed romance.

She adds, "[U]p sprung a memory of the curls and ponderous jet necklace I sported at a certain period of my existence, when John—I was silenced . . . and walked away without a word" (86). But the narrator fails to realize this utopian dream, as Mina neither leaves Zoar nor marries Gustav. Instead, readers arrive, as the narrator does, at yet another vision of a supposed utopian end—the vision of an afterlife.

When the narrator proposes again to accompany Mina to the city, Mina refuses and instead marries the widowed baker. The following year, upon returning to Zoar, the narrator learns that Mina has "gone to the Next Country" (89). Twice refusing the possibility of freedom to marry based on romantic love in the outside world, Mina settled for a dystopian practical marriage within Zoar, only to move on to the happier world of the afterlife. Readers who hold such a view of the afterlife may agree, and the story concludes with the narrator consoling herself with such a message—that Mina has found now "not rest, not peace, but an active, living joy" (89). This idyllic vision of the afterlife reverberates with Sedgwick's Bessie Lee in *The Linwoods* and Julia Ward Howe's untitled and unpublished Lawrence manuscript (ca. 1844). The afterlife as another "Country," or utopian "possible world," may prompt readers to contemplate how Woolson employs this vision. Is this other world a straightforward comment on the afterlife, to be embraced by Christian readers? Or is it an ironic and dystopian message about the impossibilities for happiness in the material world, mocking nineteenth-century works with such scenes?

I would argue that this unresolved opening, similar to the openings that Wagner-Lawlor notes in women's speculative fiction, nudges readers less certain of an afterlife as the only hope, to imagine another, improved material world yet to be brought about. The Civil War had born numerous changes in women's roles, as many men were killed and single women took on new tasks. The unsettling scene asked readers of the *Atlantic Monthly* or *Castle Nowhere*, the collection in which "Wilhelmina" and "Solomon" appeared in 1875, to set aside the presumed limits of women's roles and marriage to envision other possibilities. Perhaps Woolson hoped her audience, having traveled inside and outside of Zoar and "see[ing] the world differently," might "act decisively" to create worlds where "justice and well-being" might exist for women, regardless of their marital states.[23]

Giving Utopia in "Solomon"

Alternative worlds, highlighted by a traveling narrator, Theodora, and her friend, Erminia, present a slightly different picture in "Solomon," which also includes a version of the marriage plot. While the narrator in "Wilhelmina" wants to help the trapped Mina by removing her from Zoar and a life void of sensuality and knowledge, in "Solomon" the narrator learns the value of giving within—rather than removing from—what appears to be a dystopian world. Solomon and Dorcas, once young, determined to create their own utopia by following their passions rather than society's expectations. Aged, depressed, and marginalized from both Zoar and sensual urban life at the story's opening, the couple in their ramshackle home now epitomize dystopian despair with their paucity of pleasure. Art, artistic vision, and gift exchange emerge as the foremost utopian footholds that may renew and transform their dystopian realities. These footholds for small steps toward social change crystalize after the couple's death and in the tale's final lines—when the younger travelers Erminia and Theodora receive a beautiful portrait of an idealized Dorcas, which Solomon drew after receiving artistic tips from Erminia. The women realize the depth of Solomon's and Dorcas's love for each other and the ways in which gifts of art from these young visitors have enriched and revitalized that love.

The story unfolds as Ohio urbanites Erminia and Theodora vacation with the German Separatists, a utopian paradise for them. As the narrator explains, "The village was our favorite retreat, our little hiding-place . . . almost as isolated as a solitary island, for the Community . . . held no intercourse with the surrounding townships" and was "unmindful of the rest of the world."[24] The community's physical indulgences of food, clothing, and shelter, she explains, reveal that as they "grew steadily richer and richer," they "were no ascetic anchorites" (51). Here the idyllic community as a utopian island provides a stark contrast not only to the city that the travelers have left behind but also to the rural home of the aged couple, now isolated from both city and community. The couple's house seems haunted by memories of their past, which included not only passion but artistic drive and beauty. Their enclosed sulfur spring, which draws urban visitors to imbibe for health, also exudes an unpleasant odor, an allusion to the smell of brimstone, contributing to the gothic setting and connecting the house, for some readers, to a devil's den.

The contrast between the couple's pinched environment and the other worlds comes to life through the interchanges among Erminia, Theodora, and the couple. Here the dialogues—about the nature of marriage, sacrifices for love and relationship, commitment to art, daily toil, and life within Zoar—all push readers to realize the multiple visions of utopia and attempts to achieve them. Readers travel through time and space with Erminia and Theodora, as they visit Solomon and Dorcas, who remember their pasts, more than once. These time and space travels are punctuated by the process of gift exchange.

The gifts are multiple—first simple sulfur water, but then conversation, a scarf, a handkerchief, an overnight lodging, and even kind instructions in artistic technique. Starting with the sulfur water, the gifts almost immediately enrich the older couple's lives but in turn enrich the younger women's as well.

The tale's nuances expand in light of readings of gift exchange in feminist speculative fiction. As Wagner-Lawlor explains, hospitality and inclusion are gestures that continue to unfold possibilities for the nomadic and homeless, for those giving and for those receiving.[25] The happiest moments, what might be called utopian microcosms, occur within otherwise dystopian lives when people begin to see other metaphorical travelers differently through gift exchange. In "Solomon," what began as a diversion for the "nomadic" Erminia and Theodora reinvigorated the older couple, who have been isolated and excluded, although they have a home. The gifts help them to appreciate their longtime sacrifices for one another as gifts as well. In turn, the younger women become increasingly sympathetic to the stagnated artist and the stifled and aged housewife. The characters' awakenings to the power of love, gift exchange, and artistic vision imbue the tale with the message that these ingredients are essential to turn any setting, however dystopian, into a utopian one, if only for a fleeting moment.

Most significantly, the arrival of the portrait in the tale's final scene and the last lines leave readers once again with open-ended narration, with no single character's life being more or less exemplary than the other. As Erminia and Theodora retain their judgmental prejudices about which of the older couple had suffered more (Erminia, the artist, sympathizes with Solomon), they echo their earlier differences about the masks of life and truthfulness of fiction. "Even then we could not give up our preferences," the narrator comments, leaving an implicit question for readers to ponder in the final sentence (69). The story's ongoing debates, with the supposed utopian Zoar as a backdrop where they play out, remind us that utopia is never a literal place to be achieved. Rather, it is an imaginative experience, like Solomon's and Dorcas's, that is part of a dialectical, creative process.

This dialogic nature, most obvious in "Solomon" as Erminia and Theodora discuss in the final lines whether Solomon or his wife is the most pathetic character, also has been emphasized in utopian discourses. More's *Utopia* ends not with a definitive answer about which civilization is better—England or the island his traveling narrator Raphael Hythloday has visited—but with an open-endedness that puts the burden on readers, who are left to contemplate the possibilities of other worlds. Even Woolson's "Wilhelmina," which adheres more closely than the other two narratives to a failed marriage plot, employs this self-reflexivity and imagined dialogue between narrator and readers, as the tale closes by underscoring the narrator's travel as much as Wilhelmina's death. The burden of creativity here, as with the other works, falls upon readers. Without simple resolution, the narratives involve readers in "co-creating," to use Moylan's words; they have the "formal potential to re-vision the world," as they provide "pleasurable, probing and potentially subversive responses."[26] Woolson's traveling narrators reveal the process of utopian dialectic, as characters travel between Zoar and the world outside it and as readers realize the flaws of both worlds.

When reading these texts, if we "can manage to see the world differently," first "by becoming critically estranged and [then by becoming] engaged," the results might be, as Moylan suggests, "to make that world a more just and congenial place for all who live in it."[27] Readers may be pushed to consider alternatives, just as Woolson herself continued to imagine possible futures as she traveled through her life and career. She held on to memories, imaginatively adapting them while traveling as an uprooted, nomadic adult and looking for the perfect place in which to labor. Woolson never left behind Zoar's otherworldliness and her imagination's creative potential, as she traveled from Ohio, through the Lakes region, to Florida, the Mediterranean, and Italy. As Rioux has noted, just three years before her death, Woolson "began to look even farther back . . . , writing . . . of her father and their trips to Zoar."[28] Even her final flight—or fall—may be seen as a soaring that mirrors Wilhelmina's vision and action—prompted by her fraught position within a world whose views of women's roles were limited. More important, though, is to see what Woolson left behind—the gift of her writing—not unlike the artistic gift Solomon left for Dorcas, Erminia, and Theodora. This gift of otherworldly visions, with its tensions between the ideal and the real, continues to spur readers forward with fruitful conversations about the possibilities for social change.

NOTES

1. Constance Fenimore Woolson to Henry Mills Alden, April 8 [1881], in *The Complete Letters of Constance Fenimore Woolson*, ed. Sharon L. Dean (Gainesville: University Press of Florida, 2012), 162.

2. Victoria Brehm, "Island Fortresses: The Landscape of the Imagination in the Great Lakes Fiction of Constance Fenimore Woolson," *American Literary Realism* 22, no. 3 (Spring 1990): 51–66.

3. Jennifer A. Wagner-Lawlor, *Postmodern Utopias and Feminist Fictions* (Cambridge: Cambridge University Press, 2013), 7; Tom Moylan, *Demand the Impossible: Science Fiction and the Utopian Imagination* (Bern: Peter Lang, 2014), 10–11; Tom Moy-

lan, *Scraps of the Untainted Sky: Science Fiction, Utopia, Dystopia* (Boulder, Colo.: Westview, 2000), 7.

4. Sedgwick's *Redwood* (1824), Hawthorne's "The Shaker Bridal" (1837) and "The Canterbury Pilgrims" (1833), Harding Davis's "The Harmonists" (1866).

5. Wagner-Lawlor, *Postmodern Utopias*, 3; Moylan, *Demand the Impossible*.

6. Anne Boyd Rioux, *Constance Fenimore Woolson: Portrait of a Lady Novelist* (New York: Norton, 2016), 37.

7. Kathleen M. Fernandez, *Zoar: The Story of an Intentional Community* (Kent, Ohio: Kent State University Press, 2019), 183, 185.

8. Carolyn VanBergen, "Constance Fenimore Woolson and the Next Country," *Western Reserve Studies* 3 (1988): 88.

9. VanBergen, 87.

10. Moylan, *Demand the Impossible*, 11.

11. Moylan, 10–11, 45.

12. Moylan, 46.

13. Moylan, *Scraps of the Untainted Sky*, 4.

14. Moylan, 7.

15. Moylan, 7, 6.

16. Constance Fenimore Woolson, "The Happy Valley," *Harper's Monthly*, July 1870, 282; hereafter cited parenthetically.

17. Fernandez, *Zoar*, 182.

18. Sharon L. Dean, *Constance Fenimore Woolson: Homeward Bound* (Knoxville: University of Tennessee Press, 1995), 106.

19. Rioux, *Constance Fenimore Woolson: Portrait*, 60. Rioux cites Cheryl B. Torsney, "Zephaniah Swift Spalding: Constance Fenimore Woolson's Cipher," in *Witness to Reconstruction: Constance Fenimore Woolson and the Postbellum South, 1873–1894*, ed. Kathleen Diffley (Jackson: University Press of Mississippi, 2011), 114–15.

20. Constance Fenimore Woolson, "Wilhelmina," in *Constance Fenimore Woolson: Collected Stories*, ed. Anne Boyd Rioux (New York: Library of America, 2020), 70; hereafter cited parenthetically.

21. Fernandez, *Zoar*, 183.

22. Fernandez, 183.

23. Moylan, *Scraps of the Untainted Sky*, 5.

24. Constance Fenimore Woolson, "Solomon," in Rioux, *Constance Fenimore Woolson: Collected Stories*, 51; hereafter cited parenthetically.

25. Wagner-Lawlor, *Postmodern Utopias*, 7.

26. Moylan, *Scraps of the Untainted Sky*, 5.

27. Moylan, 5.

28. Rioux, *Constance Fenimore Woolson: Portrait*, 256.

"Dear Mr. James . . . Do Not Leave It Merely Implied"

JUPITER LIGHTS AS RESPONSE TO HENRY
JAMES'S *THE BOSTONIANS*

Kristin M. Comment

On February 20, 1886, Henry James inscribed a copy of his recently published *The Bostonians* to "Constance Fenimore Woolson, from Henry James." The two friends were living in London, and that winter James introduced Woolson to his sister Alice and her companion Katherine Loring.[1] Even without this inscribed copy of the novel, Woolson no doubt read James's unflattering portrayal of the women's rights movement in Boston. But beyond this, we know nothing of what Woolson thought of the book. No mention of *The Bostonians* appears in any of her surviving letters. Yet interesting parallels appear in *Jupiter Lights*, the first long work of fiction she published approximately three years later in 1889. Indeed, close examination of the two novels supports reading *Jupiter Lights* as a direct response to James, one that moves the "woman question" from the public to the private sphere to imagine what she believed James could not: a strong, independent woman both in love *and* loved.

On the surface, the plots of these novels appear radically different. Set mostly in the upper-class parlors of Boston, James's political satire features a simple storyline with Verena Tarrant, daughter of a shady mesmerist, as the source of conflict between distant cousins Olive Chancellor and Basil Ransom. Olive, a native Bostonian with a passion for women's rights, wants Verena to devote her speaking talent to the cause of female emancipation. Basil, a southern Civil War veteran who harbors deep-seated resentment toward Olive's "new truths" and his own inadequacies as provider, wants Verena for a trophy wife.[2] In the end, Basil wins Verena, but the narrator tells us the tears in her eyes are not "the last she was destined to shed" (419), insinuating that the marriage will not be a happy one. Woolson's more complicated narrative initially centers on Eve Bruce's plan to win custody of her dead brother's baby son from his widow, Cicely, who has remarried less than a year after Jack Bruce's death. But the focus quickly shifts when Cicely reveals that her new husband Ferdie falls into fits of drunken, abusive rage, once even breaking little Jack's arm. Shortly after this revelation, Eve witnesses one of Ferdie's rages and shoots him to protect Cicely and the baby. Cicely represses the trauma, and the crime is blamed on two Black men who had escaped from prison. When Ferdie later dies—presumably from the gunshot wound—Eve must harbor her terrible secret alone, and Eve's dilemma worsens when she falls passionately in love with Ferdie's half brother Paul. Ultimately, she confesses her crime to Paul, he forgives her, and they plan to marry, but at the last minute Eve abandons him and runs off to a convent in Italy, sure that her act of killing Ferdie would forever haunt their marriage. Then, in a contrived turn of events, Paul learns that Ferdie died not from the gunshot but by his own debauchery, and the novel ends with Paul forcing his way into the convent and taking Eve in his arms.

Despite these differences at the surface level, juxtaposing the books' broader themes, as well as a nuanced overlapping of detail in characterization and symbolism, reveals quite another picture. Broadly speaking, James and Woolson both provide a window into tensions between the North and South following the Civil War, particularly the clash between a deteriorating southern gentility resistant to changes being brought about by capitalism, industrialization, and a new social liberalism. More specifically, the two books center on a conflict between a northerner and a southerner for possession of an innocent young soul: Olive and Basil for Verena, and Eve and Cicely for little Jack. Both also interrogate the conditions of heterosexual marriage for women while offering, if only briefly, an alternate homosocial—and perhaps even homoerotic—possibility. *The Bostonians* and *Jupiter Lights* are both "queer" books in that they disrupt binaries of gender and sexuality in their search for a happy solution to the problem of heterosexual marriage for women. However, Woolson's book digs much deeper into the grayer areas of love, sexual desire, and psychology in a way that clearly offended nineteenth-century sensibilities. Horace Scudder excoriated the novel as "a conspiracy against a sane, wholesome experience of life" that leads "farther and farther away from the larger picture of human life into the windings and turnings of fictitious pathology."[3] Indeed, *Jupiter Lights*—to a much greater degree than *The Bostonians*—challenges the very core upon which nineteenth-century standards of "a sane wholesome experience of life" were founded—specifically the ideology of "true womanhood," which was aimed at keeping women subservient to their husbands within the domestic sphere.[4]

Details in characterization provide direct links between *Jupiter Lights* and *The Bostonians*. Woolson gives us Cicely, whose "silvery" singing voice captivates Eve similar to the way Verena's "lovely" voice captivates Basil.[5] Also like Verena, Cicely remains dependent on others, always seeking outside direction and protection. Verena escapes the oppressive hand of her father only by falling under Olive's and then Basil's. Cicely marries Jack Bruce as a teenager, and then marries again before she has had time even to grieve Jack's death, and while Ferdie is away, she stays under the protective roof and watchful eye of her grandfather. Moreover, Cicely remains devoted to Ferdie despite his physical abuse, just as Verena submits to Basil despite his misogynistic rhetoric. Basil and Ferdie actually have quite a lot in common: while it may be hard to imagine Basil physically striking a woman given his strong notions of southern chivalry, James's narrator notes that to Basil "the idea of meddling legislation" on temperance "filled him with rage" (45), a disturbing hint of violence just below his charming surface. Ferdie himself has all of Basil's charm and good looks when not under the influence of alcohol. In fact, Eve initially finds Ferdie so charming that she wonders if Cicely might be making up the whole story of his abuse (60).

Eve Bruce and Olive Chancellor are even more similar than Cicely and Verena. Both Olive and Eve are perceived by their southern counterparts as older than they actually are, and they share similar physical characteristics: Olive has "white skin . . . no figure . . . a certain appearance of feeling cold," and her look is one of "duty" not geniality (17); Eve is "tall, broad-shouldered, slender . . . [with] a very white face . . . eyes . . . angry & cold . . . a mouth distinctly ugly," and she has a "sullen" expression (8). Olive believes she was born to lead a crusade against the "unhappiness of women" (34); Eve feels herself "revolting, dumbly, against the injustice of all the ages, past, present, and to come, towards women" when she learns of Ferdie's abuse (61). Eve also shares Olive's obsessiveness—and possessiveness—for Verena in her desperation for custody of her brother's son Jack, and in her attempt to win little Jack with the promise of bequeathing him her fortune, a detail that echoes Olive's payment to Selah Tarrant for him to allow Verena to live with her. And both Olive and Eve profess to be committed spinsters. Olive sees the fight for women as a kind of "priesthood" that demands the sacrifice of marriage for a "great good" (127–28). Eve believes—after having a few suitors—that she is "not made of inflammable material" and develops "a strong contempt for love" as she realizes Cicely's continued loyalty to an abusive man (65). She thinks love like Cicely's "seemed almost a curse, a malediction," yet she is comforted by the notion "that she, Eve Bruce, should ever fall a victim to such miseries." She tells herself that "to love any man so submissively was weakness, but to love as Cicely loved, that was degradation!" (61). In similar self-righteous indignation, Olive Chancellor remarks to Verena that for all men, "as a matter of course, it is war upon us to the knife" (128). Perhaps not coincidentally, then, it is with a knife that Ferdie attacks Cicely and Jack.

Catherine H. Zuckert argues that James was sympathetic to the problems of American women but that he saw fundamental flaws in what he called "the agitation on their behalf" as well as all other so-called moral reform movements of the era. She finds in *The Bostonians* a reflection of James's critique of Emerson's "universal passive hospitality," manifested most obviously in the character of Miss Birdseye, who "knew less about her fellow-creatures, if possible after fifty years of humanitarian zeal, than on the day she had gone into the field to testify against the iniquity of most arrangements" (25). Likewise, Olive and Basil dwell in their ideals regarding gender politics at the expense of experiencing real passion: both see marriage only "in political terms of superiority and inferiority or economic terms of possession," which leads them both to the prospect of an unhappy future.[6] Verena falls prey to them because her innocence precludes her seeing their true natures; thus, James reveals a failed intimacy inherent in the gender politics of the era without offering any alternative beyond Dr. Prance, who embodies female empowerment and independence, but fails—in her own words—to "cultivate the sentimental side."[7] I think Woolson would have agreed with Zuckert's assessment—particularly the idea that despite his sympathy for women, James failed to imagine a relationship that could reconcile an expanded view of gender with genuine human intimacy. Even before the publication of *The Bostonians* in 1882, she criticized James's *Portrait of a Lady* for not providing "distinct expression" of Isabel's love for Osmond, "and the following agony"; he leaves "to the imagination of the reader" that which she "would rather not have 'left.'"[8] Later that same year, she praised the "true ring" of Winterbourne's love for Mme. de Katkoff in his play adaptation of *Daisy Miller*, noting that she had "found fault with [him] for not making it more evident that [his] heroes were in love with the heroines; really in love."[9] In May 1883, Woolson pleaded with James from Venice, "[W]hy not give us a woman for whom we can feel a real love . . . I do not plead that she should be happy; or even fortunate; but let her be distinctly lovable; perhaps, let some one love her very much; but, at any rate, let *her* love, and let us see that she does; do not leave it merely implied."[10] These letters further support reading *Jupiter Lights* as a coded response to *The Bostonians*, one that extends James's interest in the nexus between politics and human relations into the private sphere and that attempts to depict the "distinct expression" of real love she chastised him for eliding in his own novels.

Woolson creates Cicely and Eve as foils to test the limits of loyalty and self-sacrifice in personal relationships, especially marriage, but she also appears to create Eve as a foil to Olive Chancellor in the growth and maturity she achieves by opening herself to love. Indeed, Woolson seems to draw inspiration from a side of Emerson that James and others missed. In his essay titled "Love," Emerson recalls "being told that in some public discourses of mine my reverence for the intellect has made me unjustly cold to the personal relations." "Love" aims to correct that perception in its analysis of the way youthful passion serves the soul's development. Emerson recognizes young love as "a divine rage and enthusiasm" that "seizes on man . . . and works a revolution in his mind and body . . . enhances the power of the senses . . . [and] adds to his character heroic and sacred attributes." Maturity requires the experience of such passion because it puts us "in training for a love which knows not sex, nor person, nor partiality, but which seeks virtue and wisdom everywhere, to the end of increasing virtue and wisdom."[11] *Jupiter Lights* ends much like *The Bostonians* in leaving to the reader's imagination what lies ahead for the impending marriages. We do not see beyond the stage of "divine rage" in the love between Eve and Paul; however, their union represents—for Eve at least—a less bifurcated view of human emotions and behavior. Her own uncontrolled feelings for Paul bring her to an understanding of Cicely's loyalty toward Ferdie, despite his abuse, and Paul models for her a more discerning and compassionate view of both Ferdie and herself. Without condoning his brother's violence, Paul forgives Ferdie because he understands the mitigating circumstance of his brother's mental illness. Likewise, he accepts Eve's shooting of Ferdie as a heroic act to defend Cicely and the baby. Both Cicely and Paul enlighten Eve on the complexities of the human condition, and of love in particular. As Emerson contends, suffering is a natural part of love, and from suffering comes growth. In this Emersonian light, *Jupiter Lights* becomes a philosophical treatise on love, which far surpasses *The Bostonians* in its depth and understanding of human passion and the maturity it engenders.

Contemporary reviewers of the novel did not appreciate Woolson's daring on these topics, perhaps because of the degree to which *Jupiter Lights* transgresses nineteenth-century notions of "true womanhood." While James may be somewhat sympathetic to the cause of women, he largely adheres to reader expectations in his depiction of gender and sexuality. Woolson, on the other hand, thoroughly deconstructs these concepts. A number of critics noted particular distaste for Olive Chancellor, but they were satisfied with James's own disapproval of her, missing the equal derision aimed at Basil and even Verena. They found the "moral" of the story in Basil's perspective, articulated by one as "the true woman knows well enough that her real sphere is the home; enshrined in the affection of her husband and children, she wishes for no other, and there is certainly no other in which she could wield half her present influence over the destinies of the world."[12] By contrast, reviews of *Jupiter Lights* were scathing. In addition to Horace Scudder's attack on the novel's "fictitious pathology," a *Nation* reviewer lambasted Woolson's failure to mirror "real life," calling the book "sheer romantic nonsense," in which "every problem of conduct the people involved are as nearly irrational as possible."[13] Such accusations of "pathology" and lack of "reality" seem directed more at the book's subversion of "true womanhood" than at its sensationalism or moments of bad writing. Indeed, Eve's complicated relationships with both Cicely and Paul include scenes of gender inversion and explicit physical desire quite striking for the era.[14]

The Bostonians and *Jupiter Lights* both explore the possibility of lesbian desire; however, James's depiction of Olive's desire for Verena has dismissive echoes of the lesbian vampire trope that would have made the subject more palatable to his readers. In the scene where Olive asks Verena never to marry, she "fling[s] over the cloak that hung ample upon her own meager person, and [holds] her there with the other" until they are interrupted by Mr. Pardon, who warns that they might "freeze together" (125). The "meagerness" of Olive's person and coldness of the scene foreshadow a death of the relationship rather than any real possibility of passionate union. By contrast, Woolson depicts the possibility of female bonding as a legitimate alternative to heterosexual marriage with far more explicit homoeroticism.[15] Eve initially dislikes Cicely immensely, but their relationship soon takes on an unmistakably erotic charge as it gradually turns into a love-hate attraction, alternately tender and masochistic. The shift in their relationship begins on Christmas night, after a scene between the two women that can be read only as one of seduction. Cicely comes to Eve late that evening and says, "[Y]ou haven't touched your hair, nor unbuttoned a button . . . I should love to see you with your hair down; I should love to see you run and shriek!" (88). She leads Eve to an old moonlit ballroom and then disappears momentarily. When she returns, she is wearing a seductive "old-fashioned ball dress made of lace interwoven with silver threads and decked with little silvery stars." Apparition-like, Cicely begins to dance, "moving over the moonlit floor" with a piece of white gauze "blowing out in front of her, now waving behind her as she flew along." Then, "Suddenly she let it drop, and coming to Eve, put her arms around her waist and forced her forward. Eve resisted. But Cicely's hands were strong, her hold tenacious; she drew her sister-in-law down the room in a wild gallopade. In the midst of it, giving a little jump, she seized Eve's comb. Eve's hair, already loosened, fell down on her shoulders" (40).

The sexual suggestion in this passage is obvious, particularly the loosening of Eve's hair, which marks the beginning of her sexual awakening. The next morning Eve is "puzzled . . . [because] she had thought [Cicely] . . . a passionless, practical little creature . . . whose miniature beauty led poor Jack astray" (41). Following their "gallopade," Eve has changed her mind about Cicely: she now understands what attracted Jack to Cicely because she herself has been erotically seduced by the same woman.

Eve's feelings for Cicely grow stronger when Cicely tells her of Ferdie's abuse. Not long after the ballroom scene, Cicely comes to Eve to confess that she has "changed her mind" about telling her secret. She lets a shawl fall from her shoulder, revealing "a long purple scar, and a second one over her delicate shoulder." Cicely's eyes are "proud and brilliant," indicating a hint of sadomasochism; her scar, though a symbol of violence, remains a concrete manifestation of her connection to Ferdie. But it also furthers her seduction of Eve, perhaps as a stand-in for her late husband Jack. The shawl falling from Cicely's shoulder recalls the white gauze falling from her hand during the ballroom scene, but this time it reveals her "white breast." Like the ballroom scene, this too is filled with erotic suggestion. Cicely, now undressed, in effect submits herself to Eve by exposing the secret of her abusive marriage. Horrified by the sight of the scar, Eve takes Cicely "in her arms protectingly" (78).

From this point, Eve assumes the role of Cicely's protector as well as little Jack's, played out most obviously the night Ferdie gets drunk and chases Cicely and the baby out to the lake. Eve's cool handling of the situation, her physical strength, and of course the phallic pistol that overpowers Ferdie's knife all emphasize the conventionally masculine role she plays in relation to Cicely, later confirmed by Paul's praise of her handling of the escape "just as a man would" (104). The newly configured family with Eve as Jack's surrogate manifests symbolically when Eve places little Jack in Cicely's arms once they reach the other side of the lake. Prior to this, she had been very possessive of the child, keeping him from Cicely whenever possible, and had noticed that Cicely never took the baby directly from her. However, at this point she gives him up willingly, as if it is the natural thing to do. Her role as Jack's replacement complete, Eve maintains a protective stance toward Cicely and the baby until the end of the book, even after Cicely turns on her, and she begins to realize her physical desire for Paul.[16] Unlike other nineteenth-century narratives of "romantic friendship" that figure homoerotic desire between women as a "dress rehearsal" for marriage, Woolson balances Eve's choice between Cicely and Paul to the very end.[17]

Eve's subsequent recognition of her physical desire for Paul brings an epiphany similar to the one she has after the "gallopade" with Cicely, but this time focused on herself. She finds herself scanning Paul's "features with a sort of slow wonder . . . a wonder at herself" for feeling the way she does. She is disturbed by the feeling, but unable to check the physical transformation it produces: "Eve's cheeks showed a deep rose bloom; she was no longer the snow-white woman . . . [of] six months before. She was still markedly erect, but her step had become less confident, her despotic manner had disappeared" (107). In love, Eve understands "everything—the things she had always despised—pettiness, jealousy, impossible hopes, disgrace, shame," and more importantly, she understands Cicely (109). She labels her desire for Paul a kind of "insanity" (225), equating it with Cicely's continued devotion to Ferdie, and even Ferdie's own illness, which the novel suggests makes his abusive behavior not entirely his own fault. At first, Paul shows no romantic interest in Eve, but he does seem to admire her strength and independence. He compliments her care of Cicely: "You brought her off when she hadn't the force to come herself, poor little woman! And you did it boldly and quickly, just as a man would have done it," and "you like to do things; to be active. They tell me that you are fond of having your own way, but that is the very sort of person they need—a woman like you, strong and cool" (104). Paul's surprise at his feelings for Eve parallels Eve's own feelings in falling for him; he explains to her, "[T]he thing has come about . . . in spite of me. I never thought it would . . . I'm as helpless as anyone" (160). He waits to reveal his feelings because "I wasn't sure my time had come" (160), characterizing love in Emersonian fashion as a human inevitability.

In what may be a nod to Margaret Fuller's premature death in a shipwreck off the coast of Long Island in 1850, both *The Bostonians* and *Jupiter Lights* use boating accidents and drowning as metaphors for women's fate in marriage, but in contrasting ways. Near the end of the book while on Cape Cod, Basil takes Verena out in a sailboat. Aware that Verena has fallen for Basil, and worried that Verena has been gone too long, Olive imagines "a boat overturned—drifting out to sea, and the body of a woman, defaced beyond recognition, but washed up in some far way cove" (382). Then, in the final scene, as the crowd waits impatiently for Verena, she calls to her father, "below her breath, panting like an emergent diver" (410); she looks at Basil "with swimming eyes" as the "storm rage[s]" in the music hall (416). In Woolson's novel, the gruesome sight of a woman floating in the water interrupts the first romantic embrace between

Eve and Paul. Paul springs into action to save her but soon realizes that a whole boat has capsized, so he will not have the strength to bring all the victims in alone. He asks Eve if she can paddle, and she immediately commands the canoe that drags Paul and the victims back to shore. In his admiration and attraction to Eve, Paul provides a strong contrast to Basil, who likes women to be weak and submissive—figuratively drowning so that he can be their savior. Paul expresses respect for Eve's strength verbally, and he shows it by relying on her to help him with the rescue. The "woman" turns out to be a young girl, "lashed to a plank by somebody's hand" in a futile attempt to save her (133), perhaps a symbolic indication of the maturity lacking in women who allow men to rob them of their independence. They may look like women, but in effect they are children. When Paul's friend Hollis arrives and sees the drowned child on the beach, Eve explains how she helped, noting that Paul could not have done it alone. Hollis, who also has feelings for Eve, repeats twice, "Paul shouldn't have asked you" (135). More like Basil in his thinking, Hollis voices the more conventional view of women as weak. Eve likes Hollis, but she is not attracted to him, probably because he is passive by nature, and too traditional in his ideas. In *The Bostonians*, the drowning metaphor represents Verena's figurative death as Basil's wife; in *Jupiter Lights*, it symbolizes the fate Eve escapes by partnering with a man who treats her as an equal partner. Indeed, Woolson reimagines the prospect of drowning a second time with a different ending later in the novel when Eve saves little Jack, who has drifted out on a boat alone at sunset. Eve manages to bring him back to shore single-handedly in the dark. Thus, Woolson turns James's drowned women in a faraway cove into an independent superheroine.

From a feminist perspective, Paul's arrival at the convent to retrieve Eve disappoints, not only because of the contrived revelation that the gunshot wound did not cause Ferdie's death, thus freeing Eve to marry him. As Caroline Gebhard notes in her assessment of Woolson's otherwise important and groundbreaking depiction of wife battering, "Paul's declaration that he is willing to knock down forty women to get to Eve makes it hard to ignore the fact that a woman's body is being overpowered by a man unwilling to take no for an answer . . . her abject surrender to Paul not only fails to reassure us, but also is false to the stark realism of Woolson's own portrayal of male battering."[18] I do not disagree and would add that the ending is also "false" to details in the novel that had served to construct a much more unconventional union of equals: Paul's admiration of Eve's strength, his own surprise at falling in love, and most importantly his declaration to Cicely that "I shall never conquer her" when Cicely implores him to subdue Eve because she is "too self-willed for a woman"

(128). These details just do not jibe with Paul's final argument to Eve, in which he says, "[T]o me you are like a child; I long to take care of you, I should guard you from everything" (225). Yet, as Gebhard suggests, "Woolson obviously wants the reader to believe in Eve's happiness in such a love."[19] Reading *Jupiter Lights* as a response to *The Bostonians* offers an additional explanation. Paul's storming of the convent echoes Basil's abduction of Verena "by muscular force" (418) from the Musical Hall where an audience awaits her in Boston, but with an important contrast: Basil exerts his force directly upon a reluctant Verena as he "wrenches" her away from her mother and "thrust[s]" the hood of her cloak "over her head, to conceal her face and her identity" (418). Paul, by contrast, inflicts his force upon those blocking his entry to the convent, not Eve herself. And with Eve's only objection to marrying Paul conveniently removed, readers are left to assume there will be no reluctance on her part. Paul's physical assertion at the end—unsettling as it is within the battering context—matches Eve's own strength of both body and mind while also appealing to reader expectations. The backpedaling on gender dynamics established earlier in the book dilutes an otherwise pioneering feminist text; nonetheless, the final scene of *Jupiter Lights* provides yet another important foil to *The Bostonians*.

Woolson also puts a more positive spin—problematic though it is—on the possibility of a homoerotic alternative to heterosexual marriage. Gebhard notes that the relationship between Eve and Cicely represents a "repudiated homoeroticism that offers women an alternative to marriage" at the same time "Eve assumes the role of the battered wife in relation to Cicely . . . like the wife who remains loyal despite her husband's violence, Eve cares for Cicely tenderly although Cicely continues to lash out at her."[20] In this way, Cicely and Ferdie are matched like for like in the way that Eve and Paul are, both couples driven by forces the text suggests are beyond their control, for good or for ill. Gebhard rightly observes that in "making Cicely both seductive and cruel" in her relationship to Eve, Woolson "comes perilously close to an antifeminist blaming of the victim,"[21] but here again I would emphasize the fact that the novel *does* imagine a female homoerotic alternative to marriage. Eve believes she has a choice between staying with Cicely and Jack and marrying Paul. Both are presented as viable options, and in the end she chooses the healthier heterosexual union, healthier not because it is heterosexual but because it does not involve battering and because the desire to "possess" is balanced equally between partners. In *The Bostonians*, James couches Olive's desire for Verena in terms of morbidity and perversity, at least from Basil's point of view, which on this point James never counters. Indeed, the way Basil's cloaking of Verena mirrors Olive's directly pits homosexual against heterosexual in a way that *Jupiter Lights* does not.

Woolson scholarship has cataloged a long list of strong, active heroines who resist and reverse nineteenth-century cultural and aesthetic stereotypes of women. As a late work, *Jupiter Lights* is a culmination of this project. From an Emersonian perspective, John Pearson believes Woolson struggled with the "widespread [nineteenth-century] aesthetic philosophy that situate[d] beauty . . . in the typically lifeless object of aesthetic desire . . . especially for women, who were inevitably reified as the powerless object of the aesthetic gaze."[22] She in turn rejects the notion by finding beauty not in lifeless aesthetic objects but in women's strength and everyday life. If Olive embodies how Emersonian ideals have often been interpreted, emphasizing the intellect at the expense of human passion, Basil exemplifies another common view of an Emersonian aesthetic in his idealization of women in general as he says to Verena, "I don't listen to your ideas, I listen to your voice" (175). In *Jupiter Lights*, Hollis represents the same aesthetic: he is a nonpracticing lawyer who spends his time reading and loafing about, selling objects of little value in his failing thrift store. Eve finds Hollis likeable, but she feels no desire for him. He is a clear foil to Paul's strong, active practicality, as well as her own. Yet in the end Woolson embraces the overlooked emphasis on passion and its universalizing effects in Emerson to chastise James's inability to find "real" love for his female protagonists. In Eve, she reimagines a new first woman forging an alternative, more realistic path forward for both sexes.

NOTES

1. Anne Boyd Rioux, *Constance Fenimore Woolson: Portrait of a Lady Novelist* (New York: Norton, 2016), 180.

2. Henry James, *The Bostonians* (New York: Vintage, 1991), 19; hereafter cited parenthetically.

3. Horace Scudder, "Recent American Fiction," *Atlantic Monthly*, January 1890, 126–28, quoted in *Critical Essays on Constance Fenimore Woolson*, ed. Cheryl B. Torsney (New York: G. K. Hall, 1992), 50–52.

4. Barbara Welter, "The Cult of True Womanhood: 1820–1860," *American Quarterly* 18, no. 2, pt. 1 (Summer 1966): 151–74.

5. Constance Fenimore Woolson, *Jupiter Lights* (New York: Harper & Brothers, 1889), 28, 329; hereafter cited parenthetically.

6. Catherine H. Zuckert, "American Women and Democratic Morals: *The Bostonians*," *Feminist Studies* 3, no. 3/4 (Spring–Summer 1976): 33.

7. Zuckert, 23.

8. Sharon L. Dean, ed., *The Complete Letters of Constance Fenimore Woolson* (Gainesville: University Press of Florida, 2012), 190.

9. Dean, 213.

10. Dean, 255.

11. Ralph Waldo Emerson, "Love," Emersoncentral.com, October 12, 2020, paras. 13–15, https://emersoncentral.com/texts/essays-first-series/love/.

12. "Mr. Henry James's New Novel," *Pall Mall Gazette*, March 1886, 5, in *Henry James: The Contemporary Reviews*, ed. Kevin J. Hayes (Cambridge: Cambridge University Press, 1996), 155–56.

13. "Recent Fiction," *Nation*, March 13, 1890, 225, quoted in Torsney, *Critical Essays on Constance Fenimore Woolson*, 55.

14. See Anne Boyd Rioux, "'What! Has She Got into the "Atlantic"?': Women Writers, the *Atlantic Monthly*, and the Formation of the American Canon," *American Studies* 39, no. 3 (Fall 1998): 5–36. Rioux's analysis of the *Atlantic* during the 1980s and 1990s finds a general conservatism on "the woman question" and a push to distinguish between "high and low fiction" as a means of separating itself from the competition (19–21). Reviews of *Jupiter Lights* fit this pattern.

15. Two of Woolson's short stories, "Felipa" and "Miss Grief," have appeared in anthologies of "lesbian" literature, and I have explored the ways she encodes homosexuality in these texts elsewhere. See *Chloe Plus Olivia: An Anthology of Lesbian Literature from the Seventeenth Century to the Present*, ed. Lillian Faderman (New York: Penguin, 1995); *Two Friends and Other Nineteenth-Century American Lesbian Stories by American Women Writers*, ed. Susan Koppelman (New York: Meridian, 1994); *The Literature of Lesbianism: A Historical Anthology from Ariosto to Stonewall*, ed. Terry Castle (New York: Columbia University Press, 2003); and my "Lesbian Impossibilities of Miss Grief's 'Armor,'" in *Constance Fenimore Woolson's Nineteenth Century: Essays*, ed. Victoria Brehm (Detroit, Mich.: Wayne State University Press, 2001), 207–23.

16. Caroline Gebhard notes the way Eve's mixed feelings for Cicely seem closely tied to her feelings for her brother in "Romantic Love and Wife-Battering in Constance Fenimore Woolson's *Jupiter Lights*," in Brehm, *Constance Fenimore Woolson's Nineteenth Century*, 90.

17. Henry Wadsworth Longfellow's *Kavanagh* describes romantic friendships among girls as a "rehearsal in girlhood of the great drama of woman's life." See *Kavanagh: A Tale* (Boston: Ticknor, Reed, and Fields, 1849), 39.

18. Gebhard, "Romantic Love and Wife-Battering," 89.

19. Gebhard, 89.

20. Gebhard, 91.

21. Gebhard, 91.

22. John H. Pearson, "Constance Fenimore Woolson's Critique of Emersonian Aesthetics," in Brehm, *Constance Fenimore Woolson's Nineteenth Century: Essays*, 51.

II

Postbellum Souths

"The Ancient City" and the Ethics of Sightseeing

Susan L. Roberson

Early in a travel narrative about Florida's St. Augustine, the oldest city in the United States, Constance Fenimore Woolson writes a scene that introduces the personal dynamics among eight fictional sightseers as well as their smug, myopic gaze. As the travelers approach the city by way of the north-flowing St. Johns River, Woolson's first-person narrator translates its original Indian name, "Il-la-ka," as "'It hath its own way, is alone, and contrary to every other,'" signaling more about the forty-year-old Martha than about the river. One of her companions, Sara St. John, indifferently asks, "'[I]s there anything we ought to know about these banks?'" In response, John Hoffman lectures her about the bloody history of the location, where French Huguenots were massacred by the Spanish. Iris, the "gay school-girl of seventeen," blithely sings, "'Ye banks and bray-ass of bon-onny Doo-oon'" from a poem by Robert Burns that was set to music in 1817, a poem that connects themes of natural loveliness and hurt in the image of the "flowery thorn" the lovelorn speaker addresses. Professor Macquoid looks about for the "fresh water shell heaps" that should be close by.[1] Symbolically, even though he peers about for them, the professor can see nothing with his nearsighted eyes.

Anticipating the ways Woolson will complicate her narrative, this early vignette quickly introduces readers to several travelers in a thumbnail sketch: Sara's quiet despair, Hoffman's superior attitude, Iris's flightiness, and the professor's arrogance. The scene also demonstrates the way Woolson deploys gentle satire of tourist foibles by turning the reader's gaze on the sightseers themselves, including Aunt Diana, the wealthy Mr. Mokes, and Miss Sharp, Iris's governess, together with the narrating Martha.

Published in the December 1874 issue of *Harper's Monthly*, which enjoyed

a wide readership in part because of its emphasis on travel writing, "The Ancient City" layers modes of storytelling that mimic the layered "shell heaps"
of history and of voice in this southern city.[2] By recasting the gaze and complicating voice and genre, as Shari Stone-Mediatore has observed, Woolson "throw[s] new light on the structure of historical reality and historical
knowledge."[3] Meditating on the ways minority women's voices are heard,
María Eugenia Cotera questions assumptions about "history, agency, and
marginalization," which Woolson will also expose.[4] Following the eight
northern tourists as they go on sightseeing excursions around the city, her
narrative crafts a post–Civil War South, an imaginary geography that represents the meeting ground between the past and the present, an ancient
city overlaid with history and monuments to the dead that meet the modern tourist and the modernizing tourist industry. Told from the perspective
of Woolson's Martha, the narrative listens to the voices of others, attends to
their nuances, and ruffles complacent claims about place, history, race, and
gender. From Macquoid, the history professor who went on the journey in
part for the "pleasure of imparting information" (1), to the wistful asides by
Sara St. John and the local inhabitants who often contradict the expectations of the northern sightseers, Woolson challenges easy assumptions about
the South.

Similarly, the narrative layers textual modes—the poetic, the historic,
travel reportage, short story, and romantic love plot—that simultaneously
satisfy and confound reader expectations. Woolson uses the multiple voices
of the tourists to expose the long history memorialized in the monuments and
to satirize the careless, patronizing attitudes toward history, place, and the
Other represented by the visitors. Confronted with evidence of three hundred years of conflict in Florida, the winter sojourners often disregard the
historical memories they are meant to preserve, including those of the recent Civil War, as they pursue their own intrigues. While shaping the characters and fictional subplots of the travel narrative, Woolson shrewdly exposes
what Dennis Berthold calls "the superficiality of travelers" who lack the responsibility and productive potential of ethical sightseeing that Dean Mac-
Cannell outlines.[5] MacCannell claims, "The ultimate ethical test for tourists
is whether they can realize the productive potential of their travel desires"
in the ways they "grasp and make sense of the world" and understand "the
gap that separates them from the *other-as-attraction*."[6] As she takes readers on
an armchair tour of the city, Woolson reveals this gap when she turns their
gaze from the locals to the sightseers in a kind of reverse ethnography as both
readers and locals focus on the gazers.

Arriving by steamer in "balmy" (1) Florida after leaving New York during a January snowstorm, the band of travelers welcomes a winter's sojourn in St. Augustine, which was emerging as a major resort location for invalids and northern tourists from the increasingly elite classes. Hoping to escape the cruel winters of the North and find relief from such ailments as tuberculosis, invalids had been coming to St. Augustine at least since Ralph Waldo Emerson's stay in 1827, just six years after the United States acquired Florida from Spain. Of the climate he wrote, "The air & sky of this ancient fortified dilapidated sandbank of a town are delicious." Later, the "unrivaled salubrity" that attracted "several hundred invalids and pleasure-seekers from the North" was touted in a *New York Times* story of April 28, 1860.[8] According to Anne Boyd Rioux, Florida's mild climate attracted Woolson and her widowed mother Hannah, who suffered from rheumatism and shingles, much like the invalids in her sketch who count the number of visitors arriving in town. With an eye toward attracting "the gold-bearing Northern tourist" (3), the growing tourism industry was on the cusp of really taking off under the influence of such leaders as financier Henry Flagler. Instead of staying at the St. Augustine Hotel, one of the three large hotels in the postbellum city, Woolson's tourists, like Woolson and her mother in 1873, decide on the more familiar boarding house where John Hoffman, one of the gang of eight, has stayed for several seasons.[9] Historian Thomas Graham notes that "[r]enting rooms to invalid northern 'strangers' during the winter season had long been one of the primary ways of infusing outside money into the rickety St. Augustine economy." Such a windfall would have been particularly important, Graham observes, after the desolation brought by federal occupiers during the Civil War and Reconstruction, followed by the economic depression of the 1870s.[10] Woolson's sojourners, then, were part of a growing industry that would transform the "ancient city" that Woolson discovered.

Getting to St. Augustine during the 1870s was a complicated matter. Much like the chaotic condition of travel in the South documented in narratives like Frederick Law Olmsted's *The Cotton Kingdom* (1861), Woolson's troop takes passage on a steamer from New York to Jacksonville, transfers in Florida to a smaller steamer bound for St. Augustine, and takes a mule train from Tocoi on the St. Johns River to a rail depot shed, where an omnibus carries the party "through the ever-present and never-mended mud hole" and over the causeway (figure 4) that still functioned as a fishing spot for locals (5). The engraving of a rustic paradise no doubt appealed to readers looking for an escape from cold

HORSE RAILROAD, ST. AUGUSTINE.

Figure 4. "Horse railroad, St. Augustine."
Woolson, "The Ancient City, Part I," *Harper's Monthly*, December 1874, 15.
Wood engraving. Courtesy of the HathiTrust.

weather and harried city life. Having crossed the San Sebastian River, Miss
Sharp, Iris Carew's governess, reads from her guidebook, "'After three hours
and one-half of this torture the exhausted tourist finds himself at the San Sebastian River, where a miserable ferry conveys him, more dead than alive, to the
city of St. Augustine'" (5). Although Woolson's travelers do not take the ferry,
they are exhausted; as Graham notes, travel to Florida "remained a primitive
ordeal," even as late as 1880.[11]

     Following a night's rest, the group is ready to see the city, where the real ac-
tion begins. Equipped with a guidebook and accompanied by Professor Macquoid, who is a walking encyclopedia, the sightseers make their way around
the city, enabling Woolson to infuse her sketch with important historical facts.
When "The Ancient City" was published in 1874, there were several guidebooks, some subsidized by hotels, railroads, or land developers, designed to satisfy tourist curiosity about Florida. *Sketches of St. Augustine* by Rufus Sewell
had appeared in 1848, and a charming book, *Petals Plucked from Sunny Climes*
(1880), would describe Florida and the Caribbean in lively fashion.[12] Itself a
kind of guide to St. Augustine, "The Ancient City" participates in the ongoing
sight sacralization of the more formal guidebooks, which provided a consensus
of the sights tourists simply must see, according to MacCannell. Not only do
Woolson's travelers visit the requisite attractions, but they memorialize significant events in Florida and U.S. history even as "The Ancient City" follows the
whims and personalities of its characters.

Like most travelers, they visit Fort Marion, formerly Castillo de San Marcos, built in 1565 by the Spanish and more recently occupied by the Fourth New Hampshire Regiment during the Civil War. Its "secret dungeon" and "walled-up entrance" are reminders of the Inquisition and the Seminole chief who was imprisoned there before he made his daring escape (12). Along with the U.S. barracks at St. Francis, a former Franciscan monastery, these ancient forts testify to the three hundred years of struggle between the Spanish, French, British, and Native Americans, in addition to the Union and Confederate armies, for control of the land. The travelers peer at the quaint coquina buildings and narrow streets of Minorca Town, noting the Greek, Corsican, and Minorcan laborers who were brought as indentured servants by the Englishman Dr. Turnbull in 1767 and then mutinied against the "tyranny of their governor" (7). They visit the site where the Spanish massacred "[t]hree hundred and fifty Huguenots" (16), French Protestants who had fled Catholic Europe. Though the bones of the dead lie beneath the Mantanzas River, its name, which means "slaughter," keeps the memory of the horrific deed alive and leads Sara to ask, "Is there any place about here where there were no massacres?" (17). The group also visits a plantation in ruins, its white chimney "a monument to the past" reaching back "more than a century before Plymouth or Jamestown," which causes Hoffman to bemoan, "Poor Florida! She is full of deserted plantations" (17). These monuments are sober reminders of St. Augustine's long history of violence, colonialism, and tyranny from the Spanish invasion through the American Civil War. The latter is commemorated by a simple memorial, "a broken shaft carved in coquina," that had been erected in 1872 by the Ladies Memorial Association of St. Augustine for the Confederate dead (13). In this way, Woolson sketches a South that is haunted by the past, daily reminders built into the landscape and architecture of the city.[13]

But even as Woolson builds a text in which the past intersects with the present, she weighs the tourists' carelessness about history and the sites they visit. As she takes her troop and her readers to the usual locations and rehearses the accepted history of place, she demonstrates the traveling party's corruption of the sacred with their antics.

Satirizing her sightseers, Woolson complicates armchair perceptions by turning attention to tourists and the society they represent. John Urry argues that because the tourist gaze is socially constructed, it "is a good way of getting at just what is happening in the 'normal society,'" which in Woolson's hands is self-absorbed, unmindful of the costs of colonization.[14] They enjoy themselves during a winter's retreat, figuratively dancing on the ruins of history. Quibbling about words, mixing up historical facts, engaging in casual flirtations, and pressing, as we will see, a white male reading of history, the sightseers represent not only Berthold's "superficiality of travelers" but also the "normal" American society and the ideologies it supports.[15] Shrewdly turning the gazing eye back on the traveling and reading tourists, Woolson "manages," as Anne Boyd Rioux argues, "to decenter her text . . . in ways that challenge her northern readers' presumed cultural superiority" and to situate them and her tourists at the margins of local knowledge.[16] Deploying satire, Woolson shifts the attention of the reader and unsettles expectations about sightseeing, travel narratives, and a usable past.

One conversation that illustrates how Woolson complicates the travel sketch as a genre occurs when the group discusses the 1837 escape of Coacoochee or "Coochy," the chief who was held prisoner in Fort Marion during the Second Seminole War (1835–42). Aunt Diana confuses the chief's nickname, the Wildcat, with an actual cat. Sara confuses the chief with Osceola, his companion in escape. When Captain Carlyle explains he was the son of King Philip, Iris confuses his father with the King Philip of the New England Wampanoags. Sara references "the immortal Pontiac of the West" and "something about the Caloosahatchee," which leads John to ask primly whether she is thinking about "the distinguished chieftains Holatoochee and Taholooche, and the river Chattahoochee." That comment reminds the captain of the song lines "'with a hoochee-koochee-koochee'" and reminds Iris of her brother who plays the song on his banjo (11–12). Superficially entertaining, such banter exposes the tourists' historical ignorance and their apparent delight in it. Considering, for example, the captain whose job it is to represent and protect the country, Woolson's tale prompts disconcerted readers to reassess the thoughtless northerners.

In between these linguistic feats, the captain and Iris keep disappearing together in a flirtatious rendezvous, while Iris proposes that they "dance on the top" of the fort (9) as the love plots intersect with and disrupt the informative travel narrative and the history recounted. While the party explores the various locales of St. Augustine, Iris flirts not only with the handsome captain but also with Mr. Mokes, whose money seems to qualify him as a better choice from Aunt Diana's point of view, and with Mr. Hoffman, who gives her roses to wear in her hair. Miss Sharp pairs up with both the professor, whose arm she grasps aboard the *Oceola*, and Mr. Mokes, who gives her history lessons under the Florida trees. At almost every location, couples wander off figuratively and literally from the historical narrative. At the end of part I, as everyone is settling

in for bed, Aunt Diana informs the others that Iris has disappeared. After speculating on the whereabouts of Mokes and Hoffman, the women decide that Iris
has eloped with the young captain, leaving readers waiting until part II reveals
a month later what happens to Iris and the love plot. Although the magazine's
readers may have expected a conventional romantic ending, Woolson exposes
the superficiality of the tourist class as her narrative mimics the confused and
competing layers of Florida's historical story.[17]

Though the professor and Hoffman provide essential information about St.
Augustine and its past, their racist and sexist attitudes open them up to Woolson's quiet satire. For instance, after Hoffman has given a quick historical account of the Minorcans, he comments on their physical appearance, noting the
"dark almond-shaped eyes, now and then a classical nose, often a mass of Oriental black hair" that do not meet his standards of unified beauty, leaving them
metaphorically dismembered (7). When he remarks that the Minorcan girls remind him of Greece and Italy, Sara, who had been eager to make comparisons
to Sappho, comments that she has never been to Italy. Though he does not respond, "the reflection of an inward smile" crossing his face suggests his condescension toward the less-traveled Sara (7). Woolson also takes a swipe at what
might be called "mansplaining," a sexist mannerism employed by some men to
demean and discount women's knowledge and intellect.[18] For instance, when
the group is discussing the coquina sea wall, built in 1842, the professor cites
facts about it but does not understand, as Martha does, that the growing town
may need the wall's protection. To her statement, he replies, "'It will never be
anything more than a winter resort, Miss Martha'" (9), disregarding her understanding of St. Augustine's future. Here Woolson satirizes the microaggressions
of men like the professor and Mr. Hoffman. These instances demonstrate that,
as a woman, Woolson can appreciate the need to hear alternative histories and
knowledges, to give voice to the silenced and voiceless. As she satirizes the patriarchal travelers who, guidebooks in hand, assume their own superiority over
any gendered and racial Other, she opens spaces, gaps, between tourist and attraction so that alternatives can be heard by the attentive reader.

When most of the crew go to the North Beach on the *Osceola*, Martha visits
the St. Francis post and comes across the monument to the Confederate dead.
As she gazes upon "the broken shaft" made of the native concrete, "an old
Negro" leaning on a cane pauses nearby. Martha asks if he knew any of the
forty-four men whose names are inscribed. He did and his "ole woman" used
to take care of some when they were babies, which suggests a familial relationship between white and Black. When Martha comments on the changes for enslaved people following the Civil War, he straightens and says, "'Yas, we's free

now. . . . I breave anoder breff effer sense, mistis, dat I do'" (13–14). While the material circumstances of the elder man's life may not have changed noticeably and he may not have much time left, his sense of freedom is real. By contrast, one of the other visitors at the boarding house announced later that evening, "They do not quite know how to take their freedom yet," as if the once enslaved must be educated to breathe free air (14). By complicating the meanings associated with the monument as a memorial to both the Confederacy and emancipation, Woolson undercuts simplistic ideas about slavery, the relations between master and enslaved, and the meaning of freedom that her readers and some of Florida's tourists may have.

Despite the assertion that "the colored people of St. Augustine" were isolated and "well cared for, and led easy lives," the African Americans whom Martha encounters as narrator are proud of their freedom in ways that northern tourists do not understand. The woman thinks "their ideas take the oddest shapes" (14). However, when the boardinghouse's Black employee, the Sabre, "insists upon going and coming through the front door," and Aunt Viny, a seller of sweets, names her daughter Victoria Linkum after Abraham Lincoln, they assert their mobility and citizenship in quiet acts of defiance and equality.[19] By contrast, Sara hopes to look across the vast ocean to Africa without any obstructions such as the Canary Islands, long a site of the European imperialism and enslavement that Sara would elide. Where she looks wistfully to the Nile for a "breath" of Africa, Martha understands that Africa is here, in St. Augustine's Black section of town. Appropriately called Little Africa, though it would be renamed Lincolnville in the 1880s, it signals the residents' connection to their ancestral home and sense of community.

It is also a place to which Martha must be guided, not only because she does not know the local streets but also because Aunt Viny knows them intimately. When Viny says "[W]henebber *I* wants to go dar, I jes *goes*," she insinuates that she has something Martha lacks: an intuitive, cognitive map of place (14). The narrator is thereby positioned as the outsider, Aunt Viny as the insider; when Sara desires an unobstructed view over the ocean to Africa, Woolson positions her as someone who ignores the realities of a past that haunts St. Augustine's Black community. Woolson reveals the gaps in knowledge and perception that characterize her tourists, the spaces they thoughtlessly miss. As feminist theorist Sandra Harding declares and "The Ancient City" embodies, there are gaps in "dominant conceptual schemes" between outsider and insider, tourist and attraction, text and subtext that lie in the spaces between what is said and what is known.[20]

Having visited the Arcadian ruins of an old Florida plantation and imagined the story of the place, Sara and Martha discover some modern Arcadians in a young family living with very little in the way of material comforts, a useful example of James Cox's description of the South coalescing as a "negative identity."²¹ The modern home lacks the comforts of middle-class abodes: the house is more like an outbuilding, the dining room is situated out of doors, and "there was no window of any kind, no floor save the sand, and for a door only an old coverlet" (19). At first readers are drawn to what the Arcadians do not have. But catching the tenor of the place, Sara ventures, "[T]hey seem happy enough" (19). The couple do not work much because they live primarily off the land, and they do not intend to send their young boy to be educated. "None of us-uns goes to school, my lady" (19–20). Readers can see that Sara and Martha judge the family for what they lack: a nice home, steady work, education, ambition. But then the young mother turns the scorn on the tourists. She does not want to be like the women who visit the South, and she calls the men "wimpsy." Pondering the meaning of "wimpsy," Sara sees Mr. Mokes giving Miss Sharp a lesson on St. Augustine and observes, "He is certainly limpsy; then why not wimpsy?" (20). As the Arcadian Anita rejects northern definitions of manhood for her more virile Gaspar, Woolson shifts the gaze from the Arcadians to the northern tourists; both Anita and "The Ancient City" question assumptions about progress, knowledge, and northern consumerism. In this way Woolson critiques the careless tourists who do not comprehend what they see and demonstrates the more nuanced understanding of relations between sightseer and attraction that MacCannell would recommend, an understanding fashioned locally for Woolson's readers by residents like Anita, Aunt Viny, and the elderly Black man.²²

Deploying multiple layers of storytelling, perspective, and voice, "The Ancient City" constructs an ethics of sightseeing that models a revisionist history of place. When Woolson pauses the plot to listen to the people who populate her story, the travelers with their microaggressions and the locals who form part of their tourist experience, readers hear the personalities of both her travelers and the "attractions." Giving voice to Arcadians and African Americans, Woolson casts them as subjects with their own experiences and perspectives that counter reader and tourist expectations, rather than objects of a tour. By listening carefully to the multiple voices of place, she demonstrates what Henry James noted about the stories in *Rodman the Keeper*: "As the fruit of a remarkable minuteness of observation and tenderness of feeling on the part of one who evidently did not glance and pass, but lingered and analysed, they have a high value, especially when regarded in the light of the *voicelessness* of the conquered and reconstructed South."[23] Attending to the nuances of her subjects and letting them talk back to the northern travelers, Woolson points to alternative experiences of place and history and to an ethics of inclusion and empathy that extends beyond the usual activity of sightseeing.

This ethics is evident as well when Woolson redirects readers from the tourist attractions to the fictional travelers and the "normal society" they represent. Doing so, as Anne Boyd Rioux remarked about the short story "Felipa," Woolson "turns the tables on the northern reader and reverses the direction of the imperial gaze, modeling empathy rather than objectification."[24] Both Woolson and her narrator are outsiders glimpsing the lives of the locals, whether Black, Minorcan, or Arcadian. The northern travelers do not get to know southern cultures, nor do they attempt to dig in and find out about alternative ways of life or establish any rapport. After all, they are what Cotera calls "casual cultural colonizers" bearing northern money and northern attitudes.[25]

Yet even as she participates in promoting tourism to Florida, Woolson subtly shifts these brief cultural encounters, turning what Zora Neale Hurston calls the "spy-glass of Anthropology" back on the visitors.[26] She lets the indigenous talk back, not only to be heard but also to critique the northerners who think they represent Cotera's "ethnographic authority."[27] By deploying and then subverting the tourist's gaze, by juxtaposing touristic outsider accounts of history and placing them alongside corrective insider rebuttals, Woolson demonstrates an ethics of sightseeing that exposes the self-indulgence of the visitors and their myopic ignorance. Implying an alternate method of genuine discovery in the narrative's multimodal, polyvocal format, Woolson models a more complex, nuanced, ethical approach to seeing the South that reckons with a history of slaughter, a breath of freedom, and an Arcadia whose "sights" talk back.

NOTES

1. Constance Fenimore Woolson, "The Ancient City, Part I," *Harper's Monthly*, December 1874, 1–2; hereafter cited parenthetically. Another version of pt. 1 can be found in Victoria Brehm and Sharon L. Dean, eds., *Constance Fenimore Woolson: Selected Stories and Travel Narratives* (Knoxville: University of Tennessee Press, 2004), 91–123. Many thanks to Lisa Nais for directing me to the lyrics of the poem as song: Robert Burns, "Ye Banks and Braes o' Bonny Doon," music by R. T. Skarratt, *British Lady's Magazine*, July 1817, 84–86.

2. Sharon D. Kennedy-Nolle, *Writing Reconstruction: Race, Gender, and Citizen-*

ship in the Postwar South (Chapel Hill: University of North Carolina Press, 2015), 30. For more on *Harper's Monthly* and Woolson's travel writing about the multiple Souths of the Gilded Age, see Kevin E. O'Donnell, "'Pioneers of Spoliation': Woolson's *Horace Chase* and the Role of Magazine Writing in the Gilded-Age Development of the South," in *Witness to Reconstruction: Constance Fenimore Woolson and the Postbellum South, 1873–1894*, ed. Kathleen Diffley (Jackson: University Press of Mississippi, 2011), 266–84.

3. Shari Stone-Mediatore, *Reading across Borders: Storytelling and Knowledges of Resistance* (New York: Palgrave Macmillan, 2003), quoted in María Eugenia Cotera, *Native Speakers: Ella Deloria, Zora Neale Hurston, Jovita González, and the Poetics of Culture* (Austin: University of Texas Press, 2008), 140.

4. Cotera, *Native Speakers*, 140.

5. Dennis Berthold, "Miss Martha and Ms. Woolson: Persona in the Travel Sketches," in *Constance Fenimore Woolson's Nineteenth Century: Essays*, ed. Victoria Brehm (Detroit, Mich.: Wayne State University Press, 2001), 112.

6. Dean MacCannell, *The Ethics of Sightseeing* (Berkeley: University of California Press, 2011), 6–7.

7. Ralph L. Rusk, ed., *Letters of Ralph Waldo Emerson* (New York: Columbia University Press, 1939), 1:189.

8. "Florida; Strange Aspect of St. Augustine—Climate and Productions—Its Unequaled Salubrity—Florida Winters—Summer in St. Augustine—Hotels Crowded—St. Augustine the Resort of Invalids—The Town Three Hundred Years Old—Inducements for Emigration to Florida," *New York Times*, April 28, 1860, N10.

9. Anne Boyd Rioux, *Constance Fenimore Woolson: Portrait of a Lady Novelist* (New York: Norton, 2016), 84, 85.

10. Thomas Graham, *Mr. Flagler's St. Augustine* (Gainesville: University Press of Florida, 2014), 6, 5.

11. Graham, 34.

12. See the University Press of Florida site for digitalized versions of *Petals Plucked from Sunny Climes* by A. M. Brooks and *Sketches of St. Augustine* by Rufus Sewell. University of Florida Digital Collections, "Petals Plucked from Sunny Climes" (2017), http://ufdc.ufl.edu/AA00061997/00001.

13. For a discussion on the roles of memorials and Woolson's use of them in her fiction, see Elizabethada A. Wright, "Keeping Memory: The Cemetery and Rhetorical Memory in Constance Fenimore Woolson's 'Rodman the Keeper,'" *Studies in the Literary Imagination* 39, no. 1 (Spring 2006): 29–54.

14. John Urry, *The Tourist Gaze* (1990; London: Sage, 2002), 2.

15. Kennedy-Nolle comments on the "linguistic slapstick" and vaudeville qualities of the scene about bartizans and demi-lunes in *Writing Reconstruction*, 50.

16. Anne E. Boyd [Rioux], "Tourism, Imperialism, and Hybridity in the Reconstruction South: Constance Fenimore Woolson's *Rodman the Keeper: Southern Sketches*," *Southern Literary Journal* 43, no. 2 (Spring 2011): 13.

17. See Kennedy-Nolle, *Writing Reconstruction*, 27. The editors of *Constance Fenimore Woolson: Selected Stories and Travel Narratives* explain what happened in pt. 2 to

Iris and her possible partners as well as the reconciliation between Sara and John Hoffman, "satisfying the public expectation for a fulfilled romance, but at the expense of a woman's art" (124n58).

18. *Webster's Dictionary* defines mansplaining as what occurs when a man talks condescendingly to someone (especially a woman) about something he has incomplete knowledge of, with the mistaken assumption that he knows more about it than the person he's talking to does.

19. Kennedy-Nolle discusses the ways Woolson addresses issues of citizenship and freedom for the freed people of St. Augustine: "Through the perspective of her female tourists, Woolson accurately captured postwar interracial, gendered differences over the legacy of slavery, and even the meaning of American citizenship." See *Writing Reconstruction*, 40–41.

20. Sandra Harding, *Whose Science? Whose Knowledge? Thinking from Women's Lives* (Ithaca, N.Y.: Cornell University Press, 1991), 70–71.

21. James Cox, "Regionalism: A Diminished Thing," in *Columbia Literary History of the United States*, ed. Emory Elliott (New York: Columbia University Press, 1988), 778.

22. MacCannell, *Ethics of Sightseeing*, 6.

23. Henry James, "Miss Constance Fenimore Woolson," *Harper's Weekly*, February 12, 1887, 114, quoted in Boyd, "Tourism, Imperialism, and Hybridity," 18.

24. Boyd, "Tourism, Imperialism, and Hybridity," 22.

25. Cotera, *Native Speakers*, 61.

26. Zora Neale Hurston, *Mules and Men* (Philadelphia: Lippincott, 1935), 1.

27. Cotera, *Native Speakers*, 139.

"Sit Still and Remember"

WOOLSON'S KEEPERS AND THE PROBLEM OF THE ARCHIVE

Sidonia Serafini

By the time Constance Fenimore Woolson penned her "Southern Sketches," later collected in *Rodman the Keeper: Southern Sketches* (1880), two methodologies of archival preservation had been established in the United States. The public records tradition of the colonial era was oriented toward communally preserved, publicly accessible vital data, land records, and legislative and government proceedings. The goal of this method, as James O'Toole has observed, involved safeguarding the new democracy and the rights of its citizens.[1] Out of the public records approach grew a historical manuscripts tradition in the late eighteenth and early nineteenth centuries. Historical societies cropped up at local, state, and national levels and collected records "useful for studying and understanding the past."[2] Different from the outward-facing focus of the public records tradition, these emerging societies prioritized private papers. Then, in the aftermath of the Civil War, how, when, where, and by whom stories would be told, preserved, and made available to a public audience once again loomed large in the minds of Americans across lines of race, culture, and region. As David Blight has shown, such questions haunted the American South especially.[3] The dilemma of how to move forward with national healing helped inaugurate another kind of preservation tradition in the form of Union and Confederate cemeteries. It was at this fraught moment that Woolson took up her pen to record and fictionalize the tensions rooted in the historical memory she witnessed of southern life and culture, with a keen attentiveness to the region's "keepers" of archives.

In the late nineteenth century, Woolson anticipated questions that have increasingly come to dominate recent conversations among scholars regarding the roles of the archive and the archivist, of practices of recordkeeping, and of historical memory. Her *Rodman* stories ruminate on the ways in which history and memory are preserved in written records as well as nonprint sources, through oral history and the landscape. Storytelling occupies a central place in Woolson's oeuvre, and the summons to "sit still and remember" is the binding agent of her "Southern Sketches."[4] She was particularly interested in the figure of "the keeper"—of stories, sites, and documents—who reappears in many shapes and forms throughout the volume. In Woolson's stories, interactions with and creation of written records are often, but not always, isolated deeds that take place in seclusion and are performed by a solitary hand, most notably by the federally commissioned cemetery keeper in "Rodman the Keeper" and the self-appointed family genealogist in "Old Gardiston." While scholars such as John Lowe have gestured toward the recurrence of this figure in *Rodman the Keeper*, Woolson's ruminations on the role and practice of it remain largely unexplored.[5] Woolson examines the figure of the keeper across a spectrum of southern contexts. In doing so, she probes what is at stake in creating and preserving historical records and calls into question the power dynamics always at play with regard to an archive and its architect(s). Woolson's collection, then, is not simply a compilation of southern chronicles but also an interrogation of the act of chronicling itself.

The collection's title piece, "Rodman the Keeper," immediately signals a preoccupation with recordkeeping. Rodman, a Union veteran from New England, is the sole attendant, groundsman, recordkeeper, and (it seems) visitor of the national cemetery for Union soldiers. Manicuring the grounds, meditating among the headstones, and copying and recopying with "[i]nfinite pains and labor" the grave records and visitor logs, Rodman tends the site out of a sense of duty to the fallen soldiers, echoing Woolson's own feelings of obligation to those who have served (146). "I always go to see the soldiers' graves," Woolson wrote in an 1875 letter to Paul Hamilton Hayne, adding, "I cannot bear to think that they are so soon forgotten."[6] Characterizing the collection's primary keeper, Woolson wastes no time in presenting her readers with a dilemma surrounding historical memory: its often incomplete nature. One of two rooms in Rodman's cottage houses a "desk and the great ledgers, the ink and pens, the register, the loud-ticking clock on the wall, and the flag folded on a shelf," which "were all for the kept, whose names, in hastily written, blotted rolls of manuscript, were waiting to be transcribed in the new red-bound ledgers in the keeper's best handwriting" (143). The records, as the narrator remarks, are indicative of "those dark years among the sixties, measured now more than by anything else in the number of maidens widowed in heart, . . . who sit still and remember, while the world rushes by" (146). As keeper, Rodman, too, is among this group of rememberers. However, his recollection involves, to a certain extent, forgetting.

As Joan Schwartz and Terry Cook maintain, "Archives have the power to privilege and to marginalize."[7] Harnessed as either a mechanism of control or a weapon of "resistance," documents in any archive are not simply "bearer[s] of historical content."[8] One aspect of archival practice that has come under great scrutiny is the "myth . . . that the archivist is (or should strive to be) an objective, neutral, passive (if not impotent, then self-restrained) keeper of truth."[9] Rodman's recopying of the cemetery records positions him as a less-than-objective keeper. Through an analysis of handwriting, Woolson prompts her reader to consider what is lost in the translation of these records. Meticulous details contrast the penmanship of the "old" records that are soon to be recopied into the "new" ledgers by Rodman, signaling the ways in which these documents represent two distinct memories of the Civil War. The original "blotted rolls of manuscript" and the scribbled entries transport readers back to the visceral period of war, drawing attention to the chaotic moment when soldiers were dying and being buried with such rapidity that it was all the then-current keeper of the cemetery could do to "hastily" transcribe the name of each fallen soldier into the ledgers (143). Flash forward, then, to Rodman's moment and readers are presented with a very different scene: a quiet, still cemetery, distanced from the upheaval of war, with a new keeper who is daily in the process of replacing the original ledgers with new ones by recopying them in his own hand. The immaculately transcribed rolls evidence how, with time, memory can become romanticized and warped. Rodman's adjustments to the historical record assign a polished, controlled gloss to the war, obliterating the tumult that emanates from the original documents and the unique material qualities of the original artifact—perhaps a military seal or medical stamp, in addition to the smudged paper and the original transcriber's hurried hand. Rodman is no longer a mere custodian of the cemetery files but a tacit editor.

In addition to the rerecorded cemetery registers, the memorial site's logs do not accurately reflect its visitors. When the southerner Bettina Ward appears looking for her cousin, Rodman asks that she sign the log: "'Before you go . . . will you write your name in my register. . . . The Government had it prepared for the throngs who would visit these graves; but with the exception of the blacks, who can not write, no one has come, and the register is empty. Will you write your name?'" (169). Rodman quickly qualifies his request, asking of Bettina, "'[D]o not write it unless you can think gently of the men who lie there under the grass,'" and then speculating, "'I believe you do think gently of them, else why have you come of your own accord to stand by the side of their graves?'" (169). Bettina refuses, however, as Martin Buinicki has asserted, to become "part of the historical record."[10] A visit to the Union cemetery in search of her cousin can be excused, but defiling her loyalty to the Confederate South by inserting her name into the "locus where memory and history meet in the archive" is unforgivable.[11] Her visit to the cemetery, then, is one of utter silence—at least in terms of print. This knowledge is unearthed solely by the narrator's own telling.

Even more significant than the absence of Bettina's name on the visitor logs is the absence of the names of the freedpeople who visit the site. While Bettina is given the chance to refuse committing her name to the pages, the African American citizens who come to pay their respects are not even asked. It is not coincidental that the story does not present a similar scene in which these "other" visitors are encouraged to insert their names into a historical document. Ironically, Rodman does not prompt Pomp, the formerly enslaved servant of Bettina's cousin to whom Rodman teaches the alphabet in his downtime as keeper, to sign his name. Woolson is very much aware of the submergence of the histories and memories of people of color in the United States. The omission of their place in the historical record is facilitated both by the disadvantages of illiteracy and by the culprits Erasure and Silence. Blight has demonstrated that reconciliationist memory gave rise to narratives that cohered around the notion of reunion, inevitably suffocating memories that did not further such a vision, including African American memories of the war.[12] As a faithful servant to the government and his fallen comrades, and a keeper who is supposedly driven to recopying the cemetery records out of a deep sense of duty, Rodman himself does not transcribe the names of those who visit the site.

He is, nonetheless, at least somewhat interested in bridging historical gaps. Sometimes, as Kathleen Diffley has noted, Rodman unofficially inserts himself into archival work geared toward "recovery" when he "invents a mustering in for Blank Rodman"—a grave that rests with no name, imagined by Rodman as "——Rodman, Company A, One Hundred and Sixth New York."[13] A generous reading would grant that Rodman's reluctance is rooted in his obligation to maintain an ethical position of neutrality as recordkeeper. If he signed the names *in place of* the visitors, the logs would be in his handwriting, not that of the cemetery's visitors. Because these records would likely be recopied in his own "best handwriting," however, this hypothesis falls short (143). Rodman is a *keeper* and not a *creator* of records, and yet he exercises mastery over the cemetery archives and mars them, to a degree, with his revisions.

The sanitized cemetery rolls and the present absences that haunt the visitor logs call into question the completeness of any archive. Dead ends, omissions, and inconsistencies prompt the user of any archival document to speculate, as Rodman does regarding the sentiments behind Bettina's visit. For future cemetery visitors who might attempt to construct a portrait of the Reconstruction South from Rodman's archive, what would these records mean for their depiction? What would the pristine, carefully rewritten registers of the dead signify to them? Or, more problematically, what of the empty visitor log? Rodman's actions, or lack thereof, generate countless questions about the role of the archive and the archivist and offer a framework for thinking about such issues as Woolson's collection moves forward with a motley cast of other keeper figures.

In "Old Gardiston," Woolson crafts a counterpart to Rodman. Unlike his position in the realm of national public memory, Cousin Copeland is the self-appointed archivist of the Gardiston family papers. The family archive reveals the ways in which some records are confined to the privacy of one's own home, to a familial circle, to descendants' possession, or even to local or regional repositories. In the Gardiston mansion's isolated tower, the family documents, replete with Copeland's footnotes and references, become a self-contained archive of which Copeland is the sole arbiter, both keeper and audience.

Like the figure of the Surveyor who imagines the story of Hester Prynne in Nathaniel Hawthorne's "The Custom-House" (1850) after stumbling upon the "rubbish" of "musty papers" that have been surrendered to "oblivion," Copeland dives into the Gardiston family archive to rescue the untold and forgotten story of the "'first wife of one of the second cousins of [his] respected grandfather.'"[14] The first time Copeland speaks at length, he limns the efforts of his recovery mission, broadcasting a desire to protect his ancestral history from oblivion's threat: "A most interesting discovery—most interesting . . . the happy idea occurred to me to investigate more fully the contents of the papers in the barrel number two on the east side of the central garret—documents that I myself classified in 1849. . . . I have good hopes of finding there, too, valuable information respecting this first wife of one of the second cousins of our respected grandfather, a lady whose memory, by some strange neglect, has been suffered to fall into oblivion. I shall be proud to constitute myself the one to rescue it for the benefit of posterity," continues the little man, with chivalrous enthusiasm (235). Unlike Rodman's recordkeeping work, which at least attempted to preserve histories for the sake of public knowledge, inquiry, and memory, Copeland's historical detective work is largely circumscribed to his personal pleasure.

His analysis of the past occurs behind a veil within the private sphere, a parochial undertaking that is mirrored in the sequestered tower in which his

work takes place. On one document in the family papers, for example, Copeland scribbles in the margin, "'May we all profit by this!'" (231). Yet the "we" in
this statement never materializes, as Copeland's eyes are the only ones to view
the ostensible wisdom that radiates from the pages. Memory and history, under these circumstances, are accessible only to a select few—that is, to Copeland and to whomever he decides to divulge information. Moreover, as Leonardo Buonomo has observed, characters in Woolson's work who are "brought
to the surface . . . to be salvaged from oblivion and the omissions of historiography" are often white southern women.[15] The mysterious and fleeting ancestor in the Gardiston family genealogy whom Copeland rescues from historical
oblivion is no exception. As a white woman of a wealthy southern family, she is
in a privileged if slightly precarious position to be recorded at all.

Copeland as a keeper figure draws attention to the hierarchies of race and
class that often determine the fate and preservation of records. The intertwined
nature of power and recordkeeping is suggested in Copeland's curious shock
that the memory of a distant white southern female relative has succumbed
to "strange neglect" (235). The barrels upon barrels of the Gardiston family's records assume a towering importance that is decidedly linked to slavery,
to the wealth that forced labor enabled, and to the leisure that then ensures
both plump archives and inordinate family pride. In this regard, Copeland, who
"lived only in the past," resembles a character in Woolson's satirical sketch,
"The Bones of Our Ancestors" (231). There, a woman named Mary Ann becomes her family's self-appointed genealogist whose mission is to locate her
original ancestor—a man elusively referred to as the "original Tom"—in state
and local archives to prove her aristocratic family lineage. Living only in the
past is damaging to her health. Her "pretty hands" exist in a "chronic state of
inkiness," she "acquire[s] a slight stoop," and her hygiene and garden become
"sadly neglected."[16] The word "chronic" suggests that Mary Ann's obsession
with genealogy is a sad debility rather than an impassioned hobby. Moreover,
her sickness gestures toward the intertwined nature of archives and aristocracy, a symptom of an affliction plaguing slanted methodologies of historical
preservation that, like Copeland's, prioritize the records of wealthy, upper-class
society.

The act of salvaging stories from anonymity also prompts questions about
the functions and meanings of "rescue" and "recovery" regarding historical
subjects. Copeland's investigation of the unnamed woman's story, for example, is framed by the narrator in terms of masculine valor: Copeland describes
with "chivalrous enthusiasm" his work as a "rescue" mission (235). He imagines
himself an honorable knight, interceding to save a damsel from falling off the

cliff into historical amnesia. Copeland's conception of historical recovery as a grand display of chivalry elicits questions about the difference between "rescuing" and "uncovering." The former implies a self-aggrandizing motive; the latter suggests an ethical responsibility to the past. What is at stake in recovery work? Who is "saved" and who is "saving"? However these questions are answered, recovery work, especially when painted in terms of historical rescue, involves certain roles of authority and privilege, and those who take on this work deem what is and is not worthy of preservation.

The story's conclusion, however, seals the documents' oblivion. First, Copeland's abrupt death halts the resurrection of the woman's story; then, a fire consumes the mansion. Copeland has spent his life keeping watch over an archive that is ultimately lost to the world. To add insult to injury, the family history is further submerged when Gardis Duke, Copeland's niece and the sole surviving descendant of southern aristocracy, marries into a commonplace northern family. While it may initially seem that Woolson suggests a conflagration is all it takes to destroy the plantation and everything it represents, the rest of her collection does not confirm a similar ease in doing away with the Old South.

Although print records like Copeland's may disappear, stories live on through oral history, as in "In the Cotton Country." When an outsider from the Midwest visits South Carolina, she stumbles upon the decaying cabin of a destitute Confederate widow named Judith who, as Caroline Gebhard points out elsewhere in this volume (108–19), lives secluded in the woods with her adolescent nephew. The anonymous narrator has come to the South presumably to record its history and lore, recollecting Woolson's own visits to the region during the 1870s. The visitor lends a listening ear to Judith, a poor white counterpart to Copeland's aristocratic distant cousin. Embodied by these two women of distinct generations and regions is a collaborative approach to memory that differs from Rodman's and Copeland's roles as solitary archivists.

Immediately the traveling narrator remarks of Judith, "How still she was!," describing her as shrouded in a "great silence."[17] In her "stillness," the aged southerner resembles a concrete monument akin to the cemetery gravestones in "Rodman the Keeper." Yet Judith is a living repository, a memorial come alive. The narrator transcribes Judith's tale of familial, spousal, and property loss in the aftermath of the Civil War, periodically inserting parenthetical asides to her imagined, future audience, such as "(Impossible to put on paper her accentuation . . .)" (298). Such authorial intrusions remind the reader that the print record at hand—stripped of the atmosphere of Judith's ramshackle home as well as the intonation and emotion of her words—is not unaffected by its pen-to-paper rendering.

Yet, as Judith's oral history is transcribed, Woolson complicates the "persistence and immutability" and, further, the "stability" of "the transmission of memory and knowledge" that Margaret Hedstrom has attributed to written records.[18] Judith's narration and the story itself close with a melancholy hope that the "'errors,'" "'sins,'" and "'sufferings'" of the South will be lost to memory (307). She ends her story with one final, fatalistic word: "'forgotten'" (307). But where one story ends, another begins—or is continued. Judith's nephew, John, who sits nearby in a corner while she resuscitates her family's past and "play[s] all by himself hour after hour with two little wooden soldiers," has at his young age likely memorized the family lore and rehearses the history of the war through the actions of his toy figures (296). Judith surrenders her nephew to the traveling narrator, and John leaves with the midwestern visitor to be taken to the North, where presumably he will regenerate his family's tale to audiences outside of the South, in the same way that Faulkner's Quentin Compson divulges his southern family saga to the Canadian Shreve in their Harvard dorm in *Absalom, Absalom!*[19]

Other keeper figures often skirt the edges of Woolson's stories. African American and Native American characters reappear as living repositories of the past and as knowledgeable, intuitive guides in navigating the southern landscape, yet they seldom occupy a central narrative role. One of these characters in "The South Devil" is Scipio, a formerly enslaved African American cook working for a northern visitor, Mark, who has come to Florida in search of a healing climate for his ill stepbrother, Carl. The two rent a decaying orange plantation on the outskirts of the South Devil swamp. Unlike Judith, whose account is relayed firsthand, and more like the cemetery procession of African American individuals whose names go unrecorded in Rodman's visitor log, Scipio is not given the privilege of a direct narration. Even his expert ability to decipher and navigate the tricky swamp landscape is disseminated secondhand by Carl and mocked by Mark. "Oh, Africanus has seen several centuries," Carl observes; "the Spaniards were living here only fifty years ago, you know, and that's nothing to him. He remembers the Indian attack."[20] Having firsthand knowledge of the Indian Wars, likely the Seminole Wars of Florida, Scipio is a beacon of history. He may have just one eye, but he has seen (and he understands) much more than both Mark and Carl combined. A similar disregard characterizes a second seemingly peripheral figure in the story: an unnamed elderly hunter of mixed Spanish, African, and Seminole descent who resides in the swamp. Mark demeans both Scipio and the hunter, referring to them as "'[t]he old black rascal'" and "the mongrel" (282, 283). While Scipio's voice is heard periodically in conversations with Mark or

Carl, Woolson never provides the voice of the hunter. Readers can assume, however, that the hunter also bears more knowledge of Florida's history and landscape than is acknowledged by the northern brothers.

Except through the lens of Carl, Scipio's and the hunter's stories go untold and unwritten. Scipio, in particular, remains an untapped storehouse of history, even though he is acknowledged as one. The disregard of his wisdom calls attention to those whose voices are marginalized from historical and national memory, especially in comparison with Copeland's unnamed female cousin, whose memorial preservation is rooted in her ancestral wealth and privilege as a white subject. Such a glaring omission is condemned in "The South Devil." Reflecting on the "traces of former cultivation in Florida," the narrator remarks that such remnants are unsurprising, "if one stops to remember" the state's colonial and imperial history (261). "But," the narrator goes on, "one does not stop to remember it; the belief is imbedded in all our Northern hearts that, because the narrow, sun-bathed State is far away and wild and empty, it is also new and virgin, . . . whereas it is old—the only gray-haired corner our country holds" (261). It is no coincidence that Scipio, also described as "gray-headed," is aligned with the land's history and, like the disregarded and unwritten record of the landscape, northern visitors like Mark do not "stop to remember" his story, perspective, or knowledge (262, 261).

Yet even as Scipio and the hunter remain peripheral against the overarching story of Mark and Carl, Woolson crafts a narrative trajectory that is ultimately dependent on how they read the swamp. In traversing its waterways to find Carl, for instance, Mark's first instinct is to decide "which outlet to take" by consulting his compass—that is, until "his eye rested upon the skin of a moccasin nailed to a cypress on the other side of the pond," placed there by the hunter (285). Mark then elects to follow "the mongrel's . . . guidepost," the narrator tells us, "[w]ithout hesitation, although the direction was the exact opposite of the one he had selected" according to the compass (285). But for the knowledge imparted by Scipio and the hunter, Mark and Carl might very well have died multiple times in the murky landscape. At the end of the story, the northern brothers flee the swamp: the ailing Carl heads for San Miguel, where he dies, and Mark heads "northward" toward home, abandoning the rented plantation on the outskirts of the South Devil. Woolson concludes with a seemingly ironic, yet fitting, end: the hunter, the most overlooked character of the story, assumes the position as the final keeper of the house.

Like a soil stain that alerts an archaeologist to the spot where a wooden post once stood, the past lives on in traces as history manifests itself in the

southern landscape, which becomes perhaps the most objective archive in
Woolson's collection. Memories embedded in the earth remain long after
a human keeper, recorder, or witness is gone but nonetheless lend insights
into lived experience. Building from French historian Marc Bloch's theory of
historical observation and his work on historicizing agricultural landscapes,
Paul Ricoeur has stated that "there are traces that are not 'written testimo-
nies' and that are equally open to historical observation, namely, 'vestiges of
the past.'"[21] Woolson calls attention to the landscape as an archive of "vestiges" when the narrator of "The South Devil" uses the language of subjuga-
tion to catalogue the environment surrounding Mark's rented plantation.

Through Florida's flora and fauna, the state's colonial history is made visible. The narrator points to the "orange-trees, crape-myrtles, oleanders, gua-
vas, and limes planted by the Spaniards" which, over the course of half a
century, were "*conquered* and partially *enslaved* by a wilder growth—androm-
edas, dahoons, bayberries, and the old field loblollies, the whole *bound* together by the *tangled* vines of the jessamine and armed smilax" (260, emphasis
added). Further, the entangled tops of the orange trees above the plantation
are described as a "blossoming network," an invocation of colonial routes
during conquest and the transatlantic slave trade, events that ensnared peoples from across the globe together onto one continent under brutal conditions (288). Explored by Anne Boyd Rioux as central to the colonial project
of northern traveler tourism in Woolson's "Southern Sketches," such imperi-
ally charged images reveal that even the earth, a great equalizer that absorbs
all tissue with the same indifference regardless of race, gender, and class, reflects the history that is responsible for the silences in archives and historical
memory.[22]

The lighthouse in "Sister St. Luke" serves as another archive of the landscape that offers an alternative to the "myth" of the "objective, neutral, passive . . . keeper of truth" that Schwartz and Cook explore.[23] The cultural
layers of the lighthouse, an architectural focal point of the northern Florida
coast, stand as a testament to the state's fraught transnational, multiethnic
history, or, as the narrator terms it and Aaron Rovan discusses in this volume
(120–30), the "vast, many-raced, motley country" that is America: "[The
lighthouse] was originally a lookout where the Spanish soldier stood and
fired his culverin when a vessel came in sight outside the reef; then the British
occupied the land, added a story, and placed an iron grating on the top. . . .
Finally the United States came into possession, ran up a third story, and put
in a revolving light."[24] Its various stories and additions embody the various
occupations of the Florida coast by Spain, Britain, and the United States. In

Woolson's stories, vestiges of the landscape—whether centuries-worn paths, remnants of orange groves, forgotten graveyards, or architectural layers of lighthouses—are historical portals. Woolson decentralizes print productions, prompting readers to consider the spectrum of sources—both human-made structures and natural landscapes—that constitute an archive.

No one (myself included) is exempt from the pitfalls of the archive, and the questions that these "Southern Sketches" urge readers to wrestle with are salutary reminders to all scholars, architects, and interpreters of archives to be attuned to the power dynamics inherent in history making. Woolson herself understood that archives are heavily curated objects, her own archive included. As Anne Boyd Rioux has observed, Woolson made agreements with at least two of her correspondents—her friend Henry James and her sister Clara—to burn their letters to one another.[25] Because such an arrangement existed with more than one of her confidants, Rioux hypothesizes, the practice "was probably her idea."[26] In this sense, Woolson's own archive resonates with the sanitized cemetery rolls and empty visitor logs of the Union cemetery over which Rodman keeps watch. Depending upon how the "Southern Sketches" are read, Woolson's own participation in curating an archive of the South after the Civil War might be interpreted as an indictment of or complicity in the absences and omissions in historical records and memory. Holding up a mirror to such pitfalls, Woolson's stories are necessarily complicit, and her indictment of the archive is a quiet one. Her characters do not recognize their own myopic obsessions and the glaring ironies of their actions, but readers do.

A central message of Woolson's keeper stories is a cautionary one: the telling of history must be multidimensional and polyvocal, calling on diverse repositories (print records, oral history, and the landscape) as well as diverse communities to bring about an understanding of the past that yields precision and truth. Woolson's stories whisper: how and by whom is history remembered? Such questioning of historical memory resonates not simply with the ongoing recent efforts among scholars at making eclipsed stories visible through archival recovery work but also with national debates about the commemoration of U.S. history, or certain parts of it—inquiries that have become urgent in ongoing national dialogues about the preservation or removal of Confederate monuments across the South. Woolson's *Rodman the Keeper* foregrounds as well as questions what it means to "sit still and remember."[27] When the historical record falls short, the literary imagination steps in to interrogate those gaps.

NOTES

1. James O'Toole, *Understanding Manuscripts and Archives* (Chicago: Society of American Archivists, 1990), 30.

2. O'Toole, 31.

3. David W. Blight, *Race and Reunion: The Civil War in American Memory* (Cambridge, Mass.: Harvard University Press, 2001).

4. Constance F. Woolson, "Rodman the Keeper," in *Constance Fenimore Woolson: Collected Stories*, ed. Anne Boyd Rioux (New York: Library of America, 2020), 146; hereafter cited parenthetically.

5. John Wharton Lowe, "Constance Fenimore Woolson and the Origins of the Global South," in *Witness to Reconstruction: Constance Fenimore Woolson and the Postbellum South, 1873–1894*, ed. Kathleen Diffley (Jackson: University Press of Mississippi, 2011), 41.

6. Woolson, letter to Paul Hamilton Hayne, September 12, 1875, in *The Complete Letters of Constance Fenimore Woolson*, ed. Sharon L. Dean (Gainesville: University Press of Florida, 2012), 51–52.

7. Joan M. Schwartz and Terry Cook, "Archives, Records, and Power: The Making of Modern Memory," *Archival Science* 2, no. 1/2 (2002): 13.

8. Schwartz and Cook, 3.

9. Schwartz and Cook, 5.

10. Martin T. Buinicki, "Imagining Sites of Memory in the Post–Civil War South," in Diffley, *Witness to Reconstruction*, 171.

11. Buinicki, 171.

12. Blight, *Race and Reunion*, 285–88, 361–70.

13. Kathleen Diffley, "Numbered, Numbered: Commemorating the Civil War Dead in Woolson's 'Rodman the Keeper,'" *American Literary History* 30, no. 3 (Fall 2018): 497.

14. Nathaniel Hawthorne, *The Scarlet Letter*, in *Hawthorne: Collected Novels*, ed. Millicent Bell (New York: Library of America, 1983), 142, 143; Woolson, "Old Gardiston," in Rioux, *Woolson: Collected Stories*, 235; hereafter cited parenthetically.

15. Leonardo Buonomo, "The Other Face of History in Constance Fenimore Woolson's Southern Stories," *Canadian Review of American Studies* 28, no. 3 (1998): 15.

16. Woolson, "The Bones of Our Ancestors," *Harper's Monthly*, September 1873, 537.

17. Constance F. Woolson, "In the Cotton Country," in Rioux, *Woolson: Collected Stories*, 296; hereafter cited parenthetically.

18. Margaret Hedstrom, "Archives, Memory, and Interfaces with the Past," *Archival Science* 2, no. 1/2 (2002): 28.

19. William Faulkner, *Absalom, Absalom!* (1936; repr., New York: Vintage, 1990).

20. Woolson, "The South Devil," in Rioux, *Woolson: Collected Stories*, 263; hereafter cited parenthetically.

21. Paul Ricoeur, *Memory, History, Forgetting*, trans. Kathleen Blamley and David Pellauer (Chicago: University of Chicago Press, 2004), 170.

22. Anne E. Boyd [Rioux], "Tourism, Imperialism, and Hybridity in the Reconstruc-

tion South: Woolson's *Rodman the Keeper: Southern Sketches*," in Diffley, *Witness to Reconstruction*, 56–72.

23. Schwartz and Cook, "Archives, Records, and Power," 5.

24. Woolson, "Sister St. Luke," in Rioux, *Woolson: Collected Stories*, 172, 174.

25. Anne Boyd Rioux, *Constance Fenimore Woolson: Portrait of a Lady Novelist* (New York: Norton, 2016), 216.

26. Rioux, 216.

27. Woolson, "Rodman the Keeper," 12.

The Confederate Widow of Myth and Artistry

"IN THE COTTON COUNTRY"

Caroline Gebhard

I doubt if history affords a parallel to the deep and bitter enmity of
the women of the South. No one who sees them and hears them
but must feel the intensity of their hate.

—WILLIAM TECUMSEH SHERMAN, 1863

Years ago we in the South made our women into ladies. Then the
War came and made the ladies into ghosts. So what else can we do,
being gentlemen, but listen to them being ghosts?

—WILLIAM FAULKNER, *Absalom, Absalom!*, 1936

Even in the twenty-first century, competing narratives about the causes and
meanings of the Civil War still dominate American life. The ongoing centrality
of the war to our national narrative is the premise of *The New York Times Disunion*, a series looking back one hundred fifty years prior to America's blood-
iest war.[1] Indeed, this war has forever marked not only our history but our
literature as well. As Cody Marrs argues, "[I]f the stories we tell about the
Civil War reveal who we are—not only who we have been, but who we wish
to become—then literature is indispensable."[2] The work of Constance Fenimore Woolson, a northern writer who lived in the South less than a decade after Appomattox and before the end of Radical Reconstruction marked by the
disputed election of Rutherford B. Hayes as president in 1877,[3] is vital to understanding how warring narratives emerged about the South's defeat. One of
the most pertinent of her books in this regard is *Rodman the Keeper: Southern
Sketches* (1880). Indeed, the fundamental split between how white southerners saw the war and its aftermath as opposed to how well-intentioned northern
contemporaries perceived it is encoded in the very structure of "In the Cotton
Country," one of the most unusual stories in this volume. First published in *Ap-

pletons' Journal in April 1874, this story features a split-frame narrative begun by a white woman whose voice and outlook seem close to Woolson's own. The northern narrator's jaunty tone and sure judgments, however, are disrupted midway into the tale by the southern woman who takes over the story and does not relinquish it until she expresses the full depth of her bitterness and grief. Strikingly, however, the story that the Confederate widow tells is backed by a claim that appears nowhere else in Woolson's fiction: "I have written stories of imagination, but this is a story of fact, and I want you to believe it. It is true, every word of it, save the names given."[4] The storyline of Judith Cotesworth Kinsolving, with its backdrop of ruined cotton fields, presages what would become staples of the southern myth of the Lost Cause: Sherman's ruthless soldiers, a young Confederate widow on the verge of starvation, and the staggering loss of a noble generation of southern white men fighting for their homes, not slavery.

Representing white southerners' implacably clinging to the Confederacy as their country still, Woolson's remarkable tale also forecasts the way southern white women would become the driving force in memorializing the Confederacy. As Caroline E. Janney shows, Ladies' Memorial Associations sprang up everywhere in the South as early as May 1865, laying the groundwork for the "public rituals of Confederate memory" that would follow.[5] David Blight probes the critical role white southern women played in perpetuating and magnifying the myth of the Lost Cause in their successful efforts "to write and control the history of the war and its aftermath"; he underscores as well how this crusade for the Lost Cause carried out by successor organizations, most notably the United Daughters of the Confederacy, was underpinned by white supremacy "as both means and ends."[6] However, Woolson's choosing a widow to recount the losses of the "dark, cruel war" reflects a part of the mythology that was there from the beginning.[7] In *The Lost Cause: A New Southern History of the War of the Confederates* (1866), the book that named the myth, Edward A. Pollard entrusts to women the safekeeping of the South's "own memories, its own heroes, its own tears, its own dead," believing that "[u]nder these traditions, sons will grow to manhood, and lessons sink deep that are learned from the lips of widowed mothers."[8] Woolson's widow brings to life the southern woman storyteller.

The tonal shift could not be more striking between the gently ironic first-person narrator who jokes about nervous northern passengers on trains crossing "quaking, spongy" swamps "prophesying accidents as certain some time— when they are not on board" (294) and the humorless, quasi-biblical lament of Judith. She tells of how she lived through the war's last year: "Our servants had left us, all save one, old Cassy, who had been my nurse or 'maumee,' as we called her. . . . The poorest slaves in the old time had more than we had then; but we did not murmur, the greater griefs had swallowed up the less. I said, 'Is there any sorrow like unto my sorrow?' But the end was not yet" (303). Troublingly, Woolson's divided narrative, which gives so much weight to the story of the suffering woman on the other side, makes room for those who doubted the wisdom of destroying the old order and enabling the rise of formerly enslaved people—although emancipation was a cause in which Woolson herself deeply believed. However, Woolson's southern woman storyteller does more than play the role that Pollard and others expected of her; Woolson's Judith Kinsolving is an uncanny precursor to the compelling female characters William Faulkner created more than fifty years later. Like him, Woolson lays bare the ferocity of the southern attachment to white supremacy—even on the part of southern white ladies—that so many southern apologists for the Old South have tried to obfuscate.[9] And despite the story's projected hope of a national reconciliation achieved when "a new generation will come to whom these questions will be things of the past" (307), this fractured narrative instead powerfully registers unbridgeable regional and racial divides that even now bedevil our nation. This story, like so many that we still tell about the Civil War, tests the limits of empathy and plumbs the politics of grievance.

Confederate Widows and Southern Mythology

Woolson's "Southern Sketches" depict southern neighborhoods after the war as populated by "sonless mothers and the widows who lived shut up in the old houses with everything falling into ruin around them, brooding over the past."[10] All those Confederate widows were not figments of her imagination but a grim reality for a generation of women who reached marriageable age during the war. The work of social historians like J. David Hacker reflects the emerging historical consensus that the once accepted death toll of some 618,000 male war casualties on both sides was too low; the number of war dead is now believed to be approximately 750,000.[11] This revised estimate means that there were even more war widows and orphans than previously thought. A study by Hacker, Libra Hilde, and James Holland Jones, on the effect of the Civil War on southern marriage patterns, finds that southern white women in the 1870s—the decade in which Woolson first published her story—did face much more difficulty in finding husbands or in remarrying if they were widowed by the war. For one thing, the authors point out, unlike the North, the South "had mobilized between 75 and 85% of its white male population of military age by the end of the war." Not surprisingly, the study concludes that "the

Civil War had a major impact on the incidence of widowhood," for in 1880, the year Woolson republished "In the Cotton Country" in *Southern Sketches*, one southern-born woman in five was a widow, as compared to just one in nine for northern women. In this age cohort (women of Woolson's own age who would have been in their twenties during the war), one out of every three white southern women was a widow.[12]

In many respects, Woolson's Confederate widow narrates a story that southern women had begun to tell even before the war had reached its bloody conclusion. Indeed, Sarah E. Gardner argues that southern women were "key disseminators of southern stories of the Civil War."[13] In their diaries and novels, biographies and histories, she explains, they generally "eschewed glorifying warfare," instead emphasizing the war's brutal aspects (29). When Woolson's narrator at last succeeds in gaining the southern woman's confidence, she hears the widow's tale of unbearable losses. Plunging into an account of her brother's death at Fredericksburg, she dwells on the cold and miserable state of the Confederate troops: "Their old uniforms, worn thin by hard usage, hung in tatters, and many of them had no shoes" (298). Her brother is shot and buried without a marker. Her second brother is soon dispatched to "cold, corpse-strewed Virginia"; eventually he too is felled by a guerrilla's bullet "as he rode through a lonely mountain defile" (299). Then she recounts how her husband, taken prisoner in the North, is falsely accused of being a spy and summarily executed; Rayburn Moore speculates that Woolson may have based this incident on a real case that she wrote about in a travel sketch in 1873.[14] In the story, the doomed prisoner "at the last turned his face to the south, as if he were gazing down, down, into the very heart of the land for whose sake he was about to die" (303). In Judith's narrative, we see quintessential elements of the Lost Cause mythology that would come to dominate southern interpretations of the "War Between the States": these young men go off to fight bravely for their country despite its meagre resources. In other words, they fight and die to defend their homes and their states, not slavery.

By contrast, Gardner reports that "Northern soldiers were called 'perfidious,' 'treacherous,' 'murderous,' 'vile,' 'contemptible' and 'traitorous'" (20) by southern white women. Judith's retelling evokes Sherman's march and what the conquering army brought to her beloved country: "You have heard the story of the great march, the march to the sea? But there was another march after that . . . the march through South Carolina" (303). Although she tries to prevent her silver-haired father from getting involved in a "mêlée" with the advancing Yankee troops, he rushes out sword in hand and is shot through the head and breast before her eyes (304). Judith and the faithful Cassy are left to dig his grave despite orders to remain inside. Perhaps because Woolson had staunchly supported the Union, the Union soldiers do show some respect, "silent, attentive, and with bared heads" (306), as Judith's father is buried.

This scene offers a striking contrast to the representation of Yankee soldiers by southern women as holding nothing sacred. According to Gardner, "most southern women reserved the harshest words for those Federal soldiers who raided southern civilians' homes"; they "found their wanton destruction of women's personal possessions most egregious," with one diarist, the wife of a planter in Augusta, Georgia, reporting that the Yankees not only burned crops and destroyed livestock but also were bent on "destroying ladies wardrobes and tearing their clothes to pieces" (21). Yet Woolson's story also corroborates this southern version of marauding Yankees who destroy the most personal of women's belongings: "But after the army came the army-followers and stragglers, carrion-birds who flew behind the conquerors and devoured what they had left," Judith explains, adding, "My own home did not escape: rude men ransacked every closet and drawer, and cut in ribbons the old portraits on the wall." The crowning blow is delivered by "a German, coming in from the smoke-house, dripping with bacon-juice" and wiping his hands upon her wedding veil, which had been pulled from its box by another intruder (306).

Judith's views are entirely in keeping with what was long taught as the "'true history' of the South" in the region's schools.[15] This version of history, that whites, especially of the "better class," were the innocent victims of lawless and corrupt Yankee carpetbaggers and Blacks, was also promoted by the Dunning School of History that long held sway and was discredited only at the end of the twentieth century.[16] Living in a decaying house that the northern narrator expects to find inhabited by "black-skinned life," amid what was once her family's richest cotton fields, the widow rails against the new order that—from her perspective—has placed the formerly enslaved above her: "'Oh! it was a great deliverance for the enfranchised people! Bitter, am I? Put yourself in my place'" (307). Anne Rowe argues that none of Woolson's Black characters rises above a conventional portrait.[17] While this is not fair to many of Woolson's stories, certainly in Judith's narrative, Cassy, the faithful mammy, conforms to the stereotype, appearing as little more than her appendage. Judith even comments sarcastically that Cassy has been forgiven by her own people "for having been so spiritless as to stay with 'young missis,' when she might have tasted the glories of freedom over in the crowded hollow where the blacks were enjoying themselves and dying by the score. . . . For, you see, madam, their masters, those villainous old masters of theirs, were no longer there to feed and clothe them" (307). Here, Woolson lets the bitter, unreconstructed southern woman vent her opinions without challenge.

But elsewhere in other southern sketches she does not. When Bettina Ward tries to lay the blame for the South's problems on the freedmen, Rodman answers that the blame must instead fall on the "mighty wrong" of slavery, which in turn is responsible for the true root of the South's ills: "the lack of general education" among both Blacks and whites is "painfully apparent everywhere throughout the South."[18] Moore pointed out that these liberal northern views were edited out of "Rodman the Keeper" when it was republished in *Southern Sketches*, and even in 1963 Moore quoted with approval Daniel Kern's suggestion, that Woolson chose to omit these views because she "thoroughly understood the bitterness that was in the hearts of the southern people during that period when short-sighted northern statesmanship was rubbing salt into old wounds."[19]

Nevertheless, even as she allows Judith Kinsolving to give full voice to her bitterness and allegiance to the past, Woolson creates a portrait of a southern elite woman that despite its resemblance to the narratives southern white women told about their defeated land is ultimately quite different. It is impossible to imagine Judith becoming one of the many southern ladies who joined memorial associations, who founded homes for destitute Confederate veterans and widows, and who were determined above all, as Karen Cox and others have shown, to vindicate Confederate values.[20] These women would go on to found the United Daughters of the Confederacy, reshaping the southern landscape with countless memorials to the Confederate dead and becoming one of the most powerful influences on twentieth-century southern culture. White women like them across the South would erect marble obelisks like the one in Harrisonburg, Virginia— dated April 1876, just two years after Woolson's story was first published. It reads, "This monument is erected by the Ladies Memorial Association in grateful remembrance of the gallant Confederate Soldiers, who lie here. THEY DIED IN DEFENSE OF THE RIGHTS OF THE SOUTH, in the War between the States, from 1861 to 1865. 1876. In memory of men, who with their lives vindicated the principles of 1776." After listing many Virginia battlefields, the last words on this monument proclaim, "THE Southern Soldier Died for his Country. Success is not Patriotism, Defeat is not Rebellion."[21] Judith embodies a similarly fierce loyalty to "her country," by which she means South Carolina and by extension the Confederacy. Yet the woman Woolson describes is barely competent to sweep her house—she sweeps "every day, never thoroughly, but in a gentle, incompetent sort of way peculiarly her own" (296)—let alone capable of mustering the energy or the determination to do what so many middle- and upper-class white southern women of the time in fact did.

Woolson's Artistry: Faulkner Avant La Lettre

If it is hard to see Woolson's Judith Kinsolving as entirely conforming to nineteenth-century white southern women's narratives, it is not hard to see her as a precursor to Faulkner's female characters. Living in her dilapidated old house, Woolson's widow, with her curiously old-young face and her haunting "dry, still eyes of immovable, hopeless grief" (296), is strikingly akin to Rosa Coldfield in *Absalom, Absalom!* The last member of her family isolated in the "airless gloom of a dead house," Rosa embodies a "grim and implacable unforgiving" as she recounts that her life "was destined to end on an afternoon in April forty-three years ago," since "anyone . . . would not call what I have had since living."[22] The parallels are striking. Like Rosa, who was engaged but never married, Woolson's Judith sees her life as over, describing herself as not really living but existing "as the palsied animal lives" (300). Woolson's storyteller states flatly that "I go to no church; I can not pray. But do not think I am defiant; no, I am only dead" (300). And just as Faulkner's Judith Sutpen is a widow before she is a bride, Woolson's Judith also never consummates her marriage, as her bridegroom is called away immediately after the ceremony. Like Faulkner's female survivors of the Civil War, Woolson's narrator is destined for a perpetual widowhood of grieving for a dead past that is somehow more alive than the present. Like them as well, Judith Kinsolving has become a ghost cut off from everyone around her except her nephew, a strange child who is said to have inherited his mother's grief. Judith Sutpen also takes charge of an odd motherless child, also a nephew.

In Faulkner's novel, the southerner's Canadian roommate, in trying to understand the South and what makes it different, says, "We dont [*sic*] live among defeated grandfathers and freed slaves . . . and bullets in the dining room table and such, to be always reminding us to never forget. What is it . . . a kind of entailed birthright father and son and father and son of never forgiving General Sherman?"[23] But Faulkner's own novel reveals it is not only southern white men but also southern white women who see themselves as irrevocably bound to the past, and in his writings they possess an even more indomitable will than the men to never forget.[24]

Unlike Faulkner, however, Woolson does not seem to have fully understood the meaning of bloodlines and family to the planter class and their descendants that Faulkner brilliantly anatomizes. Nor does she ever represent the tangled family dynamics that resulted from slaveholders sleeping with their slaves but refusing to acknowledge the offspring as their sons and daughters. Because of the lineage of his half brother, Henry Sutpen can bring himself to accept the idea of his sister committing incest but not the idea of her *marrying* a man with Black ancestry. Although Woolson's story likewise registers race as the unbridgeable divide in the South, she does not imagine a Judith determined to mold the young to revere the Lost Cause. Therefore, Woolson's ending is the most problematic aspect of the story. "Well, if—if you really wish it, I will not oppose you," Judith tells the northern woman as she gives up her nephew. "Take him, and bring him up in your rich, prosperous North; the South has no place for him" (307). It is hard to think that any southerner of the planter class would condone Judith's willingness to surrender the child of her brother to anyone, let alone a strange northern woman! Even less plausible is Judith's projection of the child's future: "Let him grow up under the new *régime*; I have told him nothing of the old" (307). Perhaps Judith's parting wish reflects instead the author's own fervent desire that the next generation of southerners would someday see the issues that had torn the nation asunder from a perspective unprejudiced by the past as well as the hope that northern values represented by the emancipation of the slaves and the efforts of the Freedmen's Bureau to educate those who had endured bondage would in time triumph in the South.

But white southerners of Woolson's time and long after would have judged Judith a traitor for not ensuring that the next generation learn to worship at the shrine of the Old South. Moreover, most southern whites of Woolson's era, and many whites in succeeding generations who approved of cementing the second-class status of Black Americans by force of law, would have doubtless thoroughly identified with Judith Cotesworth Kinsolving's aggrieved harangue: "It seems we were wrong, all wrong; then we must be very right now, for the blacks are our judges, councilors, postmasters, representatives, and law-makers. That is as it should be, isn't it? What! Not so?" (307). This jibe suggests that her northern listener is not comfortable either with the thought of Black people in powerful positions while once elite white people find themselves out of power and in dire poverty. The story indeed enacts the longing of the northern narrator—and perhaps Woolson herself?—to be a "Sister of Charity" who goes "over the field when the battle is done, bearing balm and wine and oil for those who suffer" (298). Tellingly, it is the planter's daughter whom the story casts as the war's chief victim. Of course, it is perhaps too understandable that a white, upper-middle-class woman like Woolson (who had some pretensions to aristocratic lineage herself, and who

had herself gone to school with southern girls of Judith's class) would identify more with southern white women of her own class than with the formerly enslaved. Woolson's own degree of—perhaps unconscious—identifica-
tion with Judith's investment in whiteness as inherently superior is not clear,
nor is it clear if she ultimately intends the northern narrator to be an authorial stand-in or a critical portrait of northern sympathizers. What is clear is
that as an artist she was, above all, invested in rendering a complicated reality as truthfully as she could.

Nevertheless, the implied complicity of her northern interlocutor in seeming to agree with—or if not agreeing, in letting stand without comment—Judith's vitriol directed toward the idea of Black equality raises a question that
goes beyond Woolson's personal biases. The northern narrator's tacit agree-
ment mirrors what would become northern complicity not only in Jim Crow
segregation in the South but in de facto segregation in the rest of the nation.
Leigh Anne Duck argues that the trope of the "backward South" has long
obscured the ways it allowed the North to cast itself as liberal and progressive
rather than face up to its own failings. Not until the 1930s, she suggests, did
writers and activists expose "the degree to which southern racial practices
corresponded, rather than conflicted with, those of the larger nation."[25]

"In the Cotton Country" has been called the worst and the best of
Woolson's stories.[26] Even critics who admire the story see it as a disturbing
example of an author's unhealthy relationship with her subject. Ann Douglas
Wood, for example, reads Woolson as a kind of vampire who shamefully ex-
ploits the other woman both for material and for a vicarious emotional life.[27]
Wood charges, "The Southern woman has suffered, but at least her suffering testifies that she has lived."[28] Yet rather than read "In the Cotton Country" as an allegory for the northern woman writer and her southern material,
I have argued for reading the story as Woolson's attempt to let the Confederate widow tell her own story in her own words. As Anne Boyd Rioux has put
it, Woolson's stories about the South "attempted not merely to speak for the
desolated region but to allow Southern voices to speak back."[29] Woolson's
Confederate widow with her grandiose phrases uttered in a house tumbling
down around her captures the accent, attitudes, and psychology of southern
white women whose lives had been turned upside down by the war. Although
the Lost Cause mythology had just begun to take shape, Woolson's story accurately predicts the lines along which it would harden.

But she is too good a realist not to reveal the ugly truth of a bedrock belief in white supremacy inevitably bound up with honoring "Confederate"
values—values alas not so foreign to the nation as a whole. Woolson's north-

ern interlocutor notes it is "impossible to put on paper" how this Confederate widow "accentuates" the title of "freedmen" (298), but Woolson the artist does succeed in conveying how distasteful and preposterous the former planter's daughter finds this word, an ominous sign of gathering southern resistance to African Americans exercising their rights. Not until the twentieth century would a southerner like Faulkner expose the vicious racism that was the disturbing underside of a southern lady's grief, as Woolson had the daring and artistry to do more than half a century earlier. Woolson, too, was exquisitely attuned to the spoken word and what it reveals about the speaker. When William Dean Howells commented upon the second edition of Woolson's *Southern Sketches* (1886), he wrote that her stories have an "uncommon claim to remembrance" because apart from their artistry, "she has made them necessary to any one who would understand the whole meaning of Americanism." What he particularly singled out was her portrayal of southern women in the aftermath of the Confederacy's defeat, judging her most significant achievement to be "eternizing the moment of heart-break and irreconciliation in the South when its women began to realize all their woe."[30] Even in the nineteenth century Howells could already see that this "southern" sketch is really a story not just about the South but about America.

NOTES

1. The series became a book, *The New York Times Disunion: A History of the Civil War*, ed. Ted Widmer, with Clay Risen and George Kalogerakis (New York: Oxford University Press, 2016).

2. Cody Marrs, *Not Even Past: The Stories We Keep Telling about the Civil War* (Baltimore: Johns Hopkins University Press, 2020), 10. Marrs identifies four major narratives retold about the war: "A Family Squabble," "A Dark and Cruel War," "The Lost Cause," and "The Great Emancipation."

3. The widely accepted idea that a secret deal was made with southern Democrats to approve Hayes's victory in exchange for withdrawing federal troops and other concessions has recently been challenged. Historians have pointed to the small presence of federal troops, who moreover did not leave the South in 1877. In addition, they have underscored the problems of dating the Reconstruction era, arguing that Reconstruction efforts faltered earlier than 1877 but also lasted until the turn of the twentieth century, when, as Brook Thomas observes, "any glimmer of hope for continuing the goals of Reconstruction . . . completely died out." See *The Literature of Reconstruction: Not in Plain Black and White* (Baltimore: Johns Hopkins University Press, 2017), 26. See also Michael F. Holt, *By One Vote: The Disputed Presidential Election of 1876* (Lawrence: University Press of Kansas, 2008).

4. Constance F. Woolson, "In the Cotton Country," in *Constance Fenimore Woolson:*

Collected Stories, ed. Anne Boyd Rioux (New York: Library of America, 2020), 297; hereafter cited parenthetically.

5. Caroline E. Janney, *Burying the Dead but Not the Past: Ladies' Memorial Associations and the Lost Cause* (Chapel Hill: University of North Carolina Press, 2008), 3–4.

6. David W. Blight, *Race and Reunion: The Civil War in American Memory* (Cambridge, Mass.: Harvard University Press, 2001), 259.

7. "In the Cotton Country" in some respects fits Marrs's category of retellings of the war as brutal on a scale never seen before in America, joining a lineage from Ambrose Bierce's "Chickamauga" to Ken Burns's famous documentary series *The Civil War*. Marrs, *Not Even Past*, 42–95.

8. Edward A. Pollard, *The Lost Cause: A New Southern History of the War of the Confederates* (New York: E. B. Treat, 1866), 751.

9. Many writers, especially in the Plantation School, elided the politics of white supremacy by promoting the myth of faithful slaves treated as "family," but some defenders of the Old South made plain that the South's postwar goal was to secure "the supremacy of the white man" and to keep the political influence of African Americans as limited as it had been when they were enslaved. See Edward A. Pollard, *The Lost Cause Regained* (New York: G. W. Carleton, 1868), 14. According to Jack P. Maddex Jr., however, Pollard later embraced Black suffrage and denounced the Ku Klux Klan, though he never relinquished his belief in white superiority. See *The Reconstruction of Edward A. Pollard: A Rebel's Conversion to Postbellum Unionism* (Chapel Hill: University of North Carolina Press, 1974), 74–76.

10. Woolson, "Rodman the Keeper," in *Rodman the Keeper: Southern Sketches* (New York: D. Appleton, 1880), 37.

11. Widmer, "Introduction," in Widmer, *New York Times Disunion*, 2.

12. J. David Hacker, Libra Hilde, and James Holland Jones, "The Effect of the Civil War on Southern Marriage Patterns," *Journal of Southern History* 76, no. 1 (February 2010): 3, 9–11.

13. Sarah E. Gardner, *Blood and Irony: Southern White Women's Narratives of the Civil War, 1861–1937* (Chapel Hill: University of North Carolina Press, 2004), 2; hereafter cited parenthetically.

14. Rayburn S. Moore, *Constance Fenimore Woolson* (New York: Twayne, 1963), 154–55n20.

15. W. Fitzhugh Brundage, "'Woman's Hand and Heart and Deathless Love': White Women and the Commemorative Impulse in the New South," in *Monuments to the Lost Cause: Women, Art, and the Landscapes of Southern Memory*, ed. Cynthia Mills and Pamela H. Simpson, new foreword by Karen L. Cox (Knoxville: University of Tennessee Press, 2019), 64–82, 74.

16. Eric Foner's groundbreaking *Reconstruction: America's Unfinished Revolution, 1863–1877* (New York: Harper & Row, 1988) underscored the outsized and long-term racist impact that William Archibald Dunning, a Columbia University professor of history, has had on historians' interpretations of Reconstruction; see also *The Dunning School: Historians, Race, and the Meaning of Reconstruction*, ed. John David Smith and J. Vincent Lowery, foreword by Foner (Lexington: University Press of Kentucky,

2013). Thomas has argued, however, that Dunning nevertheless made important contributions by collecting empirical evidence that historians still rely upon and by identifying the "profound" problems facing Reconstruction governments. Thomas, *Literature of Reconstruction*, 18–19.

17. Anne Rowe, *The Enchanted Country: Northern Writers in the South, 1865–1910* (Baton Rouge: Louisiana State University Press, 1978), 59.

18. "Rodman the Keeper," *Atlantic Monthly*, March 1877, 276.

19. Daniel Kern, quoted in Moore, *Constance Fenimore Woolson*, 152–53n12.

20. See Karen L. Cox, *Dixie's Daughters: The United Daughters of the Confederacy and the Preservation of Confederate Culture* (Gainesville: University Press of Florida, 2003).

21. Timothy S. Sedore, *An Illustrated Guide to Virginia's Confederate Monuments* (Carbondale: Southern Illinois University Press, 2011), 51–52.

22. William Faulkner, *Absalom, Absalom!* (1936; New York: Vintage, 1972), 14, 18.

23. Faulkner, 361.

24. From Rosa and Judith to Sutpen's unacknowledged daughter born in slavery, Clytemnestra ("Clytie"), these women live their whole lives based on never forgetting the wrongs of the past.

25. Leigh Anne Duck, *The Nation's Region: Southern Modernism, Segregation, and U.S. Nationalism* (Athens: University of Georgia Press, 2006), 7.

26. Sharon Dean labels Judith Kinsolving's language "maudlin," but Joan Myers Weimer praises the story as a "fine early tale." See Dean, *Constance Fenimore Woolson: Homeward Bound* (Knoxville: University of Tennessee Press, 1995), 37, and Weimer, "Women Artists as Exiles in the Fiction of Constance Fenimore Woolson," *Legacy* 3, no. 2 (Fall 1986): 5.

27. Weimer suggests that Woolson, like Hawthorne, felt guilty about fictionalizing others' experiences, agreeing with Ann Douglas [Wood] that Woolson created women narrators "who prey on their subject matter like vampires." Weimer, "Introduction," in *Women Artists, Women Exiles: "Miss Grief" and Other Stories / Constance Fenimore Woolson*, ed. Weimer (New Brunswick, N.J.: Rutgers University Press, 1988), xvii. However, I read Woolson's exploration of another woman's suffering as mirroring her own profound grief, for like her character, Judith, Woolson had also lost her father and her family home.

28. Ann Douglas [Wood], "The Literature of Impoverishment: The Women Local Colorists in America 1865–1914," *Women's Studies* 1, no. 1 (1972): 30.

29. Anne E. Boyd [Rioux], "Tourism, Imperialism, and Hybridity in the Reconstruction South: Woolson's *Rodman the Keeper: Southern Sketches*," in *Witness to Reconstruction: Constance Fenimore Woolson and the Postbellum South, 1873–1894*, ed. Kathleen Diffley (Jackson: University Press of Mississippi, 2011), 61.

30. William Dean Howells, "Editor's Study" (review of *Castle Nowhere: Lake Country Sketches* and *Rodman the Keeper: Southern Sketches*), in *Critical Essays on Constance Fenimore Woolson*, ed. Cheryl B. Torsney (New York: G. K. Hall, 1992), 49, repr., *Harper's Monthly*, February 1887, 482.

"This Vast, Many-Raced, Motley Country of Ours"

CATHOLICISM, MINORCANS, AND
DIFFERENCE IN "SISTER ST. LUKE"

Aaron J. Rovan

In the climactic scene of Woolson's 1877 story "Sister St. Luke," Andrew Keith and George Carrington, two men from the North who are sojourning on Florida's Atlantic coast, find themselves trapped on a reef as a tornado approaches. The remnants of their boat lie shattered nearby, leaving the men stranded on a tiny jut of land. Miraculously, a "black-robed little figure"—the eponymous Sister St. Luke—arrives seemingly out of nowhere, captaining a small boat to rescue the men.[1] As if driven by supernatural aid, the nun grips the sail rope until the rescue of Keith and Carrington is complete. This heroic act contradicts everyone's expectations since the nun is a "fragile little creature" and "so timid a fly could frighten her" (172, 199). These descriptors not only mark her personality but also hint at her racialized Otherness. Although Woolson never specifies Sister St. Luke's heritage, readers are led to believe that she could be one of Florida's imported Minorcans, a group who trace their ancestry back to the Spanish island of Menorca. Minorcans are described in the story as "too indolent to do anything more than smoke, lie in the sun, and eat salads heavily dressed in oil" (175). Although Sister St. Luke is not lazy, other characters bristle at her languid personality and thus find her surge of bravery particularly inscrutable. They finally attribute the stunning rescue to her unwavering Catholic piety: "[T]he good Lord helped her to do it," one character remarks (199). The tension between her physical timidity and her stalwart adherence to the Catholic religion peaks in this baffling behavioral change and points to Woolson's central concern in the story: how to embody difference in a rapidly changing American South.

First published only weeks after the last Union troops left Florida during Reconstruction, "Sister St. Luke" destabilizes physical markers of difference to emphasize divergent cultural practices. The story illustrates how, as John Lowe writes, Woolson "embraces cultural difference and takes her readers beyond the usual racial binary of reconstruction fiction and mythology."[2] This happens in "Sister St. Luke" by virtue of the nun's hybrid American heritage, which places her, in Anne Boyd Rioux's phrase, into a "kind of middle ground between whites and blacks."[3] Extending Lowe and Rioux's focus on hybridity in Woolson's Florida stories, this essay recenters attention on the enigmatic nun by more fully charting the connection between racial hierarchy and religious difference. At a time when anti-Catholic sentiment was reaching a fever pitch in northern literary magazines, Woolson began to re draw the boundaries between "us" and "them" by shifting the idea of difference away from racial traits toward a modern articulation of ethnicity and culture.

Rather than focusing solely on physical traits, as race was often constructed in the 1870s, Woolson highlights the folkloric distinctions between groups. In her hands, as Rioux observes, Florida becomes "a site of racial and cultural mixing that raises questions about how difference is incorporated into the national narrative."[4] Florida's setting allows Woolson to exchange physical attributes for cultural markers. In "Sister St. Luke," Woolson creates a space that she names "Pelican Island," a fictitious composite of historical locations around St. Augustine. This technique suggests a reading in which the story's characters all become strangers who negotiate social hierarchies. Woolson's depictions of religious practices therefore pry apart traditional racial categories and anticipate later social movements that would result in the concepts of ethnicity and culture. In this way, Woolson's depiction of Sister St. Luke illustrates her quiet subversion of the American racial hierarchy of the 1870s.

By foregrounding the folkloric practices of her characters, Woolson tests the boundaries of difference in the post-Reconstruction South. At the time her story first appeared in the New York literary magazine the Galaxy (April 1877), both southerners and northerners were coming to terms with increasingly heterogenous demographics. Sharon Kennedy-Nolle points out that in Florida, freed African Americans were "grappling with the possibilities of citizenship" and encountering significant obstacles to full civic participation.[5] New Englanders, too, were facing a challenge to racial hierarchies with a new influx of European immigrants. Woolson's writing addresses the immediate concerns of both regions. If, as Stephanie Foote suggests, the "strangers with accents" whom readers encountered in regional literature paralleled the "accented strangers in the form of immigrants [who] were clamoring for recognition and representation in the political arena" of the northern states, Woolson unites these diverse regional contexts by focusing on her title character, whose depiction as an orphan and a nun blurs any racial binary.[6]

Sister St. Luke's ambiguous ancestry upsets the established ways of defining identity through racial or ethnic backgrounds. In fact, no one, either in the story or among its scholarly readers, can come to terms with the nun's family background. Sister St. Luke's heritage is unknown because she was abandoned as a baby on the steps of a convent, where she was raised. As a result, other characters infer—perhaps incorrectly—that her ancestry is Spanish, frequently addressing her as "señora." Scholars also disagree about the nun's heritage. Lowe claims that the nun is a "descendent" of Spanish sailors, which differentiates her from Minorcans.[7] Alternately, Rioux leaves her ancestry unsettled, pointing out that she "speaks Spanish but could be Minorcan or even Creole."[8] Sister St. Luke thus poses a clear problem in a story whose other characters have no difficulty tracing their lineages.

Reading the nun as Minorcan would certainly resonate with Woolson's depictions of those imported laborers in other stories, particularly in terms of their parallels with Florida's freed Black population. Minorcans had been indentured upon their Florida arrival in 1768 but eventually escaped servitude to establish an enclave in St. Augustine in 1777. The similarities between Florida's Minorcans and the state's newly freed Black population are hard to miss. These parallels gain even more significance when considering that the mid- to late nineteenth century witnessed, as Matthew Frye Jacobson remarks, a "new epistemological system of difference—a new visual economy keyed not only to cues of skin color, but to facial angle, head size and shape, physiognomy, hair and eye color, and physique."[9] The definitions of difference in this era were quickly expanding, and Woolson's story explodes even beyond these physical differences. With the Minorcan heritage as freed servants, Woolson's use of the ethnic group to negotiate "the muddied waters between voluntary servitude and slavery" highlights the fraught relationship between physical markers of difference and divergent cultural practices.[10]

Woolson's rapt attention to her characters' ethnic backgrounds challenges the precepts of postbellum white supremacy, particularly if Sister St. Luke is read as other than Spanish. If she is Minorcan, Woolson's title character figures as a direct challenge to Anglo hegemony, especially when she saves the two visitors from the North. Lowe argues that the story "gradually erode[s] any concept of a 'superior' Anglo 'race.'"[11] But rather than completely dismantling these established hierarchies, Woolson's ambiguous depiction of the nun's heritage prefigures a shift away from classifying humans based on static categories of race. Through the end of the nineteenth century, the concept of race "not only delimited particular populations," according to Brad Evans, "but also denoted an unchanging and untraversable space between them."[12] Despite this prevailing practice, Woolson incorporates folkloric language and tropes, particularly depictions of religious traditions, as she foregrounds the ambiguities of identity and the inability of the race concept to account for these differences.

Texts like "Sister St. Luke" poked at these static categories of race, and Woolson attends to shared social practices as a foundational factor of identity, foreshadowing the later concept of ethnicity, even though that particular term was not yet in linguistic circulation at the time Woolson wrote her "Southern Sketches." The *Oxford English Dictionary* records the earliest usage of "ethnicity"—in the sense of "having a common national or cultural origin"—in 1920, nearly three decades after Woolson's death. Although her contemporary readers would have been familiar with the concept of an "ethnic group"—defined simply as "relating to a group that has common descent"—the practice of a defining identity based on common cultural origin was not yet in wide circulation. Since, as Brad Evans explains, "the anthropological concept of culture became useful when race no longer described type but denoted biology," Woolson's profile of life in St. Augustine is an early example of a movement toward understanding difference as rooted in national heritage *and* shared traditions.[13]

The character of Sister St. Luke becomes the discursive site for Woolson to work through this shift from racial binary to cultural difference. In the story, other characters—as well as the narrator—use the nun like a blank canvas for modeling the emerging relationship between race and culture. While Lowe suggests that the naïve Sister St. Luke "stands in for the reader" while the two "city men" from the North "educate her about the Florida world that seems so strange," the nun also acts as a metaphor for the shifting perceptions of group identity in the post-Reconstruction South, particularly because she would have seemed exotic to many northerners.[14] The nun is first glimpsed through the perspective of those two men from New England, Keith and Carrington. As they arrive on the story's Pelican Island, Carrington notes "'seven pairs of Spanish eyes'" watching them (172). Keith corrects this hyperbole but still attaches a racialized signifier: "'Three pairs . . . and one if not two of the pairs are Minorcan'" (172). The nun in particular strikes them as a "large-eyed, fragile little creature" standing behind Pedro, the keeper of the island's lighthouse, and Melvyna, his wife (172). Although Woolson quickly supplies the backgrounds of Melvyna (a Vermont Calvinist) and Pedro (a Minorcan), readers are left to conjecture the nun's background. Certain physical markers do suggest her difference: Sister St. Luke's "small brown hand" (180) and her "timid dark eyes"

(194) point to a perceived racial Otherness. Echoing her physical differences, the narrator describes certain behavioral tics that make Sister St. Luke unique. Her steps, for example, are like "a series of quick, uncertain little paces over the sand like bird-tracks" (182). While Woolson's physical descriptors mark her as nonwhite, these odd, eccentric traits make her appear strange and backward.

But rather than identifying the nun as a racialized Other, Woolson establishes her Catholic faith as the fundamental signifier of her identity. This difference comes to the fore as Melvyna, an unabashed New England Protestant, describes the nun: "Is she a good Catholic, do you say? Heavens and earth, yes! She's *that* religious. . . . She believes every word of all that rubbish those old nuns have told her" (176). Later, Melvyna explains that the nun "loves the [convent], and feels lost and strange anywhere else" (177). For the Protestant, the nun is a stranger not because of her physical difference but rather because she follows a strict Catholic tradition.

Sister St. Luke's religious difference is further reinforced when the other characters trip over how to address her. In the Catholic tradition, novitiates to women's religious communities typically renounce their given names and adopt a religious name. This action, as Nancy Sweet makes clear, sets the Catholic sister "apart from Protestant strictures" to become "an agent in her own right, constructing a new identity through the very proclamation of her vows."[15] In the story, the nun's full name is simply St. Luke. Through the choice of her religious name, Sister St. Luke has renounced any racial or ethnic signifiers associated with her birth name and crafted a new, religious identity. Yet her name becomes a site of contested identity for the other characters who struggle over how to address her. Melvyna, for example, refuses to call the nun by her chosen name: "Sister St. Luke is her name; and a heathenish name it is for a woman, in my opinion. *I* call her Miss Luke" (177). Although Melvyna acknowledges that she should call the nun by her full name, "Sister St. Luke," or simply "Sister," she nonetheless refuses to do so because it would infringe upon her own Calvinist beliefs. Keith and Carrington are also confused about the nun's name, betraying their preconceived notions of race. When first addressing her, Carrington falters, "'Miss, Miss—Miss Luke—I should say, Miss St. Luke. I am sure I do not know why I should stumble over it when St. John is a common enough name'" (178). Carrington links the nun's religious name to a common Western European surname, inscribing an ethnic dimension to her identity. This false equivalence illustrates the humorous awkwardness of the situation and, more importantly, points to the shifting perceptions of identity from racially based to culturally based.

The inability of racial signifiers to account for the full range of identity is further reflected in the unusual setting of the story. Woolson's invention of Pelican Island creates a significant site for exploring these contested identities. From the beginning, Sister St. Luke is characterized as a stranger, as someone who does not belong to the island community. The nun herself voices this characterization, saying, "Here, so lost, so strange, am I" (180). Yet despite the other characters' attempts to fit Sister St. Luke into a recognizable form—and thereby set themselves apart as superior to her—Woolson reveals that all the characters in her story have similarly "strange" backgrounds. In fact, she uses the term to describe both Melvyna and Pedro. Pedro is a man "of strange and varied experiences," and Melvyna is a victim of the "strange chances of this vast, many-raced, motley country of ours" (172, 175).

While Keith and Carrington are the only characters who are not explicitly tied to the descriptor "strange," their indirect characterization underlines their status as foreigners. Their relationship to the island's environment, in particular, reveals their unfamiliarity with the locale. Although the two men appear well suited to the rigors of living on Pelican Island, Rioux points out that "the landscape itself warns [Keith and Carrington] of its recalcitrance" and that "the land itself seems . . . to reject them."[16] Significantly, none of the characters identify the island as "home." Instead, every character functions, in some way, as a displaced representative of their heritage. Sister St. Luke has left her convent. Keith and Carrington are separated from their northern residences in New England, though they have left of their own accord. Melvyna, a nurse whose patient died in Florida, still calls Vermont home, identifying herself by her maiden name Sawyer despite her marriage to the Minorcan Pedro Gonsalves. Even Pedro is separated from his Minorcan kin, visiting their community on the mainland every other week. As every character is uprooted from the places each calls home, the island environment acts to balance their differences.

Woolson's creation of the imaginary Pelican Island illustrates how these characters negotiate social hierarchies and further complicates Sister St. Luke's perceived ancestry. In the lengthy description of the island's lighthouse that opens the narrative, Woolson appears to be sketching an area close to St. Augustine. She writes that "the old square tower" of the lighthouse was "founded by the Spaniards, heightened by the English, and now finished and owned by the United States" (173). This historical outline roughly matches the actual history of the St. Augustine lighthouse: the original tower built by the Spanish in 1737 was square, constructed from coquina, and situated on Anastasia Island, just outside the city.

Yet Woolson's description casts doubt on this easy appropriation. Most pointedly, the name given to the setting in the story is unmistakably "Pelican

Island," not the recognizable Anastasia Island. Woolson would have certainly known where the lighthouse was located from her lengthy stays in the city. Substituting a new name would seem to place the site much farther south than St. Augustine, perhaps a reference to the Pelican Island National Wildlife Refuge in the Caribbean. But this sanctuary was officially established decades after Woolson wrote her story. Instead, Woolson most likely modeled the story's environment on the area surrounding present-day Daytona. An 1821 history by James Grant Forbes calls the area "the Pelican Islands," and this location seems to mirror Woolson's description of a narrow strip of land about twenty miles long that separates the Atlantic Ocean and the mainland.[17] The topography of this island chain is also reflected on contemporary maps of the Florida coast, which indicate a small, five-acre strip of land in the Halifax River as Pelican Island.

Moreover, Woolson's uses of Minorcan characters and Sister St. Luke's Catholicism further suggest that she had the Halifax River location in mind. For one thing, Pedro visits a Minorcan community every two weeks when he "managed to row over to the village, and return with supplies" (175). Given that the majority of Minorcans settled between St. Augustine and New Smyrna Beach, the Daytona-area island would provide the opportunity to make these frequent trips. Perhaps more convincingly, Sister St. Luke is identified as coming from a convent that is, according to Melvyna, about fifty miles away from their house on Pelican Island. It seems likely, then, that the nun came from the convent of the Sisters of St. Joseph in St. Augustine, which was established in 1866 and is roughly fifty-five miles north of Daytona. Using these contradictory details, Woolson creates a composite image of locations around the Florida coast, an imagined space that becomes a testing ground for contested identities. By creating an ambiguous place away from any recognizable city or settlement, Woolson sets up Pelican Island as an isolated space suited for negotiating the foundational understanding of the factors that determine identities.

Taking advantage of a fictitious location to explore hybrid identities, the story posits how religious customs complicate traditional definitions of difference. Since, as Jacobson writes, "religion was sometimes seen as a function of race" in the late nineteenth century, Sister St. Luke embodies this theory.[18] By using this story to explore a stark religious contrast, Woolson invites readers to consider difference as something other than—or in addition to—physical traits. Woolson's characterization of her title character as a reclusive Catholic is therefore not a value-neutral choice. In fact, "Sister St. Luke" represents a radical intervention in the entrenched literary tradition of anti-Catholic sentiment that circulated in northern publications throughout the nineteenth century. In

foregrounding her nun, Woolson refutes the established tropes that characterized Catholics as untrustworthy, subversive to democracy, and—particularly in
the case of nuns—victimized by abuse. As Maura Jane Farrelly observes, "Catholicism was at all times seen as antithetical to freedom. Freedom, in turn,
was seen as the foundation of 'American' identity."[19] Melvyna echoes these
fears early in Woolson's story when she acknowledges her own anti-Catholic
bias: "'I don't love 'em yet, and don't know as I ever shell'" (176). But Sister St.
Luke presents a thorny ethical issue for the Vermont nurse. Keith explains that
she "'feels a professional pride in curing, while as a Calvinist she would almost
rather kill than cure, if her patient is to go back to the popish convent'" (177).
Woolson's depiction of the nun counters the more virulent depictions of Catholics as malevolent actors in civil society, a sentiment that satisfies Melvyna.

Considering the larger context of anti-Catholic writings, Woolson's linking of religious practice to ethnic difference is not necessarily novel. Although
anti-Catholicism in the 1870s revolved mainly around questions of education,
Woolson pushes back against the literary tradition rooted in "convent narratives" that told stories of trapped young women abused by Catholic priests.
The Calvinist Melvyna alludes to these perceived dangers, saying, "'There
wasn't any man about their old convent, as I can learn, and so Miss Luke, she
hain't been taught to run away from 'em like most nuns'" (176). Although the
popularity of stories about the kidnapping and mistreatment of women peaked
between 1830 and 1850, the residue of these literary depictions lingered into
the Reconstruction era.[20] These narratives conflated two anxieties felt by
Anglo-Americans, which Sweet identifies as rooted in both "religious and ethnic intolerance."[21] By the late nineteenth century, in fact, anti-Catholicism was
most often reflected in anti-immigrant rhetoric.

A stark example of this fusion of anti-Catholic and anti-immigrant rhetoric
is everywhere apparent in an article from the same issue of the *Galaxy* in which
"Sister St. Luke" was published. Penned by Charles Wyllys Elliott, "The Hard
Times" is a conservative screed against "Cheap Labor" and the immigrant labor force of the late 1870s. Written with a sarcastic bite, the essay triangulates
economic anxiety, religious difference, and diverse national heritages. Elliott
first articulates the long-standing fear that Catholics are unable to participate
fairly in American civil democracy since they are under the thumb of the pope:
"There are people now who are getting up a scare about the wonderful growth
of the Holy Catholic Church, claiming that that church demands of all its members (as it does) allegiance *first* to the Church, and then *second* to the government where its subjects happen to be."[22] Articulating the fear that Catholics
would obey their priests in all things, including civil matters, Elliott is one of

the writers amplifying this threat since he links the fear of papal rule to immigration and the concomitant destruction of American prosperity. Claiming that over two-thirds of the population of Massachusetts is foreign-born, including many he supposes to be Catholic, Elliott writes acerbically that the "blessing" of Catholics has "reached us incidentally through our cheap labor; that is, it is a sort of superadded bliss."[23] He finally completes the link: "We have got cheap labor and we have got the Catholic church crowning every hill and blooming in every valley."[24] Although writing about Catholic immigrants and their effect on public economics, Elliott echoes many other anti-Catholic writers from the 1870s by linking Catholicism and non-Anglo immigrants to social problems. As Jacobson concludes, the "gravest objection" to new European immigrants was "their incapacity, as Catholics, to participate in a democracy."[25]

Woolson's depiction of a heterogeneous South quietly disarms Elliott's scathing critique. Because Elliott's essay ends just before Woolson's story begins, their literal juxtaposition mirrors the divergent approaches of the two authors to religious and cultural difference. Whereas Elliott's rhetoric parrots that of many northerners concerned about Catholics crowding into the political sphere, Woolson presents an episode in which a Catholic, far from diluting American democracy inside an abusive convent, serves as a model of quiet bravery. In the story's climax, when the nun captains the small paroquet across the turgid waters to Keith and Carrington, her religious identity is foregrounded. When Melvyna protests that the weather makes it too dangerous to search for the men, Sister St. Luke replies, "'The saints would help me, I think'" (197). Once the rescue is complete, she returns to her typical behavior: she "remained unconscious of the fact that she had done anything remarkable. Her black gown was spoiled, which was a pity, and she knew of a balm which was easily compounded and which would heal their bruises. . . . Then she grew timorous again, and hid her face from the sight of the waves" (198–99). Arresting the common nineteenth-century belief that Catholics would crush American government and culture, Sister St. Luke is nonthreatening (perhaps disturbingly so) but also altruistic and, most importantly, agential.

Examining Woolson's story within the context of earlier anti-Catholic writers makes the nun's rescue of Keith and Carrington—and the eventual changes brought to all these characters—even more significant. The only person who conquers the island's perils in pursuit of saving the northern Anglo men is the "strange" nun. Sister St. Luke's surprising heroism overturns earlier perceptions of her. No longer inferior, she is simply different. When the characters eventually leave the isolation of Pelican Island, they reenter the wider American society having been changed in some way by their experiences. In an act of

uncharacteristic charity, Carrington sends an ornate crucifix to the nun's convent. Keith "bares his head silently in reverence to all womanhood, and curbs
his cynicism as best he can, for the sake of the little Sister" (200). In this way,
he comes to appreciate the nun *because* of her difference, which resonates with
Woolson's other Florida fiction. In *East Angels*, Lowe notes, she "describes
throughout her novel a site of cultural independence, hybridity, and often harmony" based on religious difference.[26] Likewise, in "Sister St. Luke," diverging
island identities finally arrive at a point of harmony.

"Sister St. Luke" demonstrates how Florida's heterogeneous coast could
serve as a metonym for the United States writ large. As Foote contends, writers like Woolson, who centered their works on American regions, were en-
sconced in a literary form whose goal was to communicate difference. "Because it is a form that works to preserve local customs, local accents, and local
communities," Foote writes, "regional writing is a form *about* the representation of difference."[27] Woolson's story pushes the boundaries of what it means
to be "different" while foregrounding cultural and ethnic distinctions at a time
when neither was encountered in broad social conversations. Woolson's literary innovations also point to the hunger of her contemporary readers for this
kind of imaginative disarming of dangerous foreign figures. Her melding of religious difference to physical traits opens a space for gradations of racial "color,"
a necessity for a quickly stratifying nation. In her linguistic moves that anticipate later writers and social movements, Woolson demonstrates how difference
is both valuable and regularly misunderstood.

NOTES

1. Constance Fenimore Woolson, "Sister St. Luke," in *Constance Fenimore Woolson:
Collected Stories*, ed. Anne Boyd Rioux (New York: Library of America, 2020), 198;
hereafter cited parenthetically. The story initially appeared in the *Galaxy*, April 1877,
489–506.

2. John [Wharton] Lowe, "Constance Fenimore Woolson and the Origins of the
Global South," in *Witness to Reconstruction: Constance Fenimore Woolson and the
Postbellum South, 1873–1894*, ed. Kathleen Diffley (Jackson: University Press of Missis-
sippi, 2011), 38.

3. Anne E. Boyd [Rioux], "Tourism, Imperialism, and Hybridity in the Reconstruction South," in Diffley, *Witness to Reconstruction*, 69.

4. Rioux, 61.

5. Sharon D. Kennedy-Nolle, *Writing Reconstruction: Race, Gender, and Citizenship
in the Postwar South* (Chapel Hill: University of North Carolina Press, 2015), 32.

6. Stephanie Foote, *Regional Fictions: Culture and Identity in Nineteenth-Century
American Literature* (Madison: University of Wisconsin Press, 2001), 5.

7. Lowe, "Constance Fenimore Woolson," 42.

8. Rioux, "Tourism, Imperialism, and Hybridity," 62.

9. Matthew Frye Jacobson, *Whiteness of a Different Color: European Immigrants and the Alchemy of Race* (Cambridge, Mass.: Harvard University Press, 1998), 46.

10. Kennedy-Nolle, *Writing Reconstruction*, 64.

11. Lowe, "Constance Fenimore Woolson," 40.

12. Brad Evans, *Before Cultures: The Ethnographic Imagination in American Literature, 1865–1920* (Chicago: University of Chicago Press, 2005), 1.

13. Evans, 6.

14. Lowe, "Constance Fenimore Woolson," 42.

15. Nancy F. Sweet, "Renegade Religious: Performativity, Female Identity, and the Antebellum Convent-Escape Narrative," in *Nineteenth-Century American Women Write Religion: Lived Theologies and Literature*, ed. Mary McCartin Wearn (Farnham: Ashgate, 2014), 16.

16. Rioux, "Tourism, Imperialism, and Hybridity," 63.

17. James Grant Forbes, *Sketches Historical and Topographical of the Floridas; More Particularly Eastern Florida* (New York: Van Winkle, 1821), 91.

18. Jacobson, *Whiteness of a Different Color*, 70.

19. Maura Jane Farrelly, *Anti-Catholicism in America, 1620–1860* (Cambridge: Cambridge University Press, 2018), xii.

20. Catherine McGowan, "Convents and Conspiracies: A Study of Convent Narratives in the United States, 1850–1870" (Ph.D. diss., University of Edinburgh, 2009).

21. Sweet, "Renegade Religious," 16.

22. Charles Wyllys Elliott, "The Hard Times: What Shall We Do with Our Cheap Labor?," *Galaxy*, April 1877, 484.

23. Elliott, 484.

24. Elliott, 484.

25. Jacobson, *Whiteness of a Different Color*, 70.

26. Lowe, "Constance Fenimore Woolson," 37.

27. Foote, *Regional Fictions*, 4.

Illustrating Race and Region in *For the Major*

Kathryn B. McKee

For the Major is a novel deeply invested in the visual. Published in 1883 at the height of postbellum regional writing devoted to thick description of physical place, the narrative depends on the North Carolina mountains to evoke the town of Far Edgerley as one at a remove both from Edgerley, its near and in-dustrializing neighbor, and from the unrest of a post–Civil War South. But the novel calls upon the visual for more than setting. The artist who created the wood engravings accompanying Woolson's text, "A. F." (Alfred Freder-icks), recognized and subtly conveyed a version of the novel's events largely at odds with contemporary reviewers' fixation on Major Carroll and his sacri-ficial wife. The artist's six illustrations likewise divert readers from a more re-cent critical preoccupation with Madam Marion Carroll's elaborate masking as a younger woman, suggesting that storyline as a distraction from the novel's deeper investment in the disguise of uncomplicated whiteness. Instead, Freder-icks guides the reader toward the relationship between Madam Carroll and her stepdaughter, finally bound by what they are willing to do "for the major." The novel's illustrations also pull to the foreground the character of Julian Dupont, whose uneasy presence this mountain community remains unable to assimilate. As a result, readers can see *For the Major* as enmeshed within the broader gen-der and racial politics of its postbellum moment.

For the Major is a slim volume, compared to Woolson's other novels, but rich in complex detail. Its installments appeared serially in *Harper's Monthly* be-tween November 1882 and April 1883 before being released as a volume later that year. Contemporary reviewers homed in primarily on what the *Atlantic Monthly* dubbed two "chief personages," Major and Madam Carroll.[1] *Lippin-cott's* in August 1883, for example, called the novel a portrait of the "complex problems which married life presents."[2] The Carroll family lives in a North Carolina mountain retreat where the past is a curiously infrequent topic despite the material shabbiness suggestive of a once more comfortable existence. Characters allude to the Civil War only a handful of times—the novel is set in 1868, a mere three years after the war's conclusion—suggesting what John Pearson characterizes as "the inefficacy of an insular identity with no connection to national contexts."[3] In Marion Carroll, however, we find a character only seemingly isolated from larger forces churning outside of the hamlet. Married to Major Carroll, a man her senior, although not by as many years as she would have him believe, Madam Carroll is quite literally a self-made woman, dressing with great care and intention to suggest herself as younger than she is. "There was," the narrator tells us, "really nothing of the actual woman to be seen save a narrow, curl-shaded portion of forehead and cheek, two eyes, a little nose and mouth, and the small fingers; that was all."[4] Madam Carroll employs artifice, styling her hair, her face, and her clothing to embody a girlish youthfulness that charms the Major and allows him to understand himself as having rescued her, a young widow with a child, from certain ruin. Although that child dies, Major and Madam Carroll have a son together, named Scarborough for his father but called "Scar" for short, all that remains of the "patriarchal authority" that Cheryl Torsney understands Madam Carroll as overwriting.[5]

Instead, Major Carroll's past reasserts itself most forcefully in Sara, his daughter from his own earlier marriage, and it is Sara's return that initiates the novel's action. Having been away at school in the Northeast for many years, she seems never to have been to her family's mountain retreat at all. Shortly after her arrival, when she takes in the view of nearby mountain peaks, she tells Madam Carroll, "'I know just where they all ought to be; I made a map from the descriptions in your letters'" (7). Although her efforts to build the world into which Sara steps are extensive, Madam Carroll's construction project is unevenly successful. Sara resents her stepmother's seeming overprotection of her father, until she, too, realizes that he is declining into the twilight of dementia, a recognition that ultimately shocks her into complicity with her stepmother's maneuvering.

The arrival in town of Louis Dupont, a peripatetic stranger with vague ties to the West Indies, seems at first a mere wrinkle in the plot's main thrust, despite the townspeople's fascination with his exoticism. It is an attachment that a suspicious Sara does not share. "To Sara Carroll," we learn, "he seemed a living impertinence" (98). Readers come later to understand that his very presence has the power to crumble the twin narratives on which the Carroll family's origin story rests: Marion Carroll's blushing youth, plus the unadulterated whiteness of the South's first families and the purity of Lost Cause romance that the region will likewise stylize into a façade lasting deep into the twentieth century. A series of events reveals Louis to be Julian, Madam Carroll's son, the product of an abusive early marriage. His presence—and his age, suggested as twenty-eight or thirty—pulls the curtain back on a complicated former life for Madam Carroll, the details of which she shares only with Sara as they nurse a mysteriously dying Julian. The townspeople never know his true identity, but the two women are bound by their secret, as such knowledge would destroy the Major's cocooned existence.

With Julian dead and her aging husband's eyesight and mental faculties declining, Madam Carroll gradually drops her stylized façade, emerging as a woman of solid middle age. Critics and readers have debated whether Madam Carroll's deceptive self-fashioning acts as commentary on society's insistence, particularly in the South, on a narrow register of beauty tied to social class or whether it functions as a bold act of self-creation. Either way, Pearson suggests, "[b]y foregrounding Southern women in their inventive artistry Woolson's narrative suggests triumph rather than tragedy."[6] Her body, writes Carolyn Hall, is "the site of both oppression and resistance."[7] Insightful conversation about the meaning of Madam Carroll's elaborate bodily architecture has understandably dominated critical analysis of the novel.

From Marion Carroll's undoing, the novel moves quickly to a resolution, concluding with two weddings. Sara is set to marry the local clergyman, Frederick Owen, whose earlier insinuations of an improper affiliation between Sara and Julian have done nothing so much as betray his own affection. Still, Owen's fixation on the two as a pair is borne out by the clandestine nature of their encounters; as readers, we can almost see how Owen gets this idea and why Sara's marriage to an upright clergyman goes a long way toward restoring her to the conventionality an association with Dupont has threatened to disrupt. Their relationship is neither romantic nor incestuous (they are not brother and sister, although Sara does call Marion "Mamma"), but the desire for secrecy about his true identity means that Sara's encounters with Julian are persistently shrouded in mystery. Owen presides over the marriage of Marion and Major Carroll in a ceremony whose practical work is never clearly defined. Either Major and Madam Carroll, in fact, never actually married or Madam Carroll was once married to two men, believing her first husband to have been dead, a bigamous act now corrected. The novel does not recount just how Marion Carroll explains this curious need for an exchange of vows to her husband whose sensibilities are already shrouded by confusion. Instead, the closing lines portend the Major's death.

The frequent use of illustrations in nineteenth-century periodicals makes it no surprise that an image accompanies each installment of *For the Major*, all drawn by one of the publishing house's regular contributors, Alfred Fredericks, a New York–based artist and a watercolor painter who exhibited his work regularly.[8] According to Eugene Exman, Fredericks was among the first staff artists at *Harper's Weekly*, where he shared his "wonderfully imaginative" work.[9] In addition to images in serial publications, he, like many of his contemporaries, among them A. B. Frost and Winslow Homer, also contributed images to—or illustrated in full—a number of books, including British works by Wilkie Collins and Alfred Lord Tennyson and those by leading American authors, among them William Cullen Bryant, Henry Wadsworth Longfellow, Harriet Beecher Stowe, and southerners John Esten Cooke, Christian Reid, and Rebecca Harding Davis.[10] Kathleen Diffley notes that postbellum artists like Fredericks worked for periodicals in part because it put their art into the hands of large audiences, even if they themselves were frequently overlooked.[11] Certainly working for the Harper establishment guaranteed broad exposure. The endorsements for the self-promotional *Harper's: The Making of a Great Magazine* credit the publication's reliance on a high number of "artistic" illustrations as among its distinguishing features and in some part responsible for its impressive monthly circulation numbers, which had reached two hundred thousand by 1885.[12]

Fredericks came to the text of *For the Major* a veteran illustrator with celebrated skills. Britain's *Art-Journal*, for instance, concentrated primarily on Fredericks's illustrations in its praise for a new edition in the 1870s of *A Midsummer Night's Dream*, observing that "his hand is that of a master, and he is obviously a student who does not grudge labour to attain accuracy, while he gives continual thought to enrich truth by fancy." The reviewer reserves particular praise for Fredericks's fairies: "[S]ome of them are so admirable that it is not too much to say no living artist can surpass them."[13] Speaking of the same edition of the play, the *Athenaeum* describes Fredericks's illustrations as "remarkable for a true perception of the spirit of the text, for grace, spirited conception, poetical propriety, and delicacy of execution," concluding that the volume's merits lay primarily in the "ability and feeling of the illustrator."[14] Certainly, Shakespeare's play itself needed little introduction to the reading public, and so reviewers not surprisingly chose to dwell on what the modern era could contribute in the way of illustrations.

Still, these observations are noteworthy for the emphasis they place on the illustrator as textual interpreter. Not only does Fredericks's technical skill earn praise here. Equally touted are his attentiveness to "accuracy" and "the spirit of the text," suggesting what are, in fact, different impulses, the first toward ren-

"I AM AFRAID, MAJOR, THAT YOU ARE GROWING INDOLENT."

Figure 5. Alfred Fredericks,
"'I am afraid, Major, that you
are growing indolent.'"
Woolson, *For the Major* (New
York: Harper & Brothers,
1883), facing p. 176.
Wood engraving. Courtesy of
the University of Mississippi
Southern Documentary
Project.

dering correctly what the text describes, the second toward grasping an element beyond literal description, one that requires illustrators to combine their
skills with those of the author to convey a meaning neither can deliver strictly
on their own—"the spirit of the text." The decision about which texts to illustrate likely belonged to Charles Parsons, head of Harper's Art Department
from 1863 to 1889, although details about the selection process are scant. There
is no evidence that Woolson herself was involved, for example, although the
Art Department did sometimes consult writers about which scenes it would
be appropriate to illustrate. "[I]ncidents which are considered the most striking," obliquely writes the unnamed in-house author of *Harper's: The Making of
a Great Magazine*, "are suggested to the artist."[15] In the world of postbellum
magazine publication, "[w]e are confronted by extensive gaps," writes Joshua
Brown, "in our ability to answer elementary questions [about] . . . who was responsible for selecting subjects to be illustrated, and how that selection process
was structured."[16] Still, given the praise Fredericks elsewhere received for his
work, readers might reasonably expect that he chose which scenes to illustrate
and that his nuanced understanding of the complex interactions between characters is on display.

In both its serialized and its book-length formats, *For the Major* includes six wood engravings that feature with varying frequency the novel's five main characters: Sara Carroll, Madam Carroll, Julian Dupont, Frederick Owen, and Major Carroll himself.[17] Fredericks's images downplay the titular "Major"; he appears only in the sixth and final illustration, bedridden, hugging the margin of the frame, and characterized as "indolent," a description that the surrounding text suggests is playful but that the caption allows to stand alone (figure 5). His son with Madam Carroll, "Scar," the heir to the declining manhood and faded fortune of his estate and by extension the legacy of "the South," is never pictured at all. Conversely, Sara shows up in all six illustrations, once alone but more often as a point of dark contrast to the figure of her stepmother, who is dressed always in white. Marion Carroll appears four times and, after the first image, in a capacity consistently diminished in comparison with Sara. Fredericks's illustrations would suggest, then, that this is a novel concentrated in the tension between the two women at its center and the shifting dynamic of their relationship. By the final drawing, we see that Sara has become complicit in her stepmother's construction of an illusory world. The image that lingers for the reader yokes the two women in a visual parallel of deceptive dress, white, frilly, and serving the Major.

In a novel so concerned with Madam Carroll's creation of herself as a young woman, there is, curiously, no artistic rendering of her once she drops her elaborate façade. When the Major's sight has so dimmed that he can no longer see her, she begins pulling her hair back rather than wearing it in ringlets and dressing in plain black rather than ruffled white so that "all her lovely bloom was gone, and the whole of her little faded face was a net-work of minute wrinkles." "[T]his was an old woman who was talking to him," concludes Reverend Owen on a visit, "and Madam Carroll had been so young" (185). Woolson's words alone trace Madam Carroll's transformation; "A. F." provides no illustration, hinting that the novel's preoccupations may actually lie elsewhere.

With significant consequences for the reader's understanding of Sara and of her relationship to her stepmother, the order of illustrations varies between the published volume and the earlier magazine installments. The serial publication begins with an image in which Sara, dressed all in black, is seated on the floor while Madam Carroll sits in a chair somewhat above her with her youthful costume on full display: long ringlets, white dress, and ruffled skirt (figure 6). It is the only image in which Madam Carroll is larger than her stepdaughter. Sara is taller every other time Fredericks couples them; in the fourth illustration, depicting the scene in which Reverend Owen confronts the women about Sara's clandestine associations with Julian, Sara positively dwarfs Madam Car-

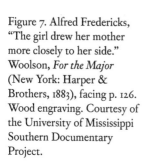

Figure 6. Alfred Fredericks,
"'Happy girl!' interpolated
Sara." Woolson, *For the
Major* (New York: Harper &
Brothers, 1883), facing p. 8.
Wood engraving. Courtesy of
the University of Mississippi
Southern Documentary
Project.

Figure 7. Alfred Fredericks,
"The girl drew her mother
more closely to her side."
Woolson, *For the Major*
(New York: Harper &
Brothers, 1883), facing p. 126.
Wood engraving. Courtesy of
the University of Mississippi
Southern Documentary
Project.

"SARA HAD PREFERRED TO WALK."—[Page 71.]

Figure 8. Alfred Fredericks, "Sara had preferred to walk." Woolson, *For the Major* (New York: Harper & Brothers, 1883), frontispiece. Wood engraving. Courtesy of the University of Mississippi Southern Documentary Project.

roll, who now appears childlike and defenseless (figure 7). The book's frontispiece, conversely, is Sara alone, the only image containing a single figure, thus underscoring her centrality to the narrative from the beginning. Fredericks situates Sara in the center of this drawing, accurately rendering her in the dark dress the text describes, her clothing slightly darker than the natural landscape tumbling around her. She stands beneath pine trees, their needles a disorderly carpet under her feet, the nearby tree trunks and branches likely twisted by the mountain winds that sweep over the very incline on which she herself stands straight, looking forward and thus directly at the reader, whom she invites with her gaze to form an attachment to her as a guide through the novel (figure 8). The illustration's caption—"Sara had preferred to walk"—describes a choice she makes rather than ride to church in the carriage with the rest of the Carroll family, a ritual that assures both Major Carroll and the town of Far Edgerley of his importance, connected as it is through unexplored allusions to prewar southern wealth and the enslavement that built it. On foot, Sara quietly separates herself from a weekly exercise in nostalgia.

In illustrating this scene, Fredericks underscores both Sara's centrality to the narrative and subterfuge as a theme in the novel, for it is here that Sara acknowledges the truth about her father's health. Fredericks draws her in the churchyard, "a beautiful rural God's-acre" donated by her ancestor and, on the side where she walks, including only a single grave "of an Indian chief, who slept by himself with his face towards the west" (71). Sara confronts in this illustrated moment what no amount of superficial window dressing can undo: her father is becoming senile and her efforts to rescue him are futile. His sense of himself and his world is vanishing, a lamented and noble past like the one suggested by the solitary grave at this site and the already prevalent narrative of the "vanishing" Indian. Eventually the "sharp personal pain, the bitter loneliness, gave way to a new tenderness for the stricken man himself" (73), and she resolves, having determined that he has some sense of what is happening to him, "to surround his life with love, like a wall, that he should never again remember anything of his loss" (74). Sara thereby abets her stepmother's scheme to hide from him both his present and, ultimately, Madam Carroll's past. What's more, her recognition that artifice powers life in Far Edgerley sets the reader up for a series of revelations, not only about the Major but also about what Madam Carroll has done for him and for herself. The novel's theme of masking only begins with her façade.

In fact, Madam Carroll's youthful masquerade may threaten to come most perilously undone through the visual rendering of Julian Dupont, who complicates her life with his sudden reappearance. A mysterious stranger alternately wooing and unsettling Far Edgerley with his alluring but inexplicable presence, Dupont is prone in the two illustrations that include him, first in a truly indolent pose (figure 9) and later on his deathbed (figure 10). In direct contrast to Madam Carroll's own meticulously assembled attire designed to convey youth, this "stranger" is "carelessly dressed, yet possessing, too, some picturesque articles of attire to which Far Edgerley was not accustomed; notably, low shoes with red silk stockings above them, and a red silk handkerchief to match the stockings peeping from the breast pocket of the coat" (91). All are captured in Fredericks's third illustration, albeit without color. Sara appears in both of the narrative moments Fredericks illustrates, further linking her to him despite her own reluctance to be in his presence. Both are disruptions to the placid present life Madam Carroll has manufactured, Sara in her yearning for the Major to be as he was and Julian in his taunting reminder of who Marion herself is.

Yet more than a sign of a repressed personal past, Julian Dupont also haunts the present text as a racialized and sexualized figure both out of place and strangely right at home. Particularly in the third illustration, Fredericks captures that tension, placing a languid Dupont in the foreground, his suitcoat falling open, his eyes cast to the sky, lines drawn on both of his cheeks and

Figure 9. Alfred Fredericks,
"He came often to their
flower garden."
Woolson, *For the Major* (New
York: Harper & Brothers,
1883), facing p. 94.
Wood engraving. Courtesy of
the University of Mississippi
Southern Documentary
Project.

Figure 10. Alfred Fredericks,
"The last look on earth."
Woolson, *For the Major*
(New York: Harper &
Brothers, 1883), facing p. 144.
Wood engraving. Courtesy of
the University of Mississippi
Southern Documentary
Project.

his forehead, across which a disorderly curl descends. Sara, by contrast, is a small figure in the background, her umbrella folded whereas Dupont's is fully extended, shading his face from the sun's darkening rays. Sara's clean, white face, conversely, pops out from the crosshatched backdrop of foliage. As Carolyn Hall suggests, Dupont perhaps most troubles the surface life in Far Edgerley with his "slender dark fingers" and the songs he plays and sings redolent of the "wild, soft, plaintive cadences of the Indian women of tribes long gone . . . of the first African slaves poling their flatboats along the Southern rivers" (98), an absence made too present in its haunting suggestion of miscegenation as Madam Carroll's most profound secret. Woolson likewise destabilizes Dupont's gender identity through extended description of his idiosyncratic dress, a character trait that Fredericks explicitly captures with Dupont's straw hat, wound round with "cream-colored gauze" (92), a ready contrast to the tint of his person. Dupont's unexplored connections to the West Indies nudge the reader here; his association with the islands connects the North Carolina mountains to deeper hemispheric souths and to the racial complications they introduce to American-styled binaries.[18]

Julian Dupont thus effectively queers the space of Far Edgerley and points toward disruptions the novel has superficially invited readers to see as far removed. As Hall explains, the "selective memory of the postbellum nation at large is echoed in the arrested life of Far Edgerley, where no one talks of race, nor of the source of the previous Carroll fortune, nor of how it was lost."[19] Although Sara eventually and perhaps grudgingly mourns Dupont, her early complaint that she is "'never sure that he is not there'" (93) means that For the Major is also a novel about Sara's uneasiness within the contradictions of a fractured postbellum world. The indeterminacies around race and gender that Julian embodies collide with a mountain retreat invested in the patriarchal hierarchies the Major represents. But in his dotage, the Major hardly seems up to the task of securing the future, leaving Far Edgerley vulnerable to Julian's threat. Julian's death and Sara and Owen's stable whiteness and their conventional marriage may be only temporary holds against the indeterminacy of a postbellum world.

Significantly, For the Major is a novel that appeared after Woolson's earlier travel sketches about the North Carolina mountains from the mid-1870s and after her collection of southern-based stories, Rodman the Keeper (1880). In fact, Woolson had been publishing work set in the South throughout much of the 1870s. Thus, she had herself witnessed the region's halting reemergence in national discourse and proven herself by 1883 a keen observer of its contradictions. Woolson wrote to Edmund Clarence Stedman from Venice that her novel was "a little genre picture of village life, with strong local color."[20] In a letter from June 1883, she labeled *For the Major* "so quiet" that it was unlikely to attract much attention; still, she observed, "it is the best piece of work I have done."[21] That combination of modesty and pride, coupled with Woolson's astute renderings elsewhere of a complex South, encourages readers to take a second look at what lies just beneath the surface, not only of the characters' self-presentations but of the narrative itself.

Although the hamlets of Edgerley and Far Edgerley are fictional, their setting is clearly the Blue Ridge Mountains. The western section of North Carolina was not immune to the postbellum conflict roiling the state, and in selecting 1868 as her setting, Woolson surely knew that she returned the plot to a convulsed moment. The initial wave of formal Reconstruction had ended, and Republicans, composed of a coalition of northern whites and Black and white North Carolinians, had the upper hand in state government. When in April 1868 voters ratified the new constitution, they did so by nearly twenty thousand votes in an electorate that included eighty thousand newly registered African American men.[22] Yet the violent legacy of the Civil War marked daily life in North Carolina much as it did elsewhere, leaving freedpeople simultaneously in "the margins of democracy and in the crosshairs of a broad campaign of terror,"[23] including in the western North Carolina counties of Rutherford and Cleveland.[24] The outmigration of Black residents that followed was the sad denouement of the optimism of 1868, the setting of *For the Major*. By century's end, coastal North Carolina would be the site of the Wilmington massacre, an exclamation point on white supremacy's role in inaugurating the twentieth century.

What Woolson subtly acknowledges in her novel is that the visible unrest of later moments is already a simmering force even in a place as seemingly removed from political life as Far Edgerley. The figure of Julian Dupont haunts the text and he haunts Sara, who is never completely sure he is out of the picture. By featuring him so prominently, Fredericks draws the reader's attention, twice, to his disruptive presence in Far Edgerley's beguiling placidity. As a precursor to later tragic mulatto figures in literature, Julian's body stands in for the twin specters of mixed race and ambiguous gender; his death emerges as the fitting resolution to a plot unable to accommodate him otherwise. Fredericks captures both moments: Dupont at his most threatening and Dupont on his death bed, in a world that will struggle to repress all that he represents, even as the patriarchs of antebellum whiteness descend to senility and the purity of white women cloaks darker stories.

Sara Carroll is enmeshed in that world. *For the Major* is only nominally about the Major, his marriage, or his faded stature. Woolson pins the future to Sara, and it is Fredericks who shows her to us as the novel's central figure. She and Marion, not the Major, understand how fully the character of Julian can unmake their existences, and they collaborate to contain his power. Although Woolson was living outside of the South by the time she wrote *For the Major*, she was unquestionably aware of the region's ongoing volatility. She does not represent it directly, but here and elsewhere she renders the South a profoundly conflicted space susceptible to misleading itself through the artifice of story-telling. Fredericks captures that "spirit of the text," and his illustrations guide readers in recalibrating their reading of *For the Major* to be a novel about the threats a postbellum world posed to its own creation myths. Fredericks's subtle images meet Woolson's subtle prose in a world whose priorities were anything but understated.

NOTES

1. "American Fiction by Women," *Atlantic Monthly*, July 1883, 120.

2. "Recent Fiction," *Lippincott's*, August 1883, 230.

3. John Pearson, "Henry James, Constance Fenimore Woolson, and the Fashioning of Southern Identity," in *Witness to Reconstruction: Constance Fenimore Woolson and the Postbellum South, 1873–1894*, ed. Kathleen Diffley (Jackson: University Press of Mississippi, 2011), 79.

4. Constance Fenimore Woolson, *For the Major* (New York: Harper & Brothers, 1883), 11; hereafter cited parenthetically.

5. Cheryl B. Torsney, *Constance Fenimore Woolson: The Grief of Artistry* (Athens: University of Georgia Press, 1989), 141.

6. Pearson, "Henry James, Constance Fenimore Woolson," 80.

7. Carolyn Hall, "An Elaborate Pretense for the Major: Making Up the Face of the Postbellum Nation," *Legacy* 22, no. 2 (2005): 148. For other discussions of Madam Carroll's acts of self-creation, see Janet Gabler-Hover, "The Portrait of a Southern Lady in Woolson's *For the Major*," in Diffley, *Witness to Reconstruction*, 215–31; Pearson, "Henry James, Constance Fenimore Woolson," 73–89; Charlotte Margolis Goodman, "Constance Fenimore Woolson's *For the Major* and Willa Cather's *A Lost Lady*," *American Literary Realism* 41, no. 2 (Winter 2009): 154–62; Torsney, *Constance Fenimore Woolson*; and Sybil B. Weir, "Southern Womanhood in the Novels of Constance Fenimore Woolson," *Mississippi Quarterly* 29, no. 4 (Fall 1976): 559–68.

8. Fredericks's book and magazine illustrations in *For the Major* are wood engravings, meaning artists' drawings that passed through the hands of engravers before their actual appearance on the page. For more on the process of wood engraving, its predecessor woodcuts, and its successor photographic images, see Kathleen Diffley, "*Harper's New Monthly Magazine*, 1866–1876: The Popular Rhetoric of Reconstruction" (Ph.D. diss., Columbia University, 1984); Theodore L. De Vinne, "The Growth of Wood-Cut Print-

ing. I.," *Scribner's Monthly*, April 1880, 860–74; and De Vinne, "The Growth of Wood-Cut Printing. II.," *Scribner's Monthly*, May 1880, 34–45.

9. Eugene Exman, *The House of Harper: One Hundred and Fifty Years of Publishing* (New York: Harper & Row, 1967), 104.

10. Sinclair Hamilton, ed., *Early American Book Illustrators and Wood Engravers 1670–1870* (Princeton, N.J.: Princeton University Press, 1968), 1:130–32, 2:82–83.

11. Diffley, *"Harper's New Monthly Magazine,"* 121.

12. For monthly circulation numbers, see *Harper's: The Making of a Great Magazine* (New York: Harper & Brothers, 1889), n.p.; for the magazine's circulation by 1885, see Charles Johanningsmeier, *Fiction and the American Literary Marketplace* (Cambridge: Cambridge University Press, 1997), 16.

13. *"A Midsummer Night's Dream*. Illustrated by Alfred Fredericks," *Art-Journal*, 1874, 63.

14. Review of "Illustrated Gift-Books," *Athenaeum*, December 13, 1873, 775.

15. *Harper's: The Making of a Great Magazine*, 22.

16. Joshua Brown, *Beyond the Lines: Pictorial Reporting, Everyday Life, and the Crisis of Gilded Age America* (Berkeley: University of California Press, 2002), 5.

17. As a serial publication later reproduced as a stand-alone volume, *For the Major* actually exists in two fairly different iterations. Scholars of print culture rightly assert that the text surrounding serialized installments of fiction likely shaped readers' encounters with the story in a way distinct from reading a self-contained text. See Charles Johanningsmeier, "Understanding Readers of Fiction in American Periodicals, 1880–1914," in *The Oxford History of Popular Print Culture*, vol. 6, ed. Christina Bold (Oxford: Oxford University Press, 2011), for a fuller discussion of this phenomenon.

18. Woolson anticipates here the havoc a character such as Charles Bon from William Faulkner's *Absalom, Absalom!* (1936) will unleash on racially ordered southern society. For explorations linking the colonial United States economically, politically, and racially to the Caribbean, see Matthew Mulcahy, *Hubs of Empire: The Southeastern Lowcountry and British Caribbean* (Baltimore: Johns Hopkins University Press, 2014); for a discussion of the postbellum South's linkages to deeper souths, see Matthew Guterl, *American Mediterranean: Southern Slaveholders in the Age of Emancipation* (Cambridge, Mass.: Harvard University Press, 2013).

19. Hall, "Elaborate Pretense for the Major," 152.

20. Constance Fenimore Woolson, "To Edmund Clarence Stedman," April 30, 1883, in *The Complete Letters of Constance Fenimore Woolson*, ed. Sharon L. Dean (Gainesville: University Press of Florida, 2012), 240.

21. Woolson, "To Hamilton Mabie," June 18, 1883, in Dean, *Complete Letters*, 258.

22. Deborah Beckel, *Radical Reform: Interracial Politics in Post-Emancipation North Carolina* (Charlottesville: University of Virginia Press, 2011), 64–65.

23. Gregory P. Downs, *Declarations of Dependence: The Long Reconstruction of Popular Politics in the South, 1861–1908* (Chapel Hill: University of North Carolina Press, 2011), 101.

24. Beckel, *Radical Reform*, 84.

"Assimilative Powers"

REGION, NATION, AND TIME IN *EAST ANGELS*

Karen Tracey

Constance Fenimore Woolson spends a substantial portion of the opening chapters of her 1886 novel *East Angels* delineating the diverse community of a town in Florida. Capturing both a historical and a contemporary perspective, her narrator explains that Gracias-á-Dios was christened by Spanish sailors three hundred years before, and "in the present day, the name had become a sort of shibboleth."[1] How the name is pronounced, and whether a full or shortened form is used, signals a character's identity in relation to the community: "To say Gracias á Dios in full, with the correct Spanish pronunciation, showed that one was of the old Spanish blood," whereas to use the shortened term "Gracias" with any suggestion of Spanish accent proved descent from English colonists of several generations back, or at least "an interest in history" or "the melody of the devout old names." But finally, and perhaps ominously, the careless pronunciation of "Grashus" indicated those entering Florida in the post–Civil War years, the latest colonizers who were seeking to profit by plundering natural resources or purchasing and developing the land, "many of the schemes dependent upon aid from Congress, and mysteriously connected with the new negro vote." This group Woolson summarizes as the "busy, practical American majority which has no time for derivations, and does not care for history" (54–55).

With her genuine interest in the past and empathy for a vulnerable community, Woolson would not seem to include herself among this "busy, practical American majority," and yet she was a latecomer to Florida, a northerner in search of respite. As a regionalist author, she took up the challenge of establishing both insider and outsider perspectives, and both historical and contemporary contexts. What emerges from her novel is a more fluid sense of what it means to be "American," especially after Florida became a state in 1845. For each moment that her narrator claims a character or viewpoint is "American," the novel as a whole, through the richly heterogeneous community of Gracias-á-Dios, suggests an alternate view. Her representations, while they would not qualify as anticipating a multiethnic and multiracial society in which all are accorded respect and treated equally, suggest a profound insight into American culture as rooted in ethnic and racial difference and inextricably tied to diverse and intersecting ways of thinking and being. *East Angels* juxtaposes a hegemonic concept of America with the complex community of Gracias-á-Dios, highlighting the dissonance between localized and nationalized understandings of the postwar nation.

Woolson's ability to work simultaneously as a regional and a national author drew attention from her earliest readers. In an 1890 review for the *Century*, Helen Gray Cone commented on Woolson's skills:

> It was a woman of the North who pictured, in a series of brief tales and sketches full of insight, the desolate South at the close of the civil war—Constance Fenimore Woolson, the most broadly national of our women novelists. Her feeling for local color is quick and true; and though she has especially identified herself with the Lake country and with Florida, one is left with the impression that her assimilative powers would enable her to reproduce as successfully the traits of any other quarter of the Union. Few American writers of fiction have given evidence of such breadth, so full a sense of the possibilities of the varied and complex life of our wide land. Robust, capable, mature—these seem fitting words to apply to the author of "Anne," of "East Angels," of the excellent short stories in "Rodman the Keeper."[2]

This early review captures the essence of Woolson's work: she is "broadly national" and also capable of a "feeling for local color [that is] quick and true." As a "woman of the North" she is still able to convey "the desolate South." The phrase "assimilative powers" suggests how effectively Woolson engages regionalism in the context of the nation as a whole. The desire to define or to capture a coherent sense of "Americanism" taking into account the "varied and complex life of our wide land" presents a paradox that has long engaged authors and critics. *East Angels* draws nation and region together in a way that is difficult to explicate using many of the critical models that have helped to shape our understanding of American literary history.

Scholars who investigate regional literature take a range of approaches to explaining how its authors negotiate the complex relationship between depictions of certain localities and the persons who inhabit them within the American nation, as well as how that tension may frame the relationship between past and present. American literature has frequently been read as centered in New England, while local color narratives offer stories of satellite regions that, as Judith Fetterley and Marjorie Pryse explain, are "minimized, ignored, and disparaged" by historians.[3] Focusing on how the American canon was shaped in the early decades of the twentieth century, Nina Baym states that literature textbooks "featured authors as culture-heroes whose lives and works displayed the virtues and accomplishments of an Anglo-Saxon United States founded by New England Puritans."[4] Despite her birth in New Hampshire, Woolson de constructs that view and challenges the white, masculine, individualist New England she seeks to replace in *East Angels*. The result is a regionalist novel with an unusual awareness of "America" emerging from diverse sources that define the present and will influence the future.

The central character, Evert Winthrop, infiltrates the society of Gracias-á-Dios and attempts to recenter it according to an American code of white male privilege that carries values connected with Puritan ancestors. "Winthrop" is a name that could not be more evocative of New England dominance. "Like most New-Englanders," the narrator states, "he had unconsciously cherished the belief that all there was of historical importance . . . was associated with the Puritans from whom he was on his father's side descended." While in many ways he comes to appreciate "a life, an atmosphere, to whose contemporary and even preceding existence on their own continent neither Puritan nor Patroon had paid heed," he takes a superior attitude toward the residents of Gracias-á-Dios (15). He is described as having "breathed so long that atmosphere of approbation which surrounded him at the North, that he had learned, though unconsciously, to rely upon it, had ended by becoming . . . smug and complacent, expectant of attention and deference" (119). He is welcomed into Gracias society, where his sense of superiority is persistently on display. By the end of the novel, however, his efforts to (re)colonize post–Civil War Florida have been absorbed into the flow of a nation that has many sources and that continuously evolves.

The title of the novel evokes not the town of Gracias-á-Dios but a specific place within that community, one with a history that is renegotiated, literally, in the present and that will continue to complicate a national future. East Angels, the home of the Spanish Dueros for generations, includes a struggling orange grove and a plantation that, because of the loss of enslaved labor, is virtually worthless after the Civil War. When Winthrop arrives, the property is occupied by Mrs. Thorne, a New England woman who has married into the Duero family and is now widowed with a daughter, Garda. She has barely enough money to subsist on and is greatly relieved when Winthrop offers to purchase East Angels and marry Garda. In that expectation, he learns "the history of the place almost back to the landing of Ponce de Leon" (197). Ownership of the property had been contested since Spain's invasion in 1585 and then England's in 1763. More recently, northern owners had temporarily laid claim, while the Dueros apparently kept possession. By contrast, the wealthy northerner Winthrop eventually boasts a clear title to this contested southern space.

The physical structure of East Angels captures this layering of history. Even as Winthrop's property, "the interior of the old house now showed its three eras of occupation": the lower level retains "the original Spanish bareness," while many of the decorations on the upper floor reveal the "attempted prettinesses of Mrs. Thorne," who tried valiantly to graft her New England sensibilities into the old rooms, and then, "last of all, incongruously placed here and there, came the handsome modern furniture which had been ordered from the North by Winthrop" (331–32). With the relocation of Winthrop and his display of wealth, Woolson shifts the narrative center from New England to Florida and in particular Gracias-á-Dios. This is one of the strategies by which she assimilates the national with the regional.

Local color authors were among the writers whom feminist critics in the twentieth century began to recuperate, and yet Woolson's work was often neglected in accounts such as those laid out in *The (Other) American Traditions*, edited in 1993 by Joyce Warren. There, Joanne Dobson simply nods to Woolson in a footnote that identifies a group of women writers who share "a new and often quite divergent ethos . . . more conscious of their feminism and more self-consciously artistic in their literary endeavors."[5] Elsewhere, Judith Fetterley proposes a provocative term to describe the regional literature of women writers such as Sarah Orne Jewett, Mary Wilkins Freeman, and Harriet Beecher Stowe: "unAmerican" is meant to foreground "the degree to which the term 'American' in the context of American literature has always referred to certain thematic content and to the values associated with that content—has, in this sense, always been political."[6] Fetterley pairs the term with the label "regional" in order to "create a category parallel to and thus potentially of equal importance to the category of realism," a category under which the women writers she studies have traditionally been subsumed and then dismissed.[7] Woolson is not included in this group of writers, perhaps because her work also deconstructs Fetterley's binary between "American" and "un-American."

Of late, critics have examined the relationship between regionalism, Americanism, and history from somewhat different perspectives. Amy Kaplan writes that "regionalists share with tourists and anthropologists the perspective of the modern urban outsider who projects onto the native a pristine authentic space immune to historical changes shaping their own lives. . . . Yet the reader of regionalism often finds less the nostalgic escape desired than a contested terrain with a complex history that ties it inseparably to the urban center."[8] As the story of *East Angels* begins, the concept of the literary tourist could well describe its narrative arc, and yet the novel takes an unexpected turn. Winthrop makes his way to Florida as a tourist in search of "blue sky" (3) but finds himself immersed in a community with a complex history that eventually becomes interwoven with his own story. He attempts to tie the region to the urban center from which he comes, but the Florida community maintains the significance of its own complications while the "urban center" remains on the periphery.

Woolson's *East Angels* also runs counter to regionalism as redefined by Stephanie Foote. Arguing that regional literature is a response to increasing immigration, Foote sees in local folk with their nonstandard dialects a stand-in for foreign intruders: "By depicting a rural folk, regional writing constructs a common national past for readers concerned with national matters." Indeed, regional literature becomes "a genre uniquely suited to imagine a homogeneous past for a heterogeneous nation."[9] Foote does not see local color writing as nostalgic, arguing that "it is no longer possible to regard regional writing as representing a common national past; rather, we must see it as helping construct a common past in the face of, and out of the raw material of, the increasing immigration and imperialism of the nineteenth century."[10] Furthermore, "for regional writing to succeed in restoring wholeness to the fragmented urban reader by offering 'authentic' experiences, it must be read as a static repository of the nation's past."[11] The past in *East Angels* is far from being a "static repository"; instead, the novel's history is constantly in flux and flows into the present in disconcerting ways.

Such a fluid treatment of a national past is also not fully accounted for in regional literature as described by Nancy Glazener, who declares that "regionalist fiction tended to depict remote and isolated ethnic communities whose inhabitants were remnants of a past social order that was inevitably passing away as a result of the advances of modern, urban-industrial-based life."[12] Gracias-á-Dios, as Woolson creates it, resists such advances by refusing to pass away. Although some of the characters struggle with their impoverishment and the diminished status resulting from their losses during the Civil War, they actively work to reestablish a community that will thrive. Within that reformulated community, disruptions to antebellum codes of race and class create tensions.

Kaplan argues that "by rendering social difference in terms of region, anchored and bound by separate spaces, more explosive social conflicts of class, race, and gender made contiguous by urban life could be effaced."[13] Yet here again Woolson's regional work takes a contrary approach. The differences of class, race, and gender simmer throughout the novel, and the region she depicts refuses to be "anchored and bound." The mixed heritage that characterizes *East Angels* derives from the past, enriches and troubles the present, and influences the future.

In her assessment of Woolson's fiction, the *Century* reviewer Cone prefigures a sense of regionalism somewhat like that developed by June Howard, whose work comes closer to explaining Woolson's fiction than some other formulations. Howard identifies a "persistent and pervasive tension between nationalism and regionalism—and the impossibility of fully separating them."[14] She points out that "the local and the global are by no means distant ends of a continuum."[15] Instead, she identifies a "fundamental tension" in scholarship on regionalism: "We are constantly shifting between what I call *substantive* and *relational* understandings of region."[16] The trend has been "broadly away from treating anything as solidly existing and toward an interest in how it is made."[17] Woolson's local/national approach to regionalism seems to incorporate similar views of place and time. She provides rich representations of a substantive place such as Gracias-á-Dios but also defines that Florida town from the perspective of its relation to other regions and times. Her mix of relationships provides the national element, while the substantive descriptions root her fiction in the local.

The places Woolson describes exist not only in relation to other physical regions but also in relation to their multiple and overlapping histories. This approach to regionalism provides an ideal vehicle for exploring a shared "Americanness," which is not "solidly existing" but instead constantly evolving. On the one hand, it is rooted in a substantive place and a certain time, but on the other it can be understood only in relation to other places and earlier times, a version of a multidimensional "America" beginning to coalesce. As a close look at *East Angels* reveals, national identity diffuses itself through history and across regions, taking temporary shape within particular moments and places before again dissolving.

The extensive glossing of the place name "Gracias-á-Dios" foregrounds the intricacy of Woolson's approach to regional literature. The unusual "color" of localities must be understood from historical and contemporary perspectives; what is "history" and what is "present" are difficult to distinguish. The characters that inhabit Woolson's novel carry identities that depend on their ancestors as well as on their current social and economic positions. Some have roots that go back to the original conquerors; the current generation has struggled through the Civil War and must face a northern occupation that only begins with Union troops. Others are postwar tourists or invalids who are encountering the ancient place for the first time. The residents of Gracias-á-Dios include two generations of descendants from the Spanish settlers (matriarchs and young men), displaced whites from the North and the South, the formerly enslaved, poor whites, Cuban immigrants, and northern travelers. Native Americans are acknowledged several times with reference to their displacement, but they are not represented by a character in the narrative. Woolson's depictions of places and characters buttress a national truth that the dominant culture would not begin to wrestle with for at least a hundred years: cultural diversity was not a discovery of the late twentieth century but the long-denied core of American history. While Woolson often reproduces the patronizing and racist assumptions of her time, she also represents diverse communities in diverse regions as "American." She privileges her genteel white characters, but they are subject to scenes in which minority voices take momentary charge of the narrative and lay their claim to be included in the stories the evolving nation tells of itself.

In Gracias-á-Dios, the genteel characters socialize together despite their varied backgrounds, but there are also many interactions between those characters and their poorer neighbors and servants, a heterogeneous group. In one key scene, a narrow version of Americanness surfaces when Winthrop commandeers East Angels and is positioned to take possession of the daughter of the Dueros. The plot potentially offers comfortable narrative closure. If the marriage of Winthrop and Garda were presented as a happy ending, New England would have successfully colonized Florida and the marriage would manifest a heartening reunion of North and South, a commonplace in postwar fiction. Glazener explains that "the most explicit and general framework for regionalist writing constructed it as a means of imaginative national unification, especially after the Civil War when regionalist fiction became a staple."[18] But the reconstituted union that Garda and Winthrop might have epitomized dissolves about halfway through Woolson's novel.

Insofar as her characters can be said to represent the regions and history from which they come, her novel's plot suggests how momentary are the versions of America that emerge from the dialectic between the national and the regional. In the novel's second half, Winthrop loses both the property and the daughter. Garda becomes bored with him and breaks their engagement, while Winthrop eventually sells East Angels to Margaret Harold, a woman he comes to passionately desire but who rejects him to remain in a loveless marriage. Ultimately, East Angels is inhabited not by a happily married couple embodying a restored nation but by a fractured northern family that has become integrated into Gracias-á-Dios. That family includes a domineering aunt (decidedly unattached) and an unloving husband and wife who, the narrator makes clear, will not produce offspring. Winthrop, the apparently powerful representative of New England, remains single and childless, denied a union with a fellow northerner. As a stand-in for New England's cultural clout in a white patriarchal country, he ends up disempowered and sullen, looking ahead to a lonely future. He certainly no longer exemplifies the masculinist imperial self.

The white privilege that Winthrop relies upon to take control of Gracias-á-Dios does not go unchallenged. As with much local color literature, in this novel people on the cultural margins are represented by characters whose appearance and language are marked as inferior. In East Angels, however, marginalized characters may reject their status in scenes that envision a more integrated nation. Rather than residing in a backwater where a people and their community have already been left behind, Woolson's characters have a present and, it is suggested, a future. They continue to play a dynamic role in the postwar nation.

The community of Gracias-á-Dios includes formerly enslaved people, most still serving in their former owners' homes. Woolson usually treats these characters as objects of amusement. There are glimpses, however, of a different possibility, as in an embedded scene narrated by Minerva Poindexter, a New England woman who has come south with her employer. Minerva finds herself "peekin'" at two Black women, Looth and Jinny, who are engaged in what is, to her, "outlandish" behavior. The narrator describes in detail the precise dance they perform: As Jinny approaches Looth and her young child, her bare feet "moved forward in a measured step, the heel of the right [foot] being placed diagonally against the toes of the left, and then the heel of the left in its turn advanced with a slow level sweep, and placed diagonally across the toes of the right. There was little elevation of the sole, the steps, though long, being kept as close as possible to the ground, but without touching it, until the final down pressure, which was deep and firm." As they come together, the two women sing, circle around each other three times, and finish with a "wild gesture" (257–58).

Realizing that Minerva has observed the dance, Looth later explains, "'We wuz *shoutin'*,' Looth went on, with gentle satisfaction. 'I's a very rilligeous 'oman, Miss Selsty, yessum. An' So's Jinny too'" (269). Woolson has presented a "ring shout," a practice described by Katrina Dyonne Thompson as "[o]ne example of West African dance persisting in the slave South . . . a religious/sacred dance that survived the Middle Passage and continued in North America."[19] This brief episode reveals an awareness of how the history of African Americans is woven into the nation's story. The dance Woolson describes had roots in Africa, became a significant element of slave culture, and was then carried forward after emancipation. In *East Angels*, the ring shout takes place in Looth and Jinny's community rather than in a space owned by whites, and the New England gaze of Minerva is incapable of comprehending its relevance. But Woolson's own knowledge enabled her to incorporate an episode in which those once enslaved and their children, their lien on the future, are establishing a region and culture of their own.

An examination of Winthrop's efforts to control the social scene in Gracias-á-Dios further demonstrates Woolson's occasionally empathetic treatment of nonwhite characters. When Winthrop is welcomed into society by Garda and family friend Dr. Kirby, they undertake a walking tour of the area and encounter two of Garda's admirers. One is Adolpho Torres, a young Cuban who has been educated in Spain, and the other is Manuel Ruiz, a descendant of an old Spanish family that was "almost as well known here in the old Spanish days as the Dueros" (40). Adolpho and Manuel participate in the society of Gracias-á-Dios and are included in various social gatherings; however, they are treated condescendingly by the town's white residents. Dr. Kirby identifies these two characters to Winthrop as "only young Torres, a boy from the next plantation" (38) and "only Manuel Ruiz" (40). Yet the narrator gives them more attention by providing detailed physical descriptions and contrasting those with Winthrop's own appearance. Torres is "a dark-skinned youth, with dull black eyes, a thin face, and black hair" (38), while Ruiz is "remarkably handsome" with hair of "little luxuriant rings, blue-black in color" (41). Winthrop's "complexion, where not bronzed by exposure, was fair; his eyes were light." Winthrop's hair is "of the true American brown," in contrast to that on the head of "the handsome young Floridian." The narrator at this moment associates "American" with Winthrop's colors and "Floridian" with Ruiz's. But a paragraph later, we are abruptly told that Manuel was "an American, and spoke English perfectly" (41). The narrator does not comment on the apparent contradiction. Instead, the close juxtaposition of these sentences establishes that the term "American" does not refer to a fixed set of characteristics but rather can have multiple associations.

The scene's dialogue reveals Winthrop's desire to elevate himself over both Torres and Ruiz. Manuel mispronounces Evert's name as "Wintup," which the narrator notes is "certainly a slight offence" especially since "owing to the mixture of races, much liberty of pronunciation was allowed in Gracias" (42). Garda invites Winthrop to look at the wild cattle, and Winthrop indicates he would find that entertaining if "one of these young gentlemen would favor us" by riding one of them. Ruiz is insulted: "What in the world are you thinking of? . . . Bull-fighting? I am afraid we shall not be able to gratify you in that way just now" (42). Neither the narrator nor Winthrop reacts to this challenge, which is left hanging when their dialogue is interrupted by the appearance of other characters. Ruiz is given the last word, and Winthrop's New England sense of superiority is briefly held in tension with the social priorities of a regional Americanism that is far less familiar.

As the narrative moves forward, Winthrop continues his efforts to belittle Torres and Ruiz. Speaking with Garda, he refers to them as "[t]hose young natives? Really, I have not observed them," to which Garda replies, "You have observed them, you observe everything. You say that to put them down—why should you put them down? You are very imperious, why should you be imperious?" (45). At a tea party where Garda is seated between Winthrop and Torres, the New Englander attempts to control Garda's interactions. She speaks Spanish fluently, he awkwardly. Garda reminds Winthrop that Torres does not speak English, but rather than be polite, Winthrop dominates the young woman's attention: "Garda and Winthrop, talking English without intermission, seemed to have forgotten his existence entirely" (108). Ruiz is angered on behalf of Torres: "he keeps you out there on the piazza for two hours in perfect silence!" (108). For much of the novel, Torres and Ruiz recede into the background, but by its end Garda has "turned her back upon her many admirers, and was about to bestow her hand upon Adolpho Torres" (591). This marriage may preview a future in which immigrants become part of the American story, whereas Winthrop's failed efforts to marry first Garda Thorne and then Margaret Harold suggest the diminishing power of New England.

Scenes in which minority characters take charge of their stories as with Looth and Jinny's dance and Ruiz's defiance of Winthrop demonstrate what Anne Boyd Rioux calls Woolson's "empathetic realism," a strategy that enables her to create "marginal or outcast characters struggling for the same things her readers did: love, dignity, and respect."[20] Although many of Woolson's scenes reproduce common cultural biases, her novel also gives marginalized characters, at times, the space for self-expression.

Woolson's insights into the continuing dialectic of nation and region in postbellum Florida are profound. Regional literature frequently creates clear distinctions and a hierarchy between urban and rural, tourist and resident, whites and nonwhites, and present and past. In *East Angels*, Woolson challenges such binaries, placing them in dialogue with each other and drawing attention to their artificiality. The result is a perception of "America" that assimilates the local into the national. She reminds readers of the country's manifold roots as a nation, placing New England on the periphery of such regions as Florida and creating a community where characters of many backgrounds mingle and merge, complicating the present and promising change in the future.

NOTES

1. Constance Fenimore Woolson, *East Angels* (New York: Harper & Brothers, 1886), 54; hereafter cited parenthetically,

2. Helen Gray Cone, "Woman in American Literature," *Century*, October 1890, 927.

3. Judith Fetterley and Marjorie Pryse, *Writing out of Place: Regionalism, Women, and American Literary Culture* (Urbana: University of Illinois Press, 2003), 4.

4. Nina Baym, "Early Histories of American Literature: A Chapter in the Institution of New England," in *Feminism and Literary History: Essays by Nina Baym* (New Brunswick, N.J.: Rutgers University Press, 1992), 81.

5. Joanne Dobson, "The American Renaissance Reenvisioned," in *The (Other) American Traditions: Nineteenth-Century Women Writers*, ed. Joyce W. Warren (New Brunswick, N.J.: Rutgers University Press, 1993), 177.

6. Judith Fetterley, "'Not in the Least American': Nineteenth-Century Literary Regionalism," *College English* 56, no. 8 (December 1994): 878.

7. Fetterley, 882.

8. Amy Kaplan, "Nation, Region, and Empire," in *The Columbia History of the American Novel*, ed. Emory Elliott (New York: Columbia University Press, 1991), 252.

9. Stephanie Foote, *Regional Fictions: Culture and Identity in Nineteenth-Century American Literature* (Madison: University of Wisconsin Press, 2001), 6.

10. Foote, 13.

11. Foote, 15.

12. Nancy Glazener, *Reading for Realism: The History of a U.S. Literary Institution, 1850–1910* (Durham, N.C.: Duke University Press, 1997), 194.

13. Kaplan, "Nation, Region, and Empire," 251.

14. June Howard, *The Center of the World: Regional Writing and the Puzzles of Place-Time* (New York: Oxford University Press, 2018), 4.

15. Howard, 42.

16. Howard, 2.

17. Howard, 3.

18. Glazener, *Reading for Realism*, 190.

19. Katrina Dyonne Thompson, *Ring Shout, Wheel About: The Racial Politics of Music and Dance in North American Slavery* (Urbana: University of Illinois Press, 2015), 114–15.

20. Anne Boyd Rioux, *Constance Fenimore Woolson: Portrait of a Lady Novelist* (New York: Norton, 2016), 79.

How "The Oklawaha" Prefigures (and Indicts) Disney World

John Wharton Lowe

Constance Fenimore Woolson was not the first (or the last) travel writer to limn the sublime aspects of the Oklawaha. Florida's tropical rivers have long offered one of the best avenues for penetrating the state's tightly woven jungle vegetation, particularly after Robert Fulton developed steamboat service on the Hudson River in 1807. By 1829, steamboats were beginning to appear in Florida's waters, and tourism was further facilitated by the invention and operation of dredges to remove fallen trees and debris. Hubbard Hart, a shrewd entrepreneur and orange grower, realized the commercial possibilities of boats that could function as both delivery vessels and tourist vehicles on the now-cleared river. His first steamer plied the Oklawaha in 1860; when the Civil War began, Hart reaped a fortune from delivering supplies for the Confederacy.[1] These profits inspired imitators, including Henry A. Gray, whose boat joined the Hart line; subsequently Sidney Lanier and Harriet Beecher Stowe would be passengers on that vessel as they voyaged up the Oklawaha. These excursions gained further popularity after visits by postwar celebrities such as Robert E. Lee and Ulysses S. Grant. But travelers remained wary of the many dangers involved: boilers often exploded, fires were frequent, and hidden debris could puncture a fragile hull and sink a vessel. While there was thus an element of trepidation in steam travel, Woolson understood that the Florida wilderness could also inspire sublime awe. In "The Oklawaha," published in *Harper's Monthly* in January 1876, she mastered a way to dramatize such exhilaration for the magazine's armchair tourists.[2]

After a traumatic war shattered the nation and devastated the South, travel writers like Woolson used the language of sublimity to explore the virtually unknown interior of Florida. In this essay, I consider earlier contributions to the development of what I am calling the "tropical sublime," before focusing on Woolson's short but complex travelogue, which took readers on the first "jungle cruise" and thereby helped inaugurate the state's tourist industry. I will then zoom forward to the development of Disney World and assess its "Jungle Cruise," one of the theme park's original attractions that is still operating today. As I demonstrate, the Florida river voyage has from the start been a composite simulacrum with disturbing racial components. In an arc of representation across several rivers and cultures, from Woolson to the Magic Kingdom, a hankering for the sublime has been transformed. Where "The Oklawaha" recalls an unexpected sense of terror in swampy jungles, Disney subsequently oom modified and diluted the tropical sublime to offer visiting families ersatz awe.[3]

For botanists John and William Bartram in the eighteenth century, the Florida swamps were a tropical labyrinth, full of a superabundance that roused bewilderment, fright at the eruptions of savage nature, and a sense of the inexpressible. Their writings engendered a tradition that Myra Jehlen has more recently linked to the early explorers and settlers of the New World: "America did not connote society or history, but . . . geography."[4] Conventional concepts of the sublime, however, did not include the flat but dense jungles and swamps of Florida and Georgia; historically, the notion of the sublime has been caught up in concepts of the high, the lofty, and the grand. But the sublime could also frighten. As Edmund Burke has noted, we are often helpless before its power, which can simultaneously impress and oppress. Volcanoes, earthquakes, and hurricanes inspire alarm, but they seem sublime only when viewed from a secure position.[5] Philip Shaw has further observed that recent acts of terrorism have reminded us of the sublime's negative manifestation, as with the feelings we experienced while witnessing the televised fall of New York's twin towers on September 11, 2001.[6] As Kant formulated, the sublime is not external but internal, and the "transcendent . . . is for the Imagination like an abyss in which it fears to lose itself."[7]

In the New World, phenomena such as swamps, rain forests, hurricanes, and alligators created the same kind of pleasure, terror, and awe that Europeans associated with the sea, the Alps, and raging storms. The Spanish found the Oklawaha early in their explorations; in our own time, a diver has discovered a cast bronze Spanish mission bell in the river, dating from the 1600s.[8] But epidemics and warfare left the area to Native Americans for centuries, a state of affairs that changed after the penetration of the first railroads during the 1830s. While cities on the coasts had developed early and prospered, the tropical interior had remained a frontier region, despite the introduction of plantations and farms along river valleys. In the nineteenth century, before decades of deforestation and urban development, primeval forests, savannahs, and swamps constituted a natural world with a dawning aesthetic appeal. Indeed, the wild Oklawaha River would become both Woolson's subject and one of Florida's most magnetic attractions in the late nineteenth century.

Postbellum Florida and the Tropical Sublime

Woolson was keenly aware that her audience would have an appetite for accounts of tropical travel, which had been popularized by publisher Josiah Gilbert Holland. Attempting to capitalize on the fevered interest in Henry Morton Stanley's account of searching for David Livingstone in central Africa, Holland employed Edward King to create, with a team of artists, a yearlong series of articles on the Reconstruction South. The 1875 compilation, *The Great South*, made extravagant claims about the novelty and "truthful picture" assembled after "the author and the artists" had "traveled," "penetrated," and "investigated" across "more than twenty-five thousand miles."[9] As Jennifer Greeson has demonstrated, both Holland and King situated the South as a kind of "domestic Africa," which was not too different from racist northern impressions of the region.[10] It bears mentioning that Florida's beaches had yet to emerge as the central attraction of the state; the tropical jungles were a much more powerful postbellum draw. The interior rather than the exterior, in other words, mattered more, thus the emphasis on penetration into previously uncharted realms, which echoed the famous accounts of African exploration that had gained unprecedented popularity. On Oklawaha steamboats, the role of the Black crew strongly suggested the parallel function of Black porters and guides in the exploration and conquest of Africa, even if it was customary to employ Black crew members during Reconstruction, when African Americans composed 40 percent of Florida's population.[11]

In the same year *The Great South* was completed, Sidney Lanier (1842–81) capitalized on the craze for southern travel by publishing his own *Complete Hand-Book and Guide* to Florida (1875).[12] Both King and Lanier were motivated by Harriet Beecher Stowe's influential *Palmetto Leaves* (1873),[13] which detailed her orange plantation life on the St. Johns River. Stowe would have agreed with Woolson, who declared the St. Johns to be "a tropical river of the dreamy kind" (162). Dreams, however, can become nightmares, replete with water moccasins, panthers, and alligators. The experience of the sublime truly requires a safe perspective, which the waterway's steamboats provided and the protection of an experienced crew ensured. As Stowe, reporting on her voyage, remarked, "[T]ourists, safely seated at ease on the decks of steamers, can penetrate into the mysteries and wonders of unbroken tropical forests."[14] Nonetheless, Stowe's description here, like Lanier's, also recalled two key components of Burke's sublime: obscurity and confusion. For Stowe, the passage of the Oklawaha through lakes, inlets, and tributaries offered a solution to the chaotic amplitude and seeming disarray of the swamp and thereby permitted a metaphorically "safe" perspective in the physical security of the boat.

Woolson, who knew these earlier treatments of the river, makes much more of the landscape in a thinly fictionalized account of her own journey through the Florida jungle. Geographer Jamie Winders has suggested that travel narratives centered on the South during and after Reconstruction featured several textual themes in "an (always imperfect) imperial holding; discourses of civilization, descriptions of nature, and discussions of whiteness."[15] All of these factors are at play in "The Oklawaha," which is enlivened by a colorful group of tourists. The "Duke" states that there are "no Gothic towers on the Oklawaha" (161); conveniently, a naturalist on board identifies species and quotes from Bartram. A veteran of the Seminole Wars provides historical context and populates the brooding landscape with ghosts of banished warriors. This is significant; Hudson River painter Thomas Cole once complained that "he who stands on Mont Albano and looks down on ancient Rome, has his mind peopled with the gigantic associations of the storied past; but he who stands on the mounds of the West, the most venerable remains of American antiquity, *may* experience the emotion of the sublime, but it is the sublimity of a shoreless ocean un-islanded by the recorded deeds of man."[16] Conversely, Woolson, who had read William Prescott's *History of the Conquest of Mexico* (1843) and appreciated the kind of deep historic structure necessary for a proper sense of the sublime, recognized the ways in which Native history—even a ghostly version of it—added to the sense of terror evoked by a tropical setting and magnified its mystery, as Native cultures and tragic destinies had become interwoven.

Édouard Glissant has pointed to the structuring devices of landscape, community, and the collective unconscious in the Caribbean world, all pertinent to Woolson's Florida as part of the Caribbean's northern rim. Nowhere is the force of the triumvirate Glissant mentions more present in her work than in her Florida novel *East Angels*; there, she demonstrates what he declares: "Our landscape is its own monument: its meaning can only be traced on the underside. It is all history."[17] This circum-Caribbean history threads its way through Woolson's response to Florida's swamps.

In "The Oklawaha," readers discover that the spectacle of the awe-inspiring river might soon vanish with the advent of industrial life. Ermine comes on the tour after seeing an engraving of the river "'so poetically beautiful in the arrangement of the tropical foliage, so full of the very spirit of untamed Florida, that the moment I saw it I resolved to come here before the wild wood gods were driven from their last hiding-places'" (165). Her rhetorical balloon is punctured, however, by a man who scoffs that these "gods" are alligators. Throughout her narrative, Woolson cleverly alternates between romantic and realistic points of view, which are rendered in appropriately divergent rhetoric. Later in the sketch, Ermine laments that "a beautiful trackless tropical wilderness" has been endangered by the growth of towns on the lakes. "'O lovely, lazy Florida!' she cries, 'can it be that Northern men have at last forced you forward into the ranks of prosaic progress?'" (175).

Words often fail spectators who view sublime sights for the first time, as Ermine does here. In "The Oklawaha," the new landscapes of the circum-Caribbean tropical zone leave others groping for a new language, which Woolson repeatedly contrives through light: "As the sun sank low in the west the red glow, which we could not see in the sky above through the dense umbrella-like tops of the cypresses, penetrated the open spaces below, and rested on the claret-colored water, as though the sun had stooped and shot under the trees . . . the water sparkled . . . the wild flowers felt a passing glory for a moment as the brilliant light swept over them" (165). This lyrical passage, situating striations of light against the sinister tangle of swamp branches, approaches the sublime while mimicking as well the fascination with light that was a familiar hallmark of the luminist and Hudson River painters of the Northeast.

Such an emphasis takes on more ominous qualities at night, when braziers of pine knots illumine the boat's passage into darkness, which is compared to the descent of Orpheus into the underworld. As the Black sailors replenish the coals they sing in "wildly sweet and natural" voices of Elijah's chariot of fire: "The whole forest lighted up, then a gleaming through the white trunks of the cypresses, then the same high-up flickering light over the tree-tops, and finally nothing save darkness. That was behind, however. In front we had our own glow, and journeyed onward into stranger and stranger regions" (167). The doubling down on "strangeness" heightens the inscrutable, inexpressible nature of this perilous yet enchanting world, which seemingly dissolves the separation between waterway and firmament while providing an Africanizing frisson.

Again and again, Woolson limns the incredible abundance of the foliage, with its fantastic forms: "Vines ran up the trees and swung downward in fantastic coils. . . . Onward we glided through the still forest, the light ever reddening in front and fading behind like a series of wonderful dissolving views set up by some wizard of the wilderness" (167). Indeed, Woolson takes this to a higher degree by asserting, "The woods through which we sailed all day were wilder than a Northerner's wildest dream of tropic forests. . . . Vegetation fairly rioted, and we almost expected to see moving about some of those strange forms of life which belonged to the age when ferns were trees, and the whole land a tropic jungle" (170–71). The passage suggests the nascent science of geology, which was rapidly bringing into consciousness a prelapsarian but very real primitive age. Nineteenth-century descriptions of landscape and waterways often employed prehistoric references that would increase the allure but also the menace of the teeming jungle on either side of the floating craft. The orderliness of Caribbean plantations and the gentility of seemingly docile natives have disap peared from this Florida account.

Here, unlike early renditions of the Caribbean, wildness is not discounted or masked, even as Woolson concludes. "Our party separated," she writes. "Their idle words and deeds will soon fade . . . but not the memory of the wild narrow river flowing on, on, through the dark tropic forests of far Florida" (179). This passage points to her sense that novel visions required a new mode of expression, a new naturalist vocabulary. Despite her reference to "idle words," Woolson's sketch draws much of its power from the lively discussions of the passengers who exclaim, wonder, and argue over so much that is bizarre, as the boat twists its way through the towering trees.

Mickey over Micanopy: The Oklawaha's Modern/Postmodern Destiny

Not far from the Oklawaha lies the mythical realm of Micanopy, a legendary Seminole chieftain who refused to give up his heritage and helped decimate the sugar plantations south of St. Augustine during the Second Seminole War (1835–42). His main legacy is a town south of Gainesville that bears his name. Even there, he has been eclipsed by a wholly imagined figure, Mickey Mouse, who presides over a new and unnatural wonder of the state—its sprawling theme park, Disney World. While many see its attraction springing full-blown from the creative mind of Walt Disney, as a natural complement to California's Disneyland, we can better understand its operations as a modern-day dismantling and ersatz reconstruction of the sublime elements of the Oklawaha cruises. This is particularly apparent in Disney's contemporary version of such a voyage, the Jungle Cruise; originally rendered along an artificial river meandering among artificial plants, robotic animals, and mechanical "natives," the nine-minute ride has gradually incorporated real tropical plants to create the impression of a bona fide jungle. The Oklawaha steamboats constituted in some ways an early version of Disney's bogus tramp steamers. While both voyages have troubling racial hints and issues with historical accuracy, Woolson's travelers are interacting with the realities of a topography and experiencing a degree of authenticity—and tropical sublimity—impossible for Disney's tourists, who are manipulated and force-fed a simulacrum of tropical penetration and discovery.

To appreciate those connections, it is worth returning to the early steamers in their final days. Railroads and then automobiles created easier paths to Florida attractions, and early parks such as Cypress Gardens, Silver Springs, and Marineland during the 1930s surpassed river cruises in popularity. Even before these developments, the Oklawaha vessels could not escape the engines of "progress." First, many of the great trees lining its banks were logged. In Nevin O. Winter's 1918 account of his voyage up the river, he notes, "Although most of the forest has been cut over, there is a stretch or two of virgin forest where the giant cypresses still stand as the monarchs of these realms."[18] Since the years of the Great Depression, the U.S. Army Corps of Engineers has also led an effort to create a cross-peninsula barge canal, which began to be built in the 1960s. As a result of this unnecessary and highly damaging project, over six thousand acres of swampland were flattened and the Rodman dam was strengthened; the sad result was the reduced flow to Silver Springs, the pollution of a major aquifer, and the separation of the Oklawaha from the St. Johns River, a "progress" that turned the former stream into a silt-filled ditch for much of its length. In 1968, construction of a new thirteen-thousand-acre reservoir, called Lake Oklawaha (aka Rodman Pool), further despoiled the fabled landscape, which eventually filled with invasive hydrilla, hyacinth, and debris.[19]

During the same decade, Walt Disney began buying property around Orlando. Soon he too was flattening the landscape to make way for the artificial tropical paradise of his "Jungle Cruise," still one of the most popular attractions at the resort.[20] George Ritzer calls the myriad shops of Disney World a "cathedral of consumption" and asserts that the conglomerate has created "magical, fantastic, and enchanted settings in which to consume."[21] The simulacrum of jungles, forests, and foreign countries is employed to ensure a sublimely safe ride, whose combination of water and foliage is carried into the lobbies of Disney hotels and the atriums of the shopping malls dotting the Magic Kingdom. Disney's inventions depart noticeably from those of earlier Florida parks centered on the state's natural flora and waters; Silver Springs touted glass-bottomed boats, for instance, and Cypress Gardens choreographed water ballets and skiing acrobats. These attractions and others like them did not attempt to transform already tropical Florida settings into imitation sites from other parts of the world. Together with Marineland, however, they did import new elements into the natural landscape, such as the "mermaids" who performed underwater ballets and the ocean denizens that would not have gravitated toward Marineland's inland waters.

In Woolson's Oklawaha narrative, Ermine laments Florida's corruption by "prosaic progress"; surely today's Sunshine State, now the country's fourth largest in terms of population, illustrates her point all too well. While we might label Disney World as a key offender in terms of imposing the "prosaic" profits on the state through its dream-inspired attractions, there is no question about the Magic Kingdom's aim: to create a simulacrum of the ecosublime that was immediately available when Woolson toured the Oklawaha.[22] Disney's technicians remembered how many consumers had been attracted to earlier spectacles such as the White City at the 1893 World's Fair in Chicago or the thrill-inducing rides at amusement parks like Coney Island two years later. But Disney World added what Henry A. Giroux and Grace Pollock call "managed exoticism," a concept produced by editing out any real-world distress, such as savage nature, dangerous minority or immigrant cultures, sexual exoticism, accumulating trash, or ambivalent replications of a national past.[23]

In a virtual whitewashing of history, Disney World "manages" the kind of narratives first produced aboard the Oklawaha steamers. There, often troubling relations with African Americans were reflected in the assigned roles of the Black crew, and contentious wars with the Seminoles found doubtful rehearsal against actual scenes of historic battles. Rather than engage Disney World's visitors with the conflicts between colonizer and colonized or the wilderness breach that eventually led to its demise, managed tour participants have been reduced to passive and protected spectators. The dangers they spot on the Jungle Cruise are manmade, whereas Woolson's tourists amid alligators and snakes could be wounded by reckless gunfire or burnt alive by exploding engines. Their voyage in "The Oklawaha" was also threatened by the possibility of running aground, which would place them at the mercy of a hostile environment. By contrast, families at Disney World have discovered that nothing really threatening or disruptive is allowed.

Instead, early promotional material for the Jungle Cruise promised a "grand tour of the world's most exotic rivers" on the park's most exotic ride: "Set sail on a 1930s tramp-steamer tour in the untamed waters of the Mekong, the Amazon and the rivers of Africa. Will your vessel . . . survive the 9-minute Jungle Cruise intact? Mother Nature is at her wildest as you pass Audio-Animatronics animals including the Bengal tiger, king cobras, elephants, lions and hyenas in their native habitats. Whether they're feasting on their prey, scaring trespassing humans or splashing water, the animals will keep you on your toes. As your

skipper leads you ever deeper into the jungles . . . be prepared for some sur-
prises. . . . Are there really piranha and headhunters lying in wait? Your skipper's sure to regale you with humorous tales of danger."[24] The "wildest" areas
of three continents central to tropical colonialism were neatly contained within
the parameters of the ride's circuit, providing in microcosm a statement of control and mastery on the part of "skippers" and, by extension, their passengers.
Entire continents and peoples are reduced to primitive representations to be
"conquered." The skipper's commentary effaces whiteness, which is nonetheless implicit in the contrast between the mostly white passengers and the ani-
matronic "natives." These racial "types" had a parallel on the banks of Woolson's Oklawaha, but there a sublime danger clung to Native Americans, real or
ghostly, and to unscripted Crackers and African Americans as well. Where the
Florida of the nineteenth century offered a version of exotic but impossibly removed Africa, now Florida is Africa through the sorcery of Disney, a simulacrum that encourages a sanitized invitation to the colonizing gaze.

As the original teaser for the Jungle Cruise suggests, the Disney company
wants to frighten visitors before reassuring them. Like Oklawaha steamers,
Disney boats are designed for the "penetration" and "trespass" of "wildest"
nature. Cruising passengers might become prey for "headhunters," bogeymen
who recall the racial stereotypes and historical allusions of earlier accounts, but
Disney World adds the drums and chanting that punctuate the scene as passengers head into simulated danger. "Natives" wielding spears mount an ambush
that is narrowly avoided, a close enough call to produce an atavistic "shudder"
at the end of the tour when Trader Sam seems to offer two of his shrunken
heads "for one of yours." Corralling global threats into the narrow limits of the
ride has been called "a playful Pacification of the third world,"[25] yet another
way in which Disney's fantasy eliminates all problems for would-be colonizers
and smothers their sublime terror of the outside world. As Baudrillard has suggested in his scathing indictment of Disney parks, they are "a perfect model of
all the entangled orders of simulations." And he adds, "When the real is no longer what it used to be, nostalgia assumes its true meaning . . . a resurrection of
the figurative where the object and the substance have disappeared."[26] Likewise, many of the original landscapes Woolson's passengers experienced have
vanished. In today's version of the Jungle Cruise, which has evolved consider-
ably over the past fifty years, the impossible combination of diverse tropicalities
has eclipsed the superabundance of Florida's swamps.

It should be noted that in recent years Disney revamped the Jungle Cruise,
eliminating racial commentary by the "skippers" such as warnings about headhunters. But the ersatz nature of the voyage remains, as voyagers view artificial

waters that are supposed to suggest a combination of the world's great rivers, ignoring the nearby tropical waters that created a true sense of awe, beauty, and danger during the era of the Oklawaha tourist vessels. True terror scarcely echoes in Disney's realm, where the tropical sublime has faded. Instead, visitors suffer an overload of stimuli; as Christophe Bruchansky explains, spectators are left feeling overwhelmed, unable to process perceptions or to discriminate among them. The wild mixture of images, puppets, artificial buildings, and contrived landscapes on a disorienting ride scrambles time, history, and cultures, leading to decontextualization. While Disney's chief aim is to create a sense of enjoyment, the voyage's "stunning effect," Bruchansky claims, blocks any real appreciation of its presentations to a reality outside the park.[27] Woolson was not immune to travelers with agendas, touring parties that scrambled time, and histories retold to satisfy elitist priorities. But during the 1870s, when she discovered the Oklawaha, jungle vegetation "rioted" in "fantastic coils" and the sublime fear of the unknown still loomed, in part because her tourists do not leave their boat. As Slavoj Žižek has declared, "The sublime object is an object which cannot be approached too closely: if we get too near it, it loses its sublime features and becomes an ordinary vulgar object—it can persist only in an interspace, in an intermediate state, viewed from a certain perspective, half-seen."[28] Safe on their steamer, the Duke and the naturalist, Ermine and the veteran, only get near enough to shiver as the mystery of the strange gives way to half-seen and chaotic vistas, never far from violence.

Both Woolson and Disney capitalized on the innate desire their readers/ passengers had for the thrill of the unknown, the tropical, and the wild. Unlike Disney, however, Woolson envisions actual—rather than ersatz—tropical abundance in the manner of Kant, who saw in the sublime the beginnings of an interior moral law. "If something arouses in us, merely in apprehension and without any reasoning on our part, a feeling of the sublime," Kant proclaimed, "then it may indeed appear, in its form, contra purposive for our power of judgement, incommensurate with our power of exhibition, and as it were violent to our imagination."[29] For him, the sublime engendered the distinction between knowing and feeling. For Disney on the Jungle Cruise, it was the threat that could be scuttled when the colonizing gaze encountered automatons. For Woolson on the Oklawaha, it was the anticipation of her extravagant fictions to come, stories and novels in which Florida's jungles provoke a compelling vision of threat and pleasure. Probing the "coils" of tangled human emotions, Woolson would translate tropical Florida into scenes of sexual longing, sublime desire swept up in a sensual landscape of "strange forms" that were dangerously charged.

NOTES

1. Bob Bass, *When Steamboats Reigned in Florida* (Gainesville: University Press of Florida, 2008), 84–89.

2. Constance Fenimore Woolson, "The Oklawaha," *Harper's Monthly*, January 1876, 161–79; hereafter cited parenthetically.

3. Monique Allewaert has suggested that swamps "are quintessentially sublime spaces, because they are vast geographies that defy measurement [and] . . . they are dangerous." See "Swamp Sublime: Ecologies of Resistance in the American Plantation Zone," *PMLA* 123, no. 2 (March 2008): 345. For my presentation of the sublime in the works of the Bartrams, see John W. Lowe, "Not So Still Waters: Early Travelers to Florida and the Tropical Sublime," in *The Oxford Handbook of the Literature of the U.S. South*, ed. Fred Hobson and Barbara Ladd (New York: Oxford University Press, 2015), 180–95.

4. Myra Jehlen, *American Incarnation: The Individual, the Nation, and the Continent* (Cambridge, Mass.: Harvard University Press, 1989), 5.

5. For the precise statement of these positions, see Edmund Burke, *A Philosophical Enquiry into the Origin of Our Ideas of the Sublime and the Beautiful*, ed. Adam Phillips (1790; repr., Oxford: Oxford University Press, 1990).

6. Philip Shaw, *The Sublime* (New York: Routledge, 2006), 2.

7. Immanuel Kant, *Critique of Judgment*, trans. Werner S. Pluhar (Cambridge: Hackett, 1983), 120.

8. Mallory O'Connor and Gary Monroe, *Florida's American Heritage Rivers: Images from the St. Johns Region* (Gainesville: University Press of Florida, 2009), 46.

9. Edward King, *The Great South: A Record of Journeys in Louisiana, Texas, the Indian Territory, Missouri, Arkansas, Mississippi, Alabama, Georgia, Florida, South Carolina, North Carolina, Kentucky, Tennessee, Virginia, West Virginia, and Maryland* (Hartford, Conn.: American Publishing, 1875), i.

10. Jennifer Rae Greeson, "Expropriating *The Great South* and Exporting 'Local Color': Global and Hemispheric Imaginaries of the First Reconstruction," *American Literary History* 18, no. 3 (Autumn 2006): 499.

11. Mark Derr, *Some Kind of Paradise: A Chronicle of Man and the Land in Florida* (New York: William Morrow, 1989), 64.

12. Sidney Lanier, *Florida: Scenery, Climate, and History, with an Account of Charleston, Savannah, Augusta, and Aiken, and a Chapter for Consumptives; Being a Complete Hand-Book and Guide* (Philadelphia: Lippincott, 1875).

13. Harriet Beecher Stowe, *Palmetto Leaves* (1873; repr., Gainesville: University Press of Florida, 1999).

14. Stowe, *Palmetto Leaves*, 247.

15. Jamie Winders, "Imperfectly Imperial: Northern Travel Writers in the Postbellum U.S. South, 1865–1880," *Annals of the Association of American Geographers* 95, no. 2 (June 2005): 392.

16. Thomas Cole, "Essay on American Scenery," *American Monthly Magazine*, January 1836, 19.

17. Édouard Glissant, *Poetics of Relation*, trans. Betsy Wing (Ann Arbor: University of Michigan Press, 1997), 11.

18. Nevin O. Winter, *Florida: The Land of Enchantment* (Boston: Page, 1918), 197.

19. Derr, *Some Kind of Paradise*, 363–64.

20. For a detailed description of the early version of the "Jungle Cruise," see Nathaniel Minnick, *The Jungle Cruise: Foray into the Faux* (Ann Arbor: University of Michigan Press, 2005).

21. George Ritzer, *Enchanting a Disenchanted World: Continuity and Change in the Cathedrals of Consumption*, 3rd ed. (Thousand Oaks, Calif.: Sage, 2010), 7.

22. Even at this date, certain clichés of the account remain; Winter notices, as most of his predecessors did, that "[a] cypress swamp is a frightful place to get into—it seems to be the very abode of snakes and everything evil" (198), a sentiment that no doubt facilitated the harmful logging. Besides, he continues, "This useful wood thrives best in stagnant black water, and the slaves who chose these swamps for concealment in their efforts to escape were certainly driven to desperation" (198). These observations underline the profit to be realized from harvesting the trees, provide history that relates to Africa through the escaped enslaved, and reiterate the terror that is so necessary to the sublime. Although Winter's title is *Florida: The Land of Enchantment*, he notes approvingly that "[t]hriving cities and resorts now exist where there was naught but sandy waste or tropical jungle a few years ago. . . . None of [Florida's] charm has been lost, while the changes have only made travel throughout the state easier and pleasanter, and comfortable and luxurious accommodations can be secured in every one of the principal resorts" (vi–vii), lines that ominously prefigure the Disneyfication of the state.

23. Henry A. Giroux and Grace Pollock, *The Mouse That Roared: Disney and the End of Innocence* (Lanham, Md.: Rowman & Littlefield, 2010), 40.

24. TalkDisney, "The Jungle Cruise" (n.d.), https://www.talkdisney.com/the-magic-kingdom/adventureland/the-jungle-cruise/.

25. Steven Watts, *The Magic Kingdom: Walt Disney and the American Way of Life* (Boston: Houghton Mifflin, 1997), 392.

26. Jean Baudrillard, "Simulacra and Simulations," in *Selected Writings*, ed. Mark Poster (Stanford, Calif.: Stanford University Press, 2001), 174.

27. Christophe Bruchansky, "The Heterotopia of Disney World," *Philosophy Now* 77 (February/March 2010): 15–17.

28. Slavoj Žižek, *The Sublime Object of Ideology* (London: Verso, 1989), 192.

29. Kant, *Critique of Judgment*, 245.

III

Through an International Lens

Woolson's Italy and Cultural Difference in *Harper's Monthly*

Lisa Nais

Setting foot in Italy for the first time in 1879, Constance Fenimore Woolson wrote, "I feel more foreign, more far away in the old world."[1] This first impression soon turned into fondness; she settled in Florence and found a home there for three years. Later she was well integrated in the American expatriate society of Venice. But for all the fondness Woolson had for Italy, she always felt a little foreign and never stopped wishing for a permanent home in Florida. Foreignness as a concept in the Anglo-American circles in Florence and Venice is hard to pin down. On the one hand, Woolson was a foreigner herself, struggling to connect with a different culture. On the other, Italians were foreigners to Woolson and her fellow American expatriates. Owing to the concept's fluidity, Woolson perceived foreignness ambivalently. In her letters she describes the Italians contrarily: they are "old-fashioned [and] sentimental" and need "so little to make them happy," or conversely, they are "deceitful" and "the most natural actors."[2] In her short story "A Pink Villa," Woolson dramatizes her ambivalent perceptions of foreignness and swaps the direction of the international theme: instead of dramatizing the lives of Americans in Europe, she renders Italy a vantage point from which Americans gaze at the western frontier in southern Florida. With an unmistakably imperial subtext, the story also engages with the rhetoric of cultural exoticism in *Harper's Monthly*.[3] Woolson appropriates this rhetoric to subvert its medium's agenda—feeding the nation's imperial appetite—to transform the story's misleading domestic subject—a mother's and daughter's rivalry for the role of the tale's protagonist—into a disquieting rendition of the international theme headed west.

Harper's Monthly, in which Woolson frequently published, put considerable emphasis on fictional and nonfictional travel writing.[4] Indeed, what the publishing house called "the profusely illustrated articles of travel and adventure" in a promotional publication constitutes a major selling point.[5] While *Harper's Monthly* amalgamated a range of material on themes such as cultural difference in the latter half of the nineteenth century, the periodical derived its fast-paced humor and great popularity from its travel sketches' colonial gaze.[6] Thus, it created a semblance of superiority of the American man, inciting its readers' imperial appetite. At several points the magazine echoed an American version of Mary Louise Pratt's "'seeing-man,' a . . . label for the white male subject of European landscape discourse—he whose imperial eyes passively look out and possess."[7] Here, I analyze the November 1888 issue of *Harper's Monthly*, using the Derridean framework of supplementarity, particularly the concept of the *parergon*, a framing device. Woolson's short story "A Pink Villa" appears in this issue alongside a generic variety of contributions that interact textually, thematically, and narratologically with the tale. I argue that the interactions among these texts reflect a cultural moment of the late nineteenth-century American imperial appetite.

"The Pink Villa" is a tale about an American mother and daughter, Fanny and Eva Churchill, who live in the titular villa on the Sorrento Coast. Fanny sees it as her duty to choose a suitable husband for Eva; in a long speech only seldom interrupted, the reader is guided through a list of suitors from different countries. Notably, the matches are described ambivalently. First is Gino, a soon-to-be Italian marques. His family has consented to Eva despite her small dowry, which leads Fanny to rave: "But not to hesitate over her mere pittance of a portion, that is very remarkable; for the marriage portion is considered a sacred point by all Italians; they are brought up to respect it—as we respect the Constitution."[8] She applauds the family's magnanimity, while describing "all Italians" as traditional. By singling out Gino's family, however, the remaining ones in Italy are automatically labeled as avaricious and small-minded. Despite his family's qualities, Gino is rejected. Second, a rich American does not meet expectations because Fanny thinks Eva would not do well in American society. "The very qualities that are admired here would be a drawback to her there" (838). Eva would be too shy, not coquettish or independent enough, as opposed to, say, a Daisy Miller.[9] Finally, Pierre, a soon-to-be Belgian count, meets all the criteria because his family has "French ideas about mothers"; mothers are the most important bar none (839). It turns out nothing had been wrong with the other men's nationalities. Fanny simply needed a husband for Eva who would not separate the two of them.

Eva, however, is more of an American girl than Fanny had originally thought. When a newcomer enters the scene, Eva quickly realizes that she had not been too besotted with her Belgian fiancé in the first place. The newcomer, David Rod, is a farmer from Florida whom Fanny and all her friends think of as commonplace. The stories he tells of Florida are too exotic and adventurous for them. In fact, one of Fanny's friends sarcastically chants, "Pioneers! oh, pioneers!," comparing Rod to Walt Whitman's poem celebrating the ostensibly inherent American pioneering spirit (845). Coming from a set of people who generically admire the more conservative poet Henry Wadsworth Longfellow, this observation is hardly a compliment. Eva decides, though, that these negatively perceived cultural differences—paradoxically as opposed to the Italian's and Belgian's positively perceived differences—do not matter. She marries Rod and leaves behind her lonely mother. The story ends with Eva's departure, while Fanny poses the unanswered question: "And the mother?" (856).

Here the physicality of the page comes into play. Fanny Churchill's rhetorical question is indented as a new paragraph, as if something were to follow. The story ends three-quarters of the way down the page, where a short horizontal line separates Woolson's contribution from the next. What dominates on the double page is an illustration featuring a few elk in a pasture, which accompanies the upcoming travel account. Similarly, the beginning of "The Pink Villa" blends in with an illustration of the Sorrento Coast, which appears to frame the story's first column. Woolson's opening is thereby merged with a visual representation of its setting, while its ending is suspended and almost overshadowed by an unrelated illustration. Jacques Derrida's concept of the parergon is useful to describe this overlap of contributions. The parergon is a kind of frame that supplements or complements or completes the work. It is an "illdetachable detachment" without which the work would display an inherent lack, much like a book would, if detached from its cover.[10] On closer inspection, however, the cover of a book essentially supplies the name of the author and the title of the collection and then, in the front matter, the date and place of publication. The purpose of these details is to root the volume firmly within its original literary historical context, leading the reader back to the magazine publication. Further, the book's title may or may not approximate the cultural moment in which its stories were first read. In order to demonstrate the relevance of the context of the magazine publication, I refer briefly to *The Front Yard and Other Italian Stories* (1895), which includes "A Pink Villa." A historical reader of Woolson's fiction who missed the November 1888 issue of *Harper's Monthly* had another chance of reading the tale seven years later in Woolson's posthumous collection. From its title, the reader learns that all of the tales included are characterized by an Italian quality. From there on, they may possibly make a connection to the international theme, which includes a notion of ambivalent foreignness. In the front matter there is also a note that indicates in which magazines the stories were originally published, pointing the reader toward *Harper's Monthly* and its imperial gaze. Overall, these clues in the book publication indicate the original cultural moment that the magazine publication generates and supplies. The meaning of this moment, then, is what is so hard to detach from and resupply to a story.

I now turn to that cultural moment in *Harper's Monthly*. Of particular interest is the magazine's "Editor's Drawer," an end section in each issue for random anecdotes, illustrations, and comics designed to elicit a laugh. Consider this example from November 1888:

A LONG TERM.

IRISH guide to American tourist: "And there is no king and nor quane nayther in America, they're tellin' me, sur?"

Indifferent Tourist: "No; we've a President there."

"And how long have you bin havin' a President, moight I ax, sur?"

I.T.: "Oh, something over a hundred years!"

Irishman, stopping, paralyzed with astonishment: "Howly saints! And do they live that long beyant there?"[11]

The reader is provoked to laugh about the apparent ignorance of the Irish guide who lacks not only education but also common sense. As the "first English colony," so Friedrich Engels puts it in a letter to Karl Marx, Ireland and the Irish were appropriated by the English.[12] The stereotypical image, as G. J. Watson argues, was that of "Paddy the Ape, violent, drunken, poor." From a "more refined" viewpoint, "the Irishman was childish, unstable, emotional, all blather and no solidity."[13] With all his stereotypes, this joke's "Indifferent Tourist" can be described as one of Pratt's "seeing-men," his indifference to the Irishman's conversation mirroring the passivity of European colonists. The joke exemplifies the "*mastery* predicated between the seer and the seen," not on a visual but on a social level. The Irishman's language is presented in eye dialect to create a semblance of the superiority of the American's educated language. According to Pratt, this strategy is used to "verify the [American's] achievement."[14] Exemplary of the type of joke generally printed in the Editor's Drawer, which compiled notes from various readers, contributors, and editors, this joke highlights a sentiment assumed to be common among readers of *Harper's Monthly*: an imperial appetite marked by condescension toward different peoples and cultures.

Similarly, Elizabeth Robins Pennell's "Our Journey to the Hebrides" pokes fun at foreignness. The four-installment piece, which concludes in the November 1888 issue, follows the writer on her travels through Scotland, from the Outer and Inner Hebrides via Inverness and the northern coastline to Aberdeen, then Edinburgh. The place is portrayed as off the beaten track, more exotic than the proximity to England tends to suggest. Its inhabitants are treated with eugenicist superiority, especially the Gaelic population. Despite these preconceived opinions, Pennell can be self-reflexive. She and her companion are intent on visiting sites related to Shakespeare's *Macbeth*, for instance, and she writes, "Macbeth seems to have shared the fate of prophets in their own country. We asked a man passing with a goat the distance to Macbeth's Hill, as it is called on the map. He didna know, he answered but presently he ran after us, Was the gentleman we spoke of a farmer?"[15] While superficially the punch line suggests the "relation of mastery" between colonizer and colonized comparable to the joke about the Irishman, Pennell draws attention to her role as a tourist by referring to the map. In Pratt's phrase, this "foregrounds the workings of her . . . subjectivity" and suggests that what for her might be the highlight of a day's travel is for the farmer an irrelevant and idle pastime. Invoking the map, this instance separates "mastery from domination, knowledge from control."[16]

Pennell, however, goes further than vaguely hinting that different societal roles and socioeconomic positions necessitate different priorities. She points to a series of issues pertaining to rural Scottish life: the protection of farmers, free trade, the lack of work, emigration, and the fishing industry. By listing these issues and empathizing with their gravity for the inhabitants of rural Scotland, Pennell legitimizes problems that the farmer who "didna know" where Macbeth's Hill was faced, and she aims to give her American readers an understanding of the hardships Scots face. She thereby attempts to do away with existing prejudices. Pennell recounts that she had been informed that Western Islanders, the inhabitants of the Inner and Outer Hebrides, are slow, of lesser intellect, and lazy. While her visit to the Hebrides seemed to confirm that stereotype, a second encounter with the Western Islanders working in the fishing industry in Fraserburgh, located at the northernmost point of Scotland's east coast, contradicts it. Pennell describes their hard, meticulous work, their long hours, and their strict work ethic. She writes in their defense that these "men and women, working incessantly by day and night, were almost all Western-Islanders, the people who, we are told, are so slovenly and so lazy!" Pennell calls out the prejudice—"the oft-repeated lies"—that her article has already operated to deconstruct.[17] As one of Pratt's "hyphenated white [wo]men" with multiple "national and civic identifications," Pennell offers an "internal critique" of the American imperialist spirit.[18]

In contrast to Pennell, the Scotsman William Black employs a form of "autoethnography," which Pratt defines as texts by "colonized subjects . . . that *engage with* the colonizer's own terms."[19] His novel *In Far Lochaber* is a love story published in magazine installments, one of which coincided with the publication of Woolson's "A Pink Villa." The protagonists are the Catholic Ludovick Macdonell and Ailie, whose father is a pastor of the Free Kirk of Scotland. Due to the religious difference, her family objects to their marriage and tries to split them up by keeping the young woman in hiding. Macdonell hires a rural lad, Johnny, who in return for a good position at Macdonell's estate observes Ailie's family home. He does not merely observe, however. The following scene casts him as the unlikely hero, who discovers Ailie's whereabouts. Johnny spots Ailie's father: "he happened to observe at a considerable distance the figure of the 'stickit minister' . . . ; and by *some lucky accident, by some flash of inspiration, a daring design* sprung into Johnny's brain. . . . [He] followed with one or two swift and stealthy steps, and then with a sudden, startling cry sprung like a wild-cat on the shoulders of the hapless probationer."[20] The melodramatic action is preceded by a passage of "verbal painting," in Pratt's terms, to describe the narratologically insignificant process of the emergence of Johnny's idea to launch an attack on Ailie's father.[21] The string of modifiers leading up to Johnny's "design" highlights the surprising nature of his inventiveness, when a little earlier in the passage the instance of eye dialect demonstrates his rural origins.[22] Then, the Scot's clear-mindedness is ironized, as his brilliant idea turns out to be physical coercion. While his actions are morally reprehensible, they advance the plot in a positive manner: Macdonell can now be reunited with his wife. Thus, Johnny's attack superficially disposes the reader toward him, but simultaneously characterizes him as a foolhardy young peasant who cannot be condemned for his actions because he is not clever enough to know better.

The contributions analyzed above act as *parerga* for one another, and the form of the magazine facilitates the interdependence of meaning among contributions. "A Pink Villa" is thus framed by the travel sketches surrounding the tale. In Derrida's words, the sketches—considered as parerga—come "against, beside, and in addition to the *ergon*, the work" under consideration.[23] Likewise, the contributions in a magazine may operate as antonymous comparisons, independent cross-references or textual supplements in relation to one another. These contributions, then, derive meaning from one another and create meaning in their interrelation, as they come to reflect and form a particular cultural landscape. This landscape is, as Derrida theorizes, "[n]either simply outside nor simply inside" any one work.[24] Instead, it is an ever-present concept on the margins and between the lines of the texts. As such, the cultural landscape that the magazine both creates and reflects is an integral part of the reading experience, in the sense that it is necessary to make a whole complete.

Along with its parerga, "A Pink Villa" functions as a meta-medial discourse on cultural difference, highlighting the notions of identity and American imperial appetite. Fanny's opening speech, occasionally interrupted by her interlocutor, Philip Dallas, suggests a predominately positive view on cultural difference. According to Fanny, Philip has little to contribute to the exceedingly difficult matter of marrying her daughter:

> "How little you have learned about some things, Philip, in spite of all your
> winters on the Nile and your Scotch shooting box!" . . .
>
> Fanny, then, with all her sense, was going to make the same old
> mistake of supposing that a bachelor of thirty-seven and a mother of thirty-
> seven were of the same age. (838)

Fanny equates being well-traveled and conversant in other cultures with being clever, sensible, or even astute. A European sojourn, therefore, contributes positively to a young person's education. Later, the reader learns that the reason the Americans think of Rod as "commonplace" is that he has never previously been abroad (844).

The example above is self-reflexive. Dallas had been bored by Fanny's long explanations about the suitability of Eva's different suitors. Fanny meanwhile had felt superior to her interlocutor, who did not show sufficient grasp of the situations without her elaborate explanations. This scene taps into a common perception of women's superficiality. Ostensibly, Fanny does not consider Dallas's intellect and wisdom (derived from his travels and, of course, his sex) when she bores him with her conversation. However, the irony about their differing ages, when they were born in the same year, prompts the reader to reflect on the two characters' different pasts. Fanny and Dallas knew one another when they were at school, but their lives have differed substantially. The woman married young to her parents' dismay. Her father then reduced her allowance significantly and ensured that none of her offspring would inherit. She gave birth at eighteen. Her husband died early, leaving Eva just a moderate inheritance. Fanny moved to Europe when the child turned three because of the cheaper living costs. The bachelor, by contrast, had probably spent some years at college or university and afterward enjoyed a life of leisure, traveling occasionally and socializing regularly. Dallas's experience of life has clearly been more carefree, whereas Fanny has had to become mature much more quickly owing to the untimely loss of her husband. In terms of responsibility and family concerns, Fanny is indeed more mature than Dallas. Woolson's self-reflexivity here prompts the reader to rethink Dallas's perceived superiority.

Fanny's opening monologue, however, also offers a more reserved view of cultural difference. This passage includes a few humorous instances of stereo-typing—the narrow-minded Italians and the flirtatious American girls—but narratologically it functions as a speech that provides the reader with necessary background information promptly. The reasons for rejecting each suitor seem shallow, providing levity and a quick pace appropriate for a magazine read. Woolson complicates the story when Fanny reaches the point at which she di-vulges the real criterion against which the suitors have been measured:

> "In addition, both father and son are extremely nice to *me*."
>
> "Ah!" said Dallas, approvingly.
>
> "Yes; they have the French ideas about mothers; you know that in France the mother is and remains the most important person in the family." As she said this, Mrs. Churchill unconsciously lifted herself and threw back her shoulders. (839)

For the first time the reader is allowed a glimpse into Fanny's consciousness. Her selection process is more egocentric than first assumed: she is more con-cerned with her own future place than with Eva's future happiness. This glimpse gives depth to Fanny's feelings and also foreshadows the tale's ironic ending. By equating herself with a French mother, Fanny becomes and remains "the most important person" for Eva before as well as after her marriage and, by extension, the most important person of the story. While the heroine of the story's marriage plot is Eva, the tale is focalized through Fanny. Thus, the two become rivals for the role of protagonist in "A Pink Villa."

The same technique is used when Fanny's circle of friends debates Rod's Tampa-made clothing. His friend, Bartholomew, defends the Floridian when his clothes are labeled "peculiar":

> "Made in Tampa, probably. And I've no doubt but that he took pains with them—wanted to have them appropriate."
>
> "That is where he disappointed me," said Gordon-Gray [an English-man]—"that very appearance of having taken pains." (844–45)

What for Bartholomew is a valid effort to fit in is ludicrous for Gordon-Gray. As the only Englishman in the circle, he embodies elegance and etiquette. His statement, then, suggests that an exotic Floridian does not have the slightest chance—despite having "taken pains"—to look appropriate, let alone fashion-able. Ridiculing the foreigner, Gordon-Gray, like Fanny, creates a pedestal for himself. Commenting on this exact phenomenon of stereotyping, Said writes about European hegemony over the Orient. He argues that the basic thought underlying the Orientalization of the Orient is "the idea of European identity as a superior one in comparison with the non-European peoples and *cultures*."[25] In this sense, he puts forward that "European culture gained in strength and identity" compared to its Oriental foil.[26] The similarity of Said's Orientalism and Woolson's characters' treatment of their southern countryman begs the question of Florida's seemingly exotic and mysterious character.

The image of Florida is linked to concepts such as pioneering the frontier and colonizing an ostensibly uncivilized land. After Gordon-Gray ridicules Rod's effort to fit in, he outlines his image of how a pioneer should look:

> "When I learned that he came from that—that place in the States you have just named—a wild part of the country, is not it [*sic*]?—I thought he would be more—more interesting. . . ."
>
> "You thought he would be more wild, you mean; trousers in his boots; long hair; knives." [speaker undetermined, potentially Bartholomew]
>
> All the Americans laughed. (845)

The joke is on both Rod and Gordon-Gray here. The Americans laugh about the stereotype, which they suspect to be exaggerated and reflects badly on both Rod, whose wildness is held in check, and Gordon-Gray, who evidently lacks knowledge about the North American continent. For the Americans in the story, therefore, Florida constitutes a frontier; for the Englishman, the supposedly uncivilized land seems a potential colony. Indeed, Gordon-Gray assumes the role of the colonizer who, according to Said, imposes his ideas of a place that cannot counteract his "superiority" on that place, which shines through as an undercurrent when Gordon-Gray responds, "Yes. I dare say you [Americans] cannot at all comprehend our penchant for that sort of thing. . . . And—er—I am afraid there would be little use in attempting to explain it to you" (845). The penchant refers to the English ambition to create an empire. Pramod Nayar locates the British colonial ambition in the so-called "cultural imaginary."[27] He defines this term as "a set of images, discourses, and narratives that enable a community to share a fantasy, an anxiety, or a collective desire, and influence the ways in which the community would acquire knowledge or interpret the world."[28] Nayar refers to the British Empire directly: because of the ambition of the English to create an empire, "'Empire' was therefore also a part of the cultural imaginary," a range of exotic lands civilized by the English and united under the British flag.[29] With his penchant for the wild and exotic, Gordon-Gray embodies the role of the colonizer.

The sinister side of colonialism, or in its American guise pioneering the frontier, is outlined by Annamaria Formichella Elsden. Dichotomizing Italy's femininity and America's masculinity by juxtaposing Fanny's maternal desire with Rod's imperial appetite, Elsden claims that "Eva falls victim to his manly power" and trades "her maternal past for a patriarchal future," which is "destined to be a tragic mistake."[30] The historical context of *Harper's Monthly* and the cultural moment it reflects, however, suggest a different reading. The imperial appetite that the magazine galvanizes mirrors Eva's fascination with Rod. Unconscious of their *"Blindness to the supplement,"* Derrida's umbrella term for *parergonal* concepts that supply or substitute what is lacking, the modern-day reader misses a reality obvious to the late nineteenth-century reader: the American expansionist project, the exciting bandwagon on which Eva jumps.[31] That choice is the solution to her feelings of inadequacy, which she betrays when she complains that she is "so useless" in comparison to Rod (851). The independence her life has thus far lacked is offered by Rod's imperialism on a silver plate and accounts for her willingness to jettison the lifestyle offered by the Pink Villa for a postlapsarian life of hard work. Indeed, the association of the Edenic life Fanny imagines for Eva—not merely by naming her thus but also through the search for a husband who would not change their lifestyle significantly—with the *Pink* Villa, suggesting an inherent connection of femininity and a life of leisure, is ironized implicitly. Eva's choice is not dissimilar to that of her mother, who also married against her family's wishes for the promise of a new and venturesome reality. In imagining an ostensibly typically feminine life of ease for her daughter, Fanny fails to notice the similarity of their characters.

Nevertheless, Fanny cannot empathize with her daughter's wishes. Likewise, Woolson remains critical of her young heroine in an authorial undercurrent enabled by the tale's narrative mode. Fanny is the story's narrative voice from beginning to close, and as such she is presumably its protagonist. As the tale proceeds, however, Eva, echoing the spirit of the biblical Eve, contests that role. Ultimately, she departs from the narrative, first by disappearing with Rod for a row along the coast, and finally as she sails for Florida. In other words, Eva rejects her mother's mediation of her life story. Woolson's initially comedic marriage plot thereby ends tragically, when Fanny expresses the same feeling of inadequacy previously voiced by her daughter by posing the final, unanswered question, "And the mother?" (856). A mother deprived of her daughter lacks purpose, the question implies, but this feeling that has incited Eva's imperial appetite does not galvanize Fanny to move on to new adventures in the New World. On the contrary, she stays in the Pink Villa by "her own arrangement," her countervision of American expansionism intact, though not without a certain feeling of ambivalence—not unlike that which Woolson expressed about being an expatriate among Italians (856). Similar to her contested protagonist who chooses to stand firm in spite of personal loss, Woolson likely valued empathy and transnationality, as opposed to mastery and dominance. Likewise, "A Pink Villa," implicitly critical of imperial appetite, is printed alongside "Our Journey to the Hebrides," *In Far Lochaber*, and the various jokes and anecdotes in the Editor's Drawer. The story provides a countervision to the lavishly illustrated contributions that regurgitate stereotypes superficially, while walking hand in hand with those that manifest often implicit but discerning criticism. Overall, "A Pink Villa" operates to infuse *Harper's Monthly* with Woolson's empathetic yet critical voice.

NOTES

1. Sharon L. Dean, ed., *The Complete Letters of Constance Fenimore Woolson* (Gainesville: University Press of Florida, 2012), 128.

2. *Complete Letters*, 324, 545, 196, 532. This kind of ambivalence was not uncommon. In *Imperial Eyes*, Mary Louise Pratt establishes that, in the eighteenth century, "Northern Europe asserted itself as the center of civilization," deducing that it is not "surprising . . . to find German or British accounts of Italy" or other Southern European countries sounding like similar accounts of ostensibly more exotic destinations, such as Africa or South America. See *Imperial Eyes: Travel Writing and Transculturation* (London: Routledge, 1992), 9. A similar argument can be found in Edward W. Said, *Orientalism* (London: Routledge and Kegan Paul, 1978). For the concept of "Oriental Italy," see Sara Blair, *Henry James and the Writing of Race and Nation* (Cambridge: Cambridge University Press, 1996), 46–59.

3. While the United States was, of course, never an empire as such, there are certain parallels between American expansionism (especially in the nineteenth century) and the imperialism of European empires. That being said, an in-depth comparison is beyond the scope of this essay.

4. The full title of the magazine at that time was *Harper's New Monthly Magazine*, which is abbreviated here for reasons of consistency.

5. *Harper and Brothers' Descriptive List of Their Publications with Trade-List Prices* (New York: Harper & Brothers, 1880), 3.

6. Frank Luther Mott approximates the U.S. circulation of *Harper's Monthly* in the period 1865–85 at 100,000 annually (3:6). The English edition of the magazine reached a circulation of 25,000 in the 1880s, outselling the competing English magazines (2:399). Frank Luther Mott, *A History of American Magazines*, vol. 2: *1850–1865* (1938; repr., Cambridge, Mass.: Belknap, 1967), and *A History of American Magazines*, vol. 3: *1865–1885* (1938; repr., Cambridge, Mass.: Belknap, 1970).

7. Pratt, *Imperial Eyes*, 9.

8. Constance Fenimore Woolson, "A Pink Villa," *Harper's Monthly*, November 1888, 837; hereafter cited parenthetically.

9. See the eponymous heroine of Henry James's 1878 bestseller *Daisy Miller*.

10. Jacques Derrida, *The Truth in Painting*, trans. Geoffrey Bennington and Ian Macleod (1978; repr., London: University of Chicago Press, 1987), 59.

11. "Editor's Drawer," *Harper's Monthly*, November 1888, 972.

12. Quoted in G. J. Watson, *Irish Identity and the Literary Revival* (Washington, D.C.: Catholic University of America Press, 1979), 18.

13. Watson, 17.

14. Pratt, *Imperial Eyes*, 204–5.

15. "Didna" is a syntactic construction for "did not" in Scottish English, here represented in eye dialect. Elizabeth Robins Pennell, "Our Journey to the Hebrides," *Harper's Monthly*, November 1888, 945.

16. Pratt, *Imperial Eyes*, 214–15.

17. Pennell, "Our Journey to the Hebrides," 951.

18. Pratt, *Imperial Eyes*, 213. Though of American origin, Pennell spent most of her adult life in Britain.

19. Pratt, 7. Note that the text differentiates between well-educated, civilized Scots, such as the protagonist Macdonell and by extension the author himself, and ostensibly less civilized Scots from rural backgrounds.

20. William Black, "In Far Lochaber," *Harper's Monthly*, November 1888, 907, emphasis added.

21. Pratt, *Imperial Eyes*, 201.

22. "Stickit minister" is a pejorative term for a cleric who fails in his position.

23. Derrida, *Truth in Painting*, 54.

24. Derrida, 54.

25. Said, *Orientalism*, 7, emphasis added.

26. Said, 3.

27. Pramod K. Nayar, *Colonial Voices: The Discourse of Empire* (Oxford: Wiley-Blackwell, 2012), 13.

28. Nayar, 13–14.

29. Nayar, 14.

30. Annamaria Formichella Elsden, "'A Modern and a Model Pioneer': Civilizing the Frontier in Woolson's 'A Pink Villa,'" in *Witness to Reconstruction: Constance Fenimore Woolson and the Postbellum South, 1873–1894*, ed. Kathleen Diffley (Jackson: University Press of Mississippi, 2011), 240, 242, 243.

31. Jacques Derrida, *Of Grammatology*, trans. Gayatri Chakravorty Spivak (1967; repr., Baltimore: Johns Hopkins University Press, 2016), 162.

Woolson's Veiled Cairo and the "Shadowing" of Jim Crow

Sharon Kennedy-Nolle

Constance Fenimore Woolson's "Cairo in 1890" opens with a startling image of Cleopatra, a carving from the Temple of Dendereh, soon followed by a sculpture of Prince Rahotep's wife. These pharaonic images of feminized, defiant power epitomize Woolson's representation of Egypt throughout this travel sketch, which first appeared in two 1891 issues of *Harper's Monthly*.[1] One of her most self-assured pieces, "Cairo in 1890" was part of a long-established gendered discourse of both imperialist and late nineteenth-century Egyptian nationalist enterprise.[2] Woolson's opening focus on Cleopatra also resonated with recent artistic appropriations of the Egyptian queen by Americans, who linked the grandeur of Egyptian civilization with the proud heritage of African Americans struggling for citizenship rights.[3]

Reconstructionist commentary underlies much of Woolson's work about the postwar American South.[4] In "Cairo in 1890" she uses the prism of gender relations, refracted through an exoticized imperial lens, to reenvision American understandings of postwar race relations and free labor ideology. By casting gendered shadows like Cleopatra's into interracial relief, Woolson affirms what Ann Laura Stoler identifies as "the centrality of women in shaping the contact zones of colonial cultures that became increasingly distinguished by race."[5] Sharply differing from contemporary travel writing that centered on empire building and Egyptian domestic reform, Woolson's writing foregrounds Egyptian women, celebrating their empowering household sororal networks. She also regenders Egyptian public spaces in ways that suggest alternative occupations of them by women. The labors of Egyptian working women prompt Woolson to revise prevailing gendered notions of American labor, which devalue women's work both at home and in the marketplace.

Moreover, Woolson capitalizes on Egypt's distinctive colonial status and its peculiar enslavement of the Sudanese to model interracial interactions for post-war Americans. At once audacious and accommodationist, Woolson's provoca-tively gendered gaze proves to be not color-blind but inextricably color-bound. Her strategic maneuverings can best be understood in the context of occupied Egypt and its relationship to the American South.

Her feminizing gaze focuses on the impact of the British military occupa-tion, commonly referred to as the Veiled Protectorate, from 1882 to 1914, when Egypt became a protectorate outright. The term "veiled" aptly captures the region's clandestine political dynamics in which Egypt, under its figurehead Khedive, was ruled by a British consul-general. Its "veiled" nature arose partly because of the British government's long-conflicted political and economic im-pulses over whether to cultivate Egypt as an imperial colony.[6] A key figure of occupation was the "all-pervasive and overdetermined figure of the (un)veiled woman" who became "central" to the contentious cultural rhetoric fueling the ongoing "divide between Islamism and western modernity."[7] An astute ob-server of this masked intrigue, Woolson launches her own "veiled" project of reenvisioning Egypt in ways that both defy and defend imperial agendas, par-ticularly in its racialist implications.

Woolson assesses the benefits of the British occupation by comparing it to American antecedents. She speculates about the implications of Urabi's cry, "Egypt for the Egyptians." She wonders "if a similar cry had been successfully raised about two hundred years ago on another coast—'America for the Amer-icans' would the Western continent have profited thereby? Doubtless the orig-inal Americans . . . raised it as loudly as they could. But there was not much listening. The comparison is stretched, . . . but there is a grain of resemblance large enough to call for reflection, when the question of occupation and im-provement of a half-civilized land elsewhere is under discussion" (258). That question's complexity continued to haunt the postwar American South, which by 1890 was dominated by "Redemptionist" governments committed to Lost Cause ideology, disfranchisement, and segregation—all of which were chal-lenged by Black Americans determined to assert their civil rights gained under Reconstruction.[8]

Woolson's detour to the Veiled Protectorate to reanimate American Recon-struction was not far-fetched. White southerners cultivated their sense of na-tionalist identity and postwar policy of segregation from British culture, par-ticularly its colonial rule.[9] Capitalizing on these ties, Khedive Ismail hired veteran Confederates to serve in his army by 1870.[10] Both regions relied on slave-cultivated cotton as the primary export crop to supply Lancashire's mills.

The year 1877 saw both America's "Compromise" officially end Reconstruction and the formal—though unevenly enforced—abolition of African slavery in Egypt. Economic interests defeated both British and American respective efforts to bring about true democratizing change in the form of land distribution.[11] Struggling to transition to free labor, Egypt's female ex-slaves, like American ex-bondswomen, faced gendered challenges that left them vulnerable to economic insecurity, violence, and exploitation. By the 1890s, Americans would again look to the Veiled Protectorate for imperial guidance.[12] Mindful of her readers' familiarity with long-standing American-Egyptian ties, Woolson strengthens them to advantage, even her lighthearted mention of the dragomen's cagey naming of donkeys after General Grant provides opportunity to reflect on his presidency's unfinished Reconstructive legacy (264).

Nevertheless, it would be misleading to map Atlantic paradigms onto the region's complex history of slavery. The hierarchies of dependency and reciprocal duties that characterize slavery in the Middle East and Mediterranean render the Black/white and slave/free dichotomies of the Atlantic model meaningless.[13] Because it evolved from complex social and religious practices in the Ottoman family, some historians have recharacterized this type of enslavement as a system of patronage. Mediterranean and Middle Eastern Muslim slavery accorded the bondsperson—considered both property and person—rights, opportunities, and responsibilities differing from those in the American South. Secular factors, too, such as the establishment of ancient agricultural patterns of small landholding and nomadism, largely precluded the need for field hands and relegated slaves primarily to soldiery and domestic service, the latter often represented by Ottomans as "mild," when compared to plantation labor.[14] Resituating Egypt's slave trade within a global capitalist network illuminates abolition's protracted nature, mainly because it clashed with international commercial interests. When Britain initiated abolition efforts in the mid-1800s, slavery and slave trading thrived.[15] Arriving in Cairo, one of the largest regional slave markets in the Ottoman Empire and home to about half of the country's slave population, Woolson reflects on an Egyptian culture still enmeshed in the slave trade to revisit the American South's recent occupation.

Distinguishing Egypt from other areas of the African diaspora was its own complex colonizing relationship with the Sudan, which it had ruled since 1821 and which was its major supplier of Sudanese and Nubian slaves. Itself informally colonized by the British and Ottomans, nineteenth-century Egypt thus emerges as a "colonized colonizer." Egyptians understood their enslavement of the Sudanese as an "ages-old trade relationship," one that was "often framed as a domestic exercise in a national 'civilizing mission.'" The inherent alterity of

Egypt's position resonates to some degree with that of the former Confederacy, itself occupied by the United States from 1865 to 1877 and yet an inextricable part of postwar America's imperialist ventures. The triangulated dynamics of Egyptian colonialism allowed for a "more fluid relationship" than that found in the Manichean binarism of colonized/colonizer as it informed Egypt's cultural identity and emergent nationalism.[16] Woolson capitalized on the potential of these labile ties to soften the polarities of American segregation.

Woolson's work can also be situated against that of the tourism industry, which was central to occupation. With the opening of the Suez Canal, tourism boomed under the aegis of cultural entrepreneurs Thomas Cook and his son, John, whose successful commercial presence provided essential economic infrastructure in the form of food, mail delivery, transportation, and boat building. John Cook was lauded as the man who "simply owns Egypt," and his enterprise was extolled for its "civilizing" benefits by his ships' ongoing military services, particularly his transport and rescue of British troops.[17] Counterpointing Cook's tours of public monuments were "hidden Egypt" tours touted by other nineteenth-century travel writers. With voyeuristic, often fantasized, prose, these writers tried to penetrate Egypt's feminized interior spaces, especially the harem. Implicitly comparing Egyptian women of all classes to the Victorian domestic ideal of the "angel of the household," these male and female writers stereotyped them as shiftless, perverse, and ignorant. Blamed for Egypt's irrational, tyrannical rulers, the oppressed figure of the veiled woman was increasingly used by travelogue writers to symbolize uncivilized society and her reform was made pivotal in justifying occupation.[18] Rather than seeking to reform and unveil those she encounters, Woolson seeks connection with them by seeing Cairo *through* their veiled perspective and by celebrating women's overlooked roles in shaping empire.

Veils function as a trope for facilitating Woolson's cross-cultural exchange with Islamic women while maintaining a façade of separation. She presents acquaintanceship with Egypt as an indirect or veiled enterprise, for Egypt "does not reveal herself to the Cook tourist" (151). Woolson's travel sketch is distinguished by its celebration of Egypt's rich Arab-Islamic cultural heritage. Admonishing her readers that "it must be remembered that Cairo is Arabian," she seeks out "gems of Saracenic taste" (155, 158). Throughout Woolson suggests that it is veiled encounters that allow for the gendered occupation of identities and sites otherwise strictly boundaried. In all her perambulations, Woolson captures the complexity of Cairene spaces, revealing that its gendered boundaries are constantly negotiated, historically specific, and distinct from colonialist fixed notions of public and private.[19]

Woolson's regendering focus is apropos as she visits Cairo on the cusp of dynamic fin-de-siècle change, a time scholars Marilyn Booth and Anthony Gorman have characterized as one of "*accelerated cross-cultural contacts and fluid
identities.*"[20] This zeitgeist was partly enabled by a burgeoning print culture.
Noting that over fifty newspapers and magazines debuted in Cairo alone between 1880 and 1889, Booth has explored how "the question of gender" then
"*saturated* the Arabic publishing scene of the 1890s," to conclude that "in one
way or another 'women and the nation' already constituted a ramified discourse."[21] Offsetting Egypt's low literacy levels, particularly for women, was
an alternative tradition of oral and visual media that circulated new ideas.[22]
Recognizing the intransigence of empire while questioning its ethos of Western
progress, Woolson emphasizes the Cairene values of relativism, context, and
cross-cultural balance in her portrayals of local women. Through them Woolson suggests strategies for women rights advocates challenging American wom-
en's subordinated status.

One source of women's emergent organizational power was the harem,
whose concubines and wives of eighteenth-century Ottoman elite households
had long operated as "political adepts" by solidifying political alliances, sta-
bilizing the household, and protecting family wealth.[23] Although the dynasty
behind these households collapsed and a new middle class arose, harem slavery nevertheless continued to be "a defining feature of nineteenth-century elite
Ottoman-Egyptian households." Precisely because of harem slavery's recognized value in supporting the household, it declined gradually, eventually making way for different socialization patterns and reconstructed social roles. Its
legacy of gender segregation provided the wellspring for Egyptian women's political involvement, which took the form of elite "women-only" organizations,
institutions, and print culture.[24]

Woolson foregrounds the empowering value of this sororal network when
she encounters a harem at the Gizeh museum, one that she linguistically extends to "their English, French, and American sisters" (178). Focusing on their
common interest in jewelry, Woolson stages her earnest desire for cross-cultural contact with them. As Woolson and an Egyptian woman pore over the
jewelry of Queen Ahhotpu, "our sister in vanity," a doting Woolson admits, "I
looked more at her than I did at the jewels, and she returned my gaze; we might
have had a conversation. What would I not have given to have been able to
talk with her in her own tongue!" (177). However, in letting a respectful silence
reign, Woolson, unlike her contemporaries, resists appropriating these women
by trying to speak for them.

Woolson unearths women's counternarratives of occupation among Cairene's "half ruined" obscure domestic spaces where "all the magnificence is kept" (197). Devoting an entire section to "Domestic Architecture," Woolson sifts through ruins, which Stoler targets as "sites that condense alternative senses of history." They can "animate new possibilities, bids for entitlement and unexpected political projects," as they do for Woolson in her treatment of the "hareem."[25] Refusing to part the harem's "gayly colored curtain" (197), Woolson demonstrates a restraint lacking in her effusive contemporaries.[26] She prosaically redefines the harem in flattening language: "The word means simply the ladies, or women, of the family, and the term is made to include also the rooms which they occupy, as our word 'school' might mean the building or the pupils within it" (253). A sketch of a Western-attired ex-Khedive's wife sitting on a sofa with her "private band" of musicians suggests that she could substitute for an entertaining Empress Eugénie, for whom Ismail decorated a special interior suite in colors to complement her complexion (251, 250). Woolson's elision of the two women allows readers to imagine utilizing the harem's empowered hierarchy, one complexly based on different races and multiple ethnicities in which slaves often occupied privileged familial places.[27] Woolson uniquely remakes harems into the most asexualized, generic haunt of her travels, rendering mundane their exoticized racial and gendered ambiguity. Ambiguity, now normalized, becomes the basis from which she challenges racial and gendered divisions of American labor.

Complementing her de-exoticizing of female-coded private spaces into public spaces, Woolson reconstructs traditionally male public spaces into feminine enclaves. The pendentives of a "sheykh's reception hall" transform into "a Persian scarf," while still others see "an India shawl" (201). Woolson regenders mosques through detail—the fretwork, patterned mosaics, oriels, exquisite minarets—that gives them "the whole appearance like that of jewelry" (160). Her feminizing gaze dwells on the mosques' silken-robed, slippered male guardians, the shawled dragomen, and the lettuce-munching Persian merchants. She notes that the merchants' "complexions" were like "cream-tinted tea-roses" while their hands and feet were "well-formed, slender, and delicate," favored Woolson words for describing women (189, 185).

Woolson's gendered description of their work helps reframe the labor question for American women, something American feminists seeking joint property reform for married women had tackled throughout the century. By detailing the "delicate" tasks of the Egyptian merchants as they "weigh incense on tiny scales" while their "taper fingers move about amid whimsically small cabinets," Woolson recasts their labors into feminized occupations akin to those Western women had long performed (186). In Cairo, she describes "beautiful gauzes, a few embroidered with the motto, 'I do this work for you,' and on the reverse side, 'And this I do for God'" (186). Their womanized work becomes a reward and a model for selfless service, much like the labors of the dutiful American wife. Recalling the strategies of antebellum feminists, Woolson's celebration of these labors asks readers to reconsider the worth of American women's labor outside the terms of its gender-biased market devaluation.

Woolson goes further in spotlighting the value and dignity of working-class Egyptian women's labors. Although Americans had made compulsory labor a cornerstone of the market and Victorian travel writers routinely condemned the Egyptian poor, particularly women, as lazy incompetents, Woolson praises them.[28] She savors the "abundant opportunity to admire the grace and strength" of women workers with their "free, effortless step" (179, 180). Their highlighted presence defies some Egyptians' "deep anxiety" heightened by occupation "over the visibility of women—-working class women, in particular—-in urban spaces."[29] Interspersed throughout her travelogue are conspicuous images of confident women workers that reflect the classed struggle in Egypt to organize against both British colonialism and capitalism.[30] Sketches of female water carriers and fruit sellers, often presented without husbands or children, paired alongside Woolson's female pharaonic images, reclaim the value of self-ownership for all women workers.

Derived from classical political economy, self-ownership discourse was long invoked by abolitionists and reformers to draw comparisons between a wife's servile condition and that of the slave. Condemning women's lack of personal and property rights under coverture, women's rights advocates applied the Lockean notion of having a property in their own personhood. With an eye to the family economy, antebellum feminists argued for the worth and importance of a wife's domestic work, which they wanted the legal right to claim. Yet when the courts grudgingly allowed that right, it was solely for wages earned outside the home, and it applied only in exceptional situations where a husband was incapacitated, imprisoned, or missing. Postwar feminists then began to endorse market-based "two-career families." They thus challenged the gendered differentiation of labor; but in doing so, they devalued women's domestic work because it was still unpaid and owned by husbands. Through reconfiguring the appearance, setting, and work of Egyptian men into feminized forms and by celebrating independent Egyptian women workers, Woolson launches a two-pronged feminist polemic that goes beyond the competing vision of her American counterparts: she challenges both the American gendered division of labor *and* the devaluation of women's domestic labors.[31]

Yet Woolson's emphasis on regendered spaces ironically reinscribes them for imperial occupation as she stages her own classist infiltration. Upon seeing one overlooked mosque "never visited by strangers," Woolson admits, "of course I dismounted" (159). Defying the "fiercely" glaring guard whom she bribes, Woolson tromps over the unprotected floor in her own "unsanctified shoes" (159). Her actions foreshadow the imperial brazenness of other Western women who attend a whirling dervish performance; these spectators perch transgressively on the balustrade, defying the repeated injunctions of a dervish, who, Woolson wryly observes, "did not conquer" (232). Her celebration of female self-assurance harbors an imperial intent to reclaim the segregated public spaces of Egypt for privileged white, Westernized women. As Stoler notes, "European women in these colonies experienced the cleavages of racial dominance and internal social distinctions very differently than men precisely because of their ambiguous positions, as both subordinates in colonial hierarchies and as agents of empire in their own right."[32] Precariously straddling these two positions, Woolson accommodates her own contrary attitudes, particularly regarding the role of Black citizens in postwar American life.

American women workers, themselves rendered partially free and partially bound in the aftermath of postwar earnings legislation, shared these race- and class-biased attitudes. Whereas the plight of lower-class tenement women working as hirelings was pitied because they necessarily neglected domestic work, for example, the claim of former bondswomen to refrain from wage work to devote themselves to family responsibilities was derided as profligate.[33] Similarly, Woolson's progressivist gendered vision in Cairo also occludes when the lens of race is added. When Woolson enters another male enclave, El Azhar University, she glimpses "a large, very black negro dressed in pure white" engaged in solitary prayer. Woolson stresses his seated position, one that avoids the supplication of the kneeling slave in abolitionist rhetoric: "[H]is feet stretched out . . . his hands placed stiffly on his knees, his eyes staring straight before him. He was motionless" (226). Woolson's observations ask readers to rethink the role allowed Black men in American public culture. In her rendering of a nonlaboring, undesiring Black man engaged in a serene pursuit, Woolson affirms the capacity and entitlement of Black men to attain a higher order of being. Yet this portrayal is qualified by her tapping into the emergent minstrel tradition as Woolson juxtaposes the meditating man to the antics of a baboon next door. To her inquiry about what the meditative man is doing, the dragoman replies, "He? Oh, he *berry* good man; he pray" (226). Woolson thus undercuts her valorizing portrait of the dignity and empowerment of Black men.

This ambivalence registers again in her presentation of the servile labors performed by Nubians, culminating in slavery's most dangerous outcome for masters: their overthrow. Retelling in gruesome detail one of the "black stories of cruelty" that swirl about Khedive Ismail, Woolson relates how he employed his Nubian servant Ishak to execute his foster-brother, Sadyk, the minister of finance (245). Losing two fingers in the murder, Ishak ultimately becomes an agent of justice when he reveals his mutilated hand and speaks of the crime and Ismail's cover-up. When Woolson visits Gezireh, the haunted palace of the murder, she embellishes this intrigue with a spectral parade that ends with Ishak stalking Sadyk. This image spotlights Ishak's capability to flawlessly serve and yet to ruin his master's reputation. Woolson thereby showcases the fearsome capacity of Black men to be their own agents of retributive justice Ishak's example endorses the power of African American self-advocacy but in a freighted context.

For many readers, Ishak's murderous stalking of Sadyk enacts an old drama of a feared Reconstruction, suggesting an untoward authority for Black men, particularly terrifying in the realm of sexuality. Managing indigenous Black men's sexuality, thought to be uncontrollable and predatory, was at the crux of social Darwinism, a race consciousness with which Egyptians were famil- iar.[34] For many Americans, the only instance allowing the symbolic coupling of white southern women and Black men on a public stage was a lynching.[35] Like the emergent Jim Crow South, occupied Egypt had stiff prohibitions in place against interracial contact between Egyptians and Britons, causing one histo- rian to categorize life under the Protectorate as under a "strict scheme of social apartheid."[36]

To challenge segregation, Woolson stages two sequential scenes of inter- racial social contact between Black slaves and harem women but in hedged, seductive terms. In both, Nubian eunuchs are key because of their castrated status, a requirement of service. Eunuchs thus allow her to challenge segrega- tion's racialist logic while accommodating the ideological demands underlying lynching dramas. She presents the eunuchs as "negroes," recognizable by "the extreme care with which they are dressed" in fashionable European clothes "with patent leather shoes" and "decorated with gold chains, seal rings, and scarf-pins" (174). Noting that some are "idling about," Woolson panders to what some white Americans condemned as Black pretensions to an unearned wealth and dandified leisure, a status that nevertheless became possible with the end-of-century's establishment of a consumer-oriented Black middle class (177). Black eunuchs, particularly those in the imperial court, enjoyed a pres- tige that allowed them to identify as equals among the powerful Ottoman elite "by virtue of being enslaved, castrated, and trained in the palace."[37] Woolson interprets the scene lightheartedly, seeing the eunuchs' casual presence as in-

citing shared mirth and allowing a fuller scene of gastronomic pleasure to unfold (177).

Yet in developing their easy intimacy, Woolson presents interracial exchange
in a paradoxically provocative but accommodating way. She invokes the one exception to segregated travel in the American South: Black women were permitted in white, first-class cars, provided they had white children under their care.
Again, Woolson uses sartorial detail to emphasize the eunuchs' touching of the
women, "their charges": "there was a general smoothing down of draperies" as
"they themselves attired the ladies in the muffling cloaks, and refastened their
veils securely, as a nurse dresses children, and with quite as much authority"
(178). By appearing infantilized, the asexualized harem women complement the
eunuchs' altered sexuality and effete mannerisms, allowing for their handling
by Black men who range in age, she notes, from seventeen to over sixty.

This casual scene builds toward another in which interracial contact is a *requirement* for upper-class traveling Egyptian women—one that flirtatiously affirms Nubian workers' desirability in language suggestive of the well-known
sexual parasitism practiced by the European aristocracy upon their servants.
Woolson concedes, "To go out without a eunuch would be a humiliation for a
Cairo wife; to her view, it would seem to say that she is not sufficiently attractive to require a guardian" (178). Occasioning "more laughter still" is the arrival of an intermediary American who escorts the women to their "hareem"
carriages. Although Woolson assures the reader that he is harmless, this elderly but racially unmarked and noncastrated man paves the way for the Nubian *sais* or running footmen who herald the carriage by carrying aloft a "long
lance-like wand" (178, 179). Leaving the status of *their* sexual potency deliberately unclear, Woolson teases that these "very handsome" men also work "occasionally" for Europeans (179). Far from the "hideous" eunuchs in the museum, the sais garner Woolson's full praise for their fleet, "admirably formed,"
and lavishly attired figures (174, 179). An otherwise proper Woolson rhapso-
dizes, "[T]heir gait is the most beautiful motion I have ever seen. The Mercury
of John of Bologna; the younger gods of Olympus—will these do for comparisons?" (179). Woolson tantalizingly posits potent interracial contact by dramatizing the flighty pleasures of desire itself. Yet for all her venturesome reporting about a complexly colonized region sizzling with possibilities for all kinds
of close encounters, Woolson retreats to the safety of innuendo. That Egyptian
asset of ambiguity hardens into ambivalence.

A mistress to compromise, Woolson balances her endorsement of occupation with sympathy for Egyptian nationalists. Ruminating on British repressive
tactics used to control their other colonies, she notes dryly "that certain per-

sons in Ireland are followed so closely by a policeman that the official might be the shadow" just as the Khedive has but a "shadowy power" (258, 261). The binarism of American racialist thinking, whether it resembles Ishak's shadow or the policeman's, stalks expatriate Woolson even as she creatively circumvents such discourse. Her successful adaptation of Cairene values to challenge American gender polarities notwithstanding, Woolson's devotion to Egypt demands absolute affections: "If one cares for it at all, one loves it; there is no half-way. If one does not love it, one really (though perhaps not avowedly) hates it" (279). The culmination of a literary career dedicated to redressing injustice, "Cairo in 1890" thus demonstrates that such reconstructions are undermined by the very veils and shadows that conceived them.

NOTES

1. Constance Fenimore Woolson, *Menton, Cairo, and Corfu* (New York: Harper and Brothers, 1896), 147–280; hereafter cited parenthetically. Reprinted from "Cairo in 1890," *Harper's Monthly*, October and November 1891, 651–74, 828–55.

2. See Beth Baron, *Egypt as a Woman: Nationalism, Gender, and Politics* (Berkeley: University of California Press, 2005).

3. Margaret Malamud and Martha Malamud, "The Petrification of Cleopatra in Nineteenth Century Art," *Arion: A Journal of Humanities and the Classics* 28, no. 1 (Spring/Summer 2020): 31–51; Charmaine Nelson, *The Color of Stone: Sculpting the Black Female Subject in Nineteenth-Century America* (Minneapolis: University of Minnesota Press, 2007), 143–79.

4. Kathleen Diffley, ed., *Witness to Reconstruction: Constance Fenimore Woolson and the Postbellum South, 1873–1894* (Jackson: University Press of Mississippi, 2011).

5. Ann Laura Stoler, "Tense and Tender Ties: The Politics of Comparison in North American History and (Post) Colonial Studies," in *Haunted by Empire: Geographies of Intimacy in North American History*, ed. Stoler (Durham, N.C.: Duke University Press, 2006), 33.

6. Robert Tignor, *Modernization and British Colonial Rule, 1882–1914* (Princeton, N.J.: Princeton University Press, 1966), 48–93.

7. Teresa Heffernan, *Veiled Figures: Women, Modernity, and the Spectres of Orientalism* (Toronto: University of Toronto Press, 2016), 14.

8. The historiography on Black resistance to Jim Crow is rich. For recent examples, see Henry Louis Gates Jr., *Stony the Road: Reconstruction, White Supremacy, and the Rise of Jim Crow* (New York: Penguin, 2019); Sarah Haley, *No Mercy Here: Gender, Punishment, and the Making of Jim Crow Modernity* (Chapel Hill: University of North Carolina Press, 2016).

9. Edward L. Ayers, "What We Talk about When We Talk about the South," in *All Over the Map: Rethinking American Regions*, ed. Ayers (Baltimore: Johns Hopkins University Press, 1998), 76.

10. P. J. Vatikiotis, *The History of Egypt: From Mohammad Ali to Mubarak*, 3rd ed. (Baltimore: Johns Hopkins University Press, 1985), 87.

11. Tignor, *Modernization and British Colonial Rule*, 80.

12. Patrick M. Kirkwood, "Lord Cromer's Shadow: Political Anglo-Saxonism and the Egyptian Protectorate as a Model in the American Philippines," *Journal of World History* 27, no. 1 (2016): 1–27.

13. Gwynn Campbell, "Slavery in the Indian Ocean World," in *Routledge History of Slavery*, ed. Gad Heuman and Trevor Burnard (London: Routledge, 2011).

14. John Hunwick, "The Same but Different: Africans in Slavery in the Mediterranean Muslim World," in *The African Diaspora in the Mediterranean Lands of Islam*, ed. John Hunwick and Eve M. Troutt Powell (Princeton, N.J.: Marcus Weiner, 2002), ix–xxiv; Bernard Freamon, "Straight, No Chaser: Slavery, Abolition, and Modern Islamic Thought," in *Indian Ocean Slavery in the Age of Abolition*, ed. Robert Harms, Bernard K. Freamon, and David W. Blight (New Haven, Conn.: Yale University Press, 2013); Terence Walz and Kenneth M. Cuno, eds., *Race and Slavery in the Middle East* (Cairo: American University in Cairo Press, 2010). On patronage, see the work of Ehud Toledano; Ron Shaham, "Masters, Their Freed Slaves, and the Waqf in Egypt," *Journal of the Economic and Social History of the Orient* 43 no. 2 (2000): 162–88.

15. Matthew S. Hopper, *Slaves of One Master: Globalization and Slavery in Arabia in the Age of Empire* (New Haven, Conn.: Yale University Press, 2015), 1–17; Alison Frank, "The Children of the Desert and the Laws of the Sea: Austria, Great Britain, the Ottoman Empire, and the Mediterranean Slave Trade in the Nineteenth Century," *American Historical Review* 117, no. 2 (April 2012): 410–44.

16. Eve M. Troutt Powell, *A Different Shade of Colonialism: Egypt, Great Britain, and the Mastery of the Sudan* (Berkeley: University of California Press, 2003), 6, 3, 8; Eve M. Troutt Powell, *Tell This in My Memory: Stories of Enslavement from Egypt, Sudan, and the Ottoman Empire* (Stanford, Calif.: Stanford University Press, 2012).

17. Cited in Lanver Mak, *The British in Egypt: Community, Crime, and Crises, 1882–1922* (New York: I. B. Tauris, 2012), 133; E. A. Wallis Budge, *Cook's Handbook in Egypt and the Sudan*, 2nd ed. (London: Thomas Cook and Son, 1906), 269–70; Piers Brendon, *Thomas Cook: 150 Years of Popular Tourism* (London: Secker and Warburg, 1991), 120–40, 182–200.

18. Lisa Pollard, *Nurturing the Nation: The Family Politics of Modernizing, Colonizing, and Liberating Egypt, 1805–1923* (Berkeley: University of California Press, 2005), 48–99; Heffernan, *Veiled Figures*, 14–46.

19. Elizabeth Thompson, "Public and Private in Middle Eastern Women's History," *Journal of Women's History* 15, no. 1 (2003): 52–69.

20. Marilyn Booth and Anthony Gorman, "Introduction," in *The Long 1890s in Egypt: Colonial Quiescence, Subterranean Resistance*, ed. Booth and Gorman (Edinburgh: Edinburgh University Press, 2014), 13.

21. Marilyn Booth, "Before Qasim Amin: Writing Women's History in 1890s Egypt," in Booth and Gorman, *Long 1890s in Egypt*, 369, 365.

22. Baron, *Egypt as a Woman*, 57–81; Hoda A. Yousef, *Composing Egypt: Reading,*

Writing, and the Emergence of a Modern Nation, 1870–1930 (Stanford, Calif.: Stanford University Press, 2016), 3–49.

23. Jane Hathaway, *The Politics of Households in Ottoman Egypt: The Rise of the Qazdaglis* (Cambridge: Cambridge University Press, 1997), 116, 109–24; Mary Ann Fay, "Women and Waqf: Toward a Reconsideration of Women's Place in the Mamluk Household," *IJMES* 29, no. 1 (1997): 33–51; Madeline C. Zilfi, *Women and Slavery in the Late Ottoman Empire* (Cambridge: Cambridge University Press, 2010), 96–215.

24. Baron, *Egypt as a Woman*, 32, 17–39.

25. Ann Laura Stoler, "Imperial Debris: Reflections on Ruin and Ruination," *Cultural Anthropology* 23, no. 2 (May 2008): 194, 198.

26. Mary Roberts, *Intimate Outsiders: The Harem in Ottoman and Orientalist Art and Travel Literature* (Durham, N.C.: Duke University Press, 2007), 59–106.

27. Troutt Powell, *Different Shade of Colonialism*, 142, 135–67; Troutt Powell, *Tell This in My Memory*, 115–47.

28. Pollard, *Nurturing the Nation*, 64–65.

29. Hanan Hammad, "Regulating Sexuality: The Colonial-National Struggle over Prostitution after the British Invasion of Egypt," in Booth and Gorman, *Long 1890s in Egypt*, 209.

30. Joel Beinin and Zachary Lockman, eds., *Workers on the Nile: Nationalism, Communism, Islam, and the Egyptian Working Class, 1882–1954* (Princeton, N.J.: Princeton University Press, 1987).

31. Reva B. Siegal, "Home as Work: The First Woman's Rights Claims Concerning Wives' Household Labor, 1850–1880," *Yale Law Journal* 103 (1994): 1075–1217; Amy Dru Stanley, *From Bondage to Contract* (New York: Cambridge University Press, 1998), 138–217.

32. Ann Laura Stoler, *Carnal Knowledge and Imperial Power: Race and the Intimate in Colonial Rule* (Berkeley: University of California Press, 2010), 41.

33. Stanley, *From Bondage to Contract*, 138–48, 187–203.

34. Troutt Powell, *Different Shade of Colonialism*, 16–19.

35. Lisa Cardyn, "Sexualized Racism / Gendered Violence: Outraging the Body Politic in the Reconstruction South," *Michigan Law Review* 100 (2002): 675–867; Elaine Frantz Parsons, "Midnight Rangers: Costume and Performance in the Reconstruction-Era Ku Klux Klan," *Journal of American History* 92, no. 3 (2005): 811–36; Martha Hodes, *White Women, Black Men: Illicit Sex in the Nineteenth Century South* (New Haven, Conn.: Yale University Press, 1997), 147–208.

36. Mak, *British in Egypt*, 58.

37. Jane Hathaway, "Out of Africa into the Palace: The Ottoman Chief Harem Eunuch," in *Living in the Ottoman Realm: Empire and Identity, 13th to 20th Centuries*, ed. Christine Isom-Verhaaren and Kent F. Schull (Bloomington: Indiana University Press, 2016), 237; Hunwick and Troutt Powell, *African Diaspora*, 99–108.

Too Light to Fall

FEMALE BODIES AND ITALIAN PRECIPICES IN "DOROTHY"

Katherine Barrett Swett

Woolson's "Dorothy" initially seems like it will be a satire of society, a Florentine retelling of *Daisy Miller* with a frivolous American girl center stage against a gorgeous Tuscan backdrop.[1] "Dorothy" has a multigenerational literary ancestry going back to James's *Daisy Miller* and *Roderick Hudson* and Hawthorne's *The Marble Faun*. But like *Daisy Miller*, "Dorothy" takes a surprising generic turn from light comedy to heavy pathos as the frivolous woman suffers a slow, lingering, and mysterious death. Initially the narrator offers a comic image of the impossibility of Dorothy falling; her physical lightness is equated with her lack of seriousness or substance as a character. The pretty, charming American flirt seems too light to fall, a characteristic she shares with Hawthorne's Hilda and James's Daisy and that distinguishes her death from the bold masculine gesture of James's Roderick Hudson. "Dorothy" explores the multiple meanings of weight and lightness to women and to writers in Woolson's society. By shifting genres from comedy to tragedy and by refusing the possibility of Dorothy's death by falling but exploring her death by self-starvation, Woolson exposes the emotional damage caused to women by being characterized as "light weight."[2] By looking at "Dorothy" as a story that explores patriarchal perceptions of the female body, literary style, the sublime landscape in Italy, and death by wasting or anorexic suicide, we can appreciate the mystery and power of this story that mid-twentieth-century male critics dismissed as sentimental and also, perhaps, come a little closer to understanding the cultural as well as the emotional causes of Woolson's final act.[3]

Published in 1894, "Dorothy" appears at the end of a long tradition of depictions of precipices in Italy. These images are familiar, but what needs to be
underscored in Woolson's inheritance is the gendered view of precipices and
weight in this iconography. In James's *Roderick Hudson*, falling from a Roman
ruin is identified with masculine romantic gestures. Roderick imagines climbing "a rugged surface of vertical wall" high in the crumbling stones of the Coliseum.[4] Roderick's aim is to pick a flower for his beloved, tellingly and femi-
ninely named Christina Light. She accuses him of intending "to kill himself";
his patron, Rowland Mallet, torn between horror and admiration, "felt a sudden, admiring glee at the thought of Roderick's doing it. It would be finely
done, it would be gallant, it would have a sort of *masculine eloquence*."[5] Such
recklessness for a man is "gallant" and "eloquent." The gesture speaks to his
dominance over the female viewer. That Rowland prevents Roderick from attempting the impossible feat speaks to an unquestioned understanding that a
male body has weight; that gravity will inevitably lead to death for a man. Although he abandons this first foolhardy, reckless escapade, Roderick later falls
to his death in the Alps. James's early scene thus functions as a quite specific
foreshadowing of Roderick's death. The sublime romantic gesture, the physical
risk associated with scaling heights, will not be available to Daisy or Dorothy;
they, like Hawthorne's Hilda in *The Marble Faun*, are too light to fall.

Hawthorne's *The Marble Faun* is an important source for all later novels and
tales of Americans in Italy, and particularly for Woolson's "Dorothy," which is
set in Bellosguardo in sight of Hawthorne's villa. For Woolson, Florence was
full of literary history. She writes to a friend during her first visit to Florence in
1880, "But Florence! here I have attained that old-world feeling I used to dream
about, a sort of enthusiasm made up of history, mythology, old churches, pictures, statues, vineyards, the Italian sky, dark-eyed peasants, opera music, Raphael and old Michael, 'Childe Harold,' the 'Marble Faun,' 'Romola,' and ever
so many more ingredients,—the whole having I think taken me pretty well off
my feet! Perhaps I ought to add *Henry James*. He has been perfectly charming
to me for the last three weeks."[6] Her rhapsody traces Florentine influence from
Byron to Hawthorne to Eliot right to her actual friendship with Henry James,
whose identity as author has been elided into his role as cicerone! It is important to acknowledge the sly ambition in that inclusion of the living pair, James
and herself, in that list of great writers. Around the time of writing "Dorothy"
Woolson was considering returning to Bellosguardo and staying in the Villa
Montanto, Hawthorne's villa. It seems likely that Hawthorne was very much
on her mind as she composed the story. She writes Samuel Mather (April 11,
1891), "I have been upset a little by the chance (offered to me) of getting Lady

Hobart's Villa 'Montanto' for the summer . . . the offer unsettled me for a day. The evenings on top of that old tower, with the vast landscape darkening slowly round me,—what an atmosphere for a novelist! Hawthorne wrote the Marble Faun there one summer you know. Perhaps one could catch a breath of his spirit."[7]

The Marble Faun is full of precipices in both Tuscany and Rome, and in Hawthorne's novel we find an early gendered formulation of heights and falls. Hilda, an American artist, is an early figure of the American innocent abroad. Hawthorne imagines his heroine's lightness as a matter of weight as well as complexion and innocence. By contrast, the character of Miriam's model—the vaguely drawn but clearly male allegory of evil who torments the beautiful and mysterious artist Miriam—has more of an imagined weight than the somewhat realistically drawn American artist Hilda, allegory of innocence. The model, pushed from the Tarpeian rock, "sank quivering downward to the earth" with the full weight of his sin landing "on the pavement, below . . . a dark mass, lying in a heap."[8] Hilda dwells both morally and physically on high; she lives in a tower in Rome. Her moral fall can be vicarious only through "the guiltiness of some trusted friend,"[9] a slight spiritual tainting through knowledge. Sin can never actually be experienced in her body. In a chapter named after her abode in a high tower, "The Virgin's Shrine," Hilda herself describes her angelic lightness to the more earthy Miriam: "A height of some fifty feet above the roofs of Rome gives me all the advantages that I could get from fifty miles of distance. The air so exhilarates my spirits, that sometimes I feel half-inclined to attempt a flight from the top of my tower, in the faith that I should float upward!" Miriam, interjecting a comic and slightly gruesome realism, dissuades her friend, "Oh pray don't try it. . . . If it should turn out that you are less than an angel, you would find the stones of the Roman pavement very hard; and if an angel indeed, I am afraid you would never come down among us again."[10] The idea of a woman having body weight is equated with a realistic, comic tone as well as with sin. Innocence is weightless.

⬦⟶

James and Woolson inherit Hilda as the archetype of the American girl abroad. James recasts Hilda as the nouveau riche Daisy Miller, light in the moral and intellectual sense as well as in the physical. Unlike Hilda, whose "purity of heart and life are . . . their own proof and security" and render her free to wander around Rome unjudged by her peers,[11] James's heroine sacrifices her reputation in order to get exercise; she tells Winterbourne and Mrs. Walker that "if I didn't walk I would expire."[12] If Hilda's archetype of innocence is allegorized to the level of pure ideal and spirit, Daisy Miller's significance is limited to the social and the national. The lightness of this rendition of the American innocent is not angelic but superficial. She is not an artist but a flirt. The danger of moving her body through space is less physical recklessness, less romantic "masculine eloquence" than social ruin.

Daisy's physical and spiritual lightness is central to her beauty and charm. She is "an indolent sylph" (158), and fairy-like "she came tripping downstairs," her gait a "little rapid, confiding step" (167). In addition to her physical weightlessness, she is also intellectually light; she has a "superficial little visage" without "irony" (147). Winterbourne "said to himself that she was too light and childish, too uncultivated and unreasoning, too provincial, to have reflected upon her ostracism or even to have perceived it" (197). But again and again we see that Daisy does perceive the snubs and judgments; no one is as dumb as observers imagine the American charmer to be. She takes social risks willfully, and James often conflates her moments of social risk with precipitous locations. First in Vevey, she learns of Mrs. Costello's snubbing her: "'You needn't be afraid,' she repeated. . . . Then she paused again; she was close to the parapet. . . . Daisy looked out upon the mysterious prospect" (160). In Rome, when she defies Mrs. Walker to meet Giovanelli and ruins herself in the eyes of Rome's expatriate community, it is "that place in front . . . where you look at the view" (179). Daisy and Giovanelli "walked towards the parapet. . . . When they reached the low garden-wall they stood a moment looking off at the great flat-topped pine clusters of the Villa Borghese" (187). Finally, Daisy, her social ruin complete in the eyes of Mrs. Costello and Mrs. Walker, is seen by Winterbourne at the Palace of the Caesars: "Daisy was strolling along the top of one of those great mounds of ruin. . . . It seemed to him that Rome had never been so lovely as just then. He stood looking off at the enchanting harmony of line and colour . . . feeling the freshness of the year and the antiquity of the place reaffirm themselves in mysterious interfusion. It seemed to him also that Daisy had never looked so pretty" (198). It is impossible for a creature as light and insignificant as Daisy to "fall." Instead, she "strolls" upon a ruin. There is no literal risk of her falling as Robert's figure does or as Roderick Hudson could have in the Coliseum. Instead, Winterbourne lyrically imagines Daisy already part of the Roman landscape; she is "the freshness of the year" already "interfus[ed]" with "the antiquity of the place" (198). This description domesticates the sublime as the pastoral and eradicates any violence even as it foreshadows Daisy's eventual burial in Rome.

In the final scene with Daisy in the Coliseum, there are significant parallels and differences from the Coliseum scene in *Roderick Hudson*. Giovanelli and Daisy do not ascend the upper tiers, so there is no precipice, no overt sublime gesture or imagery. Winterbourne, as protective as Rowland Mallet, sees the "craziness, from a sanitary point of view, of a delicate girl lounging away the evening in this nest of malaria" (202).[13] Disease, not accident, is the danger for a frail girl. Daisy is "delicate," and she "lounges," both words suggesting her passivity. The contrasts between Daisy's and Roderick's experiences in the Coliseum are telling: Roderick's grand romantic attempt at scaling the ruins as opposed to Daisy's "grave indiscretion" (203), only to fulfill a tourist's cliché. That she was "bound to see the Colosseum by moonlight" (203) confirms the trivial nature of her motives. Winterbourne, unlike Rowland, does not find anything romantic about "a clever little reprobate" "dying of the perniciosa." To his mind, Daisy's risk is threefold: her reputation in society, her sexual purity—as "grave indiscretion" and "reprobate" both suggest a sexual connotation for the fever—and her health. She retorts to Winterbourne's expression of concern at her exposing herself to the fever: "I don't look like much, but I'm healthy" (203). Yet by the end of the scene she leaves, having "perceived" quite clearly how he views her and suggesting the suicidal thought of dying from disease: "I don't care," said Daisy, in a little strange tone, "whether I have Roman fever or not" (204). She passively invites death. It is this ambiguous scene of female passive risk taking and potentially suicidal defiance that Woolson revisits and expands upon in "Dorothy."

Woolson introduces the eponymous heroine of her tale at a soiree on a high parapet outside Florence in Bellosguardo. Like Daisy, Dorothy is a pretty, young American heiress. A group of American, British, and Italian residents of Florence attend the gathering. The opening scene is satirical and "light," written in a style Woolson felt pressured to write by editors. Woolson applied that term "light" to the kind of writing that editors like Howells admired. For example, her story "A Florentine Experiment" and the beginning of "Dorothy" contain the chatty dialogue, small social interactions, and detailed descriptions characteristic of such stories. At the time of composing "The Florentine Experiment," Woolson wrote to Alden, "[H]ow much pressure has been brought to bear upon—what shall I call it?—society—about *this light delicate* highly-finished style of writing that holds itself far above subject, incident and plot. It is the worship of manner; not matter. . . . I admire it too . . . only—it seems to me that there *are* other ways of writing. *And the matter is more than the man-*

ner, though the skies fall."[14] Again, her metaphor is consistent: serious matter has weight and causes a fall.

Dorothy, like Daisy, is from the beginning perceived as physically and emotionally light. She is "like a sprite," "very slight," and "ethereal" and has "her own light swiftness."[15] Everyone laughs when they hear the slender Dorothy wishes she had "six buckwheat cakes with maple syrup!" because "the contrast between this evoked repast and the girl herself was so comical" (472). It was part of the anorexic bind that Victorian society put on women that they were expected to have healthy girlish appetites but also to be slender and almost bodiless.[16]

It is easy to overlook Woolson's obsession with weight in this story, but once one starts reading for it one finds it everywhere. For many of the female characters weight is part of their description and of the satire and distance the narrator maintains. Here is a sampling (emphasis added): "Rose Hatherbury, *attenuated* though she was . . . Rose was *thin*" (466). We hear of "an Italian countess of *large circumference* and ancient name" (466–67). During one of the exchanges with her husband that Dorothy later regrets as part of her not showing him she loved him, she subjects Miss Jane Wood to scorn, "Why do you always escort Miss Jane? She must *weigh one hundred and eighty*" (486). While, Mrs. North, Dorothy's stepmother, is "tall, *thin*" (469), Mrs. Tracy is "*stout*" (469) and comically taken aback when "she caught a glimpse of herself in the full-length mirror." "Overwhelmed," she later asks, "[D]o I look like that? Do I? *Stout*, short-nosed?" (485). So while the humor of these remarks on weight sets an initially light and satirical note, the comic tone, the lightness is exactly what Dorothy comes to regret.

When Woolson introduces precipices to her story, the tone is also comic. Whereas in *Roderick Hudson* the hero's tragic fate is foreshadowed by the dramatic scene in the Coliseum, the opening scene of "Dorothy" poses no serious risk of harm. Silly flirts are not supposed to die. Dorothy has no fear of heights, so she "herself generally led them in the dangerous experiment" of "perch[ing]" on the edge of the "parapet" (465). She does not stand or climb but, like a little bird, "perches." She faces no risk because she has no body weight in the imagination of the satirical narrator: "But one could never think of Dorothy as falling; her supple figure conveyed the idea that she could fly—almost—so lightly was it poised upon her little feet" (465). Woolson's image of Dorothy, like Hawthorne's of Hilda, voices the Victorian dream of female slenderness. Alexander Walker, a physiognomist, offered in 1840 a description of female "weightlessness" that is similar to the description of both Dorothy and Hilda on high: "[F]rom its proportions, it seems almost aerial; and we would imagine that, if our hands were placed under the lateral parts of the tapering waist of a woman thus characterized, the slightest pressure would suffice to throw her into the air."[17] In comic contrast to this ethereal floating, the narrator humorously imagines how some of the other women at the party would fall: "The case was different regarding the Misses Sebright; they too were handsome girls, but they would certainly go down like rocks" and one other character though thin "would cut the air like a needle in her swift descent" (466). The narrator offers a kind of macabre humor of gravity and female bodies.

Woolson does introduce the idea of Dorothy's suicide at this early point in her tale. Accidental falling, "one could never think of," for Dorothy but "one" could imagine her "tak[ing] the fancy to throw herself off" (465). Suicide for Dorothy's type would be an impulse, a fancy, neither a great romantic gesture nor a humorous tumble. Even if the impulse occurred, Dorothy's lightness would keep her alive as "she would float to the lower slope as lightly as thistle down" (465). The repeated use of the pronoun "one" to introduce these speculations aligns the narrator with all the people who dismiss Dorothy as lightweight, impulsive, and frivolous. When Dorothy marries Alan Mackenzie and quickly becomes his widow, all of Florence believe "what a career that little girl will have" (489). But unlike the imagining of the public at large, there is nothing "fanciful" or impulsive about Dorothy's final romantic gesture. It is a prolonged, serious, and willful abandonment of life. While Daisy Miller's death is covered in a couple of paragraphs. Dorothy's decline and death take up the last third of the tale.

The imagery of weight that initially forms part of the comic satire of women and society ends up being a defense of the capacity of "light weights" to suffer. The generic switch in the story from satire to pathos reflects a final fierceness in Woolson's insistence that fiction and women can embrace the sublime and the weighty even if their ways of achieving this redemption are limited by their gender. The contrast between Dorothy's death, a silent wasting away, possibly from anorexia, and a more violent jump is at the heart of the story itself.

As critic Victoria Coulson has observed, it is surprising that Woolson chose a girl of Dorothy's type for her final and most profound meditation on death: "Dorothy—until her husband's death—is everything that her spinster sisters have failed and refused to be: girlishly pretty, happy, sexually successful. Constance had been struggling with the temptations and the reproaches of such blithe, untroubled women throughout her life; what is she doing when she chooses to ennoble an unreflective flirt, redeeming her protagonist in death?"[18] Like Daisy, Dorothy dies unexpectedly, given the comic nature of the beginning of the story. But in "Dorothy" Woolson dramatizes more fully than James the suffering this type of woman experiences when she becomes aware of her perceived lightness. Winterbourne acknowledges in passing that Daisy "would have appreciated one's esteem,"[19] but Dorothy's mysterious, wasting illness shows that she has internalized the view of herself as light. Woolson suggests that Dorothy's suicidal depression and self-starving are ultimately an embodiment of the world's view of her.

Dorothy's death, the turn from a comic treatment of the American girl to a tragic one, answers one of Woolson's early criticisms of James's characters, including Winterbourne. Woolson was committed artistically to pressing past manners and convention to depicting strong emotion without cold irony. One of her criticisms of James was that he did not probe the emotion of love deeply. In a discussion of James's play of Daisy Miller, she writes, "You know I have found fault with you for not making it more evident that your heroes were in love with the heroines, really in love."[20] In "Dorothy," Woolson explores what she sees James as avoiding: "the killing griefs." And she gives that "killing grief" to a character who resembles lightweight Daisy.[21]

Even as Woolson echoes certain details from Daisy Miller, she reassigns the gender of the characters. Whereas in James's novella Daisy, unloved and not esteemed by Winterbourne, is the victim of Roman fever, ruined not by crumbling precipices but by disease, in Woolson's story Dorothy's dull, rich husband, Alan Mackenzie, dies of Roman fever. Thus Dorothy—whose chilly last name "North" perhaps contains an echo of Winterbourne's characteristic season—is a conflation of Daisy and Winterbourne. At the end of Daisy Miller, Winterbourne heads back to Geneva feeling only the slightest bit of remorse that he misjudged Daisy and that she would have "appreciated one's esteem" (206). In contrast, Dorothy takes full responsibility for her never having let Alan know that she loved him. Some of her last words are these: "If only I could tell him once, just once, that I did love him" (505). Unlike Winterbourne, whose emotions remain cold—"justice" and "esteem"—Dorothy's love emerges. She is the reformed flirt at the end, proving that society misjudged her lightness.

And yet Dorothy dies as the early image of her weightlessness suggests that she would: "[I]f she should take the fancy to throw herself off, she would float to the lower slope as lightly as thistle-down" (465). Dorothy's death is just such a gentle process of gradual descent. By the end, she "look[s] very childlike" (505), and in an echo of the initial image of her "float[ing] to the lower slope as lightly as a thistle-down," the doctor says she "should not have even a feather's weight of excitement" (501). She eats only "delicate nourishment" (499) and "she doesn't gain" (500). Other characters see "how thin she was; the black dressing gown hung about her like a pall" (500). Woolson shows the consequences of a young woman's internalizing the view of even her closest relatives that she is light and superficial. She gives us more insight into Dorothy's interior than James does with Daisy.

Neither the doctor nor her closest female relatives understand what is wrong with Dorothy. The doctor asks if she has "anything weighing upon her mind—weighing too much, I mean?" (499). But no one imagines Dorothy serious enough, weighty enough, to have a "killing grief." The point of the story is that the reader knows that Dorothy does have a weight on her mind, that her physical and mental states are opposite. Dorothy's stepmother tells her friend, "You have always saddled Dorothy with deeper feelings than she had ever possessed" (500). This misreading includes another telling allusion to Daisy Miller. Her relatives want to cure her by taking her to Vevey, where Daisy Miller first meets Winterbourne. They want her to become again the lighthearted girl who "used to like Vevey" (502); their language even presents Vevey as a kind of heaven: "go to sleep; you will open your eyes in Vevey" (502). But Dorothy, in Woolson's imagining, has left behind the American charmer and flirt. Dorothy dies of the very weightlessness, flightiness, lightness the world ascribed to her.

Anna Krugovoy Silver in Victorian Literature and the Anorexic Body offers context for reading Dorothy's death as a kind of anorexic sublime. Both Dorothy's healthy slimness and her wasting illness are aspects of Victorian anorexia. In the early comic portion of the story, Dorothy, despite her lightness and etherealness, exhibits a healthy appetite for pancakes and interest in exercise (riding horses). In her guilt and grief after Alan's death, Dorothy instead exhibits an anorexic logic. According to Silver, for the anorexic "disciplining her body becomes her particular arena of mastery, and she considers her capacities for self-denial and self-discipline virtuous."[22] Dorothy is punishing herself for her lightness, for not having shown Alan that she loved him. She misused her sexual power and physical vitality by teasing Alan and flirting with others. Her only revenge on herself and those who judge her rightly or wrongly is to literally embody the lightness that used to be celebrated and found charming. Silver notes that "not to eat at all was extremely disruptive of social norms, specifically middle-class norms . . . did not conform to rules of passive and obedient female behavior."[23] Refusing to eat is considered obstinate and unfeminine. Dorothy "remained passive" but not obedient. Her illness becomes her form of asserting the depth of her feelings.

Biographers have found it difficult not to read Woolson's death into "Dorothy."[24] As Henry James wrote of Woolson's suicide in a letter to Francis Boot, "*After* such a dire event, it is true, one sees symptoms, indications in the past, and some of these portents seem to me now not to be wanting."[25] The imagery of falling in "Dorothy" as well as the suicidal nature of Dorothy's death make the association inescapable. Sharon Dean responds to Edel's reading of "Dorothy" as yet another fable of Woolson's unrequited love for James. Dean observes sharply that "part of the reason that Dorothy does not want to live is because she is subjected to precisely the kind of speculation Edel engages in about Woolson and James."[26] Dean, who does see Dorothy as in some sense anticipating Woolson's death, sees that it "showed . . . how a woman who faced conflicting messages about sexuality, marriage, and gender-defined interests could embrace death as an attractive home."[27] In this story, Woolson uses light and weight as the perfect metaphor to embody this corset that enwrapped Victorian women.

At the time of writing "Dorothy," Woolson was very focused on her own body weight. At the beginning of her European sojourn, Woolson clearly associated weight gain with a comic healthiness. For example, after having regained weight lost to an illness, she wrote, "The other day I was weighed & was astounded to find that, in spite of it all, I weighed over 141 pounds! Certainly I can no longer pose as an invalid."[28] Two years later, in 1884, she wrote, "I am quite scandalously well this winter. Haven't had an ill moment; and am as stout as can be."[29] At the time of her imagining Dorothy, and shortly after, however, she had been trying to lose weight. She wrote to her nephew in 1893, "You must be prepared to see me a good deal changed. I looked very well while I was stout. But now that I have lost some of the flesh, I have also lost the stronger look. And just now I am very tired over 'Horace C.'"[30] As much as she preferred being thin, she also saw thinness as a sign of illness and fragility. "Stout" suggests strength.

Woolson gave her heroine exactly the kind of death she most dreaded for herself. She wrote to James in 1883, "I don't in the least mind dying, you know, if one could be sure to die, & have it over; but I have a horror of being ill—ill a long time, over here all alone."[31] Woolson feared a lingering illness such as Dorothy or Alice James, Henry's sister, experienced. There is significant parallel language in "Dorothy" and the letters that suggests Dorothy's wasting away was connected in Woolson's imagination with Alice James's lingering illness with cancer.[32] Woolson wrote Dorothy a sickbed scene that she had imagined for Alice James eight years earlier in a letter to Katherine Loring written from Villa Castellani Bellosguardo: "I am grieved to hear that Miss James has been suffering. Tell her that an exclamation burst from me irresistibly, night before last,—namely—'I wish she were here this minute!' Mrs. Duveneck was paying me a visit, & we were speaking of Miss James. *The broad doors stood wide open; the moonlight outside lighted* up my old garden, & the dark, rugged outline of Hawthorne's tower. . . . It seemed to me, then, that if *Miss James' couch could be drawn across that door*, she should enjoy it so much."[33] Here is the setting she provides the dying Dorothy: "A month later Dorothy, *lying on a couch in her room*, put out her hand to Nora . . . 'take the lamp out, Nora, please, and *let in the moonlight; I like to see it shining across the floor.*' She lay in silence for some minutes looking at the radiance" (504–5). The last thing Katharine Loring read to Alice James was "Dorothy," and at that moment this story should have taken its place as a major meditation on nineteenth-century women facing death.

But as Emily Dickinson puts it, "a nearness to tremendousness" is where her society located women. They could be next to the sublime but not part of it. When a woman transcended the physical, a component of Kant's definition of the sublime, her lightness caused her to evaporate, not to ratiocinate. When she had a heavy enough body to fall, she did so into the gross and comic materiality that men strove to transcend when experiencing that state. This story about a lingering death that embodied society's views of women's bodies was entwined with Woolson's view of her own body and her fear of a long lingering illness, which she did not aestheticize as "floating to the end like thistle-down." Instead Woolson's seemingly impulsive jump rewrote the comic image of "a woman going down like rocks" as a tragic, eloquent, female gesture.

NOTES

1. Lyndall Gordon makes a similar point in her analysis of "Dorothy": "a comedy of manners turns into a mystery . . . the challenge is similar to the death of Daisy Miller." Gordon, *A Private Life of Henry James: Two Women and His Art* (New York: Norton, 1998), 242.

2. I have found this sense of light as early as Spenser's *Fairy Queen* (I, I, 55): "Much grieved to think that gentle Dame so light, / For whose defense he was to shed his blood." Hugh MacLean, ed., *Edmund Spenser's Poetry* (New York: Norton, 1968), 19. More contemporaneous with James and Woolson is Mark Twain's description of his Rowena in "Those Extraordinary Twins" as a "silly young miss" and "light-weight heroine." Mark Twain, *Those Extraordinary Twins* (Project Gutenberg, etext no. 3185), preface.

3. Rayburn S. Moore dismissed this as "exactly the sort of fiction that Miss Woolson opposes in 'At the Château of Corinne'" and noted that John Kern called it "an exceedingly sentimental tale." Moore, *Constance Fenimore Woolson* (New York: Twayne, 1963), 75.

4. Henry James, *Roderick Hudson*, in *Novels 1871–1880* (New York: Library of America, 1983), 337.

5. James, 338, emphasis added.

6. Sharon L. Dean, ed., *The Complete Letters of Constance Fenimore Woolson* (Gainesville: University Press of Florida, 2012), 134.

7. *Complete Letters*, 448–49. Additional mentions of Hawthorne occur in letters from the late 1880s when she lived in Bellosguardo: "I have taken a villa . . . at Bellosguardo, for a year, perhaps two. Bellosguardo is just outside the Roman Gate of Florence; it is the hill of Galileo; of Hawthorne (where he wrote 'The Marble Faun')" (332). Her familiarity with the text is clear from her writing on December 8, 1889, to Samuel Mather, "This is Hawthorne's villa, you know. Here he wrote 'The Marble Faun'; he gives an account of his life here in the 'Italian Notebooks,' and he introduces the villa & its old tower into the romance as the home of Donatello" (388).

8. Nathaniel Hawthorne, *The Marble Faun*, in *Novels* (New York: Library of America, 1983), 995–96.

9. Hawthorne, 1021.

10. Hawthorne, 896.

11. Hawthorne, 897.

12. Henry James, *Daisy Miller*, in *The Complete Tales of Henry James*, vol. 4, ed. Leon Edel (Philadelphia: Lippincott, 1962), 183; hereafter cited parenthetically.

13. In *Henry James and the "Woman Business"* (New York: Cambridge University Press, 1989), Alfred Habegger asks, "Why is Daisy Miller the one who dies of malaria, even though Giovanelli and Winterbourne are also exposed? Behind James's narratives there is found the ancient theory that women are weaker than men" (26). Woolson corrects this view.

14. *Complete Letters*, 179, emphasis added.

15. Constance Fenimore Woolson, "Dorothy," in *Collected Stories*, ed. Anne Boyd Rioux (New York: Library of America, 2020), 467, 472, 487; hereafter cited parenthetically.

16. Anna Krugovoy Silver, *Victorian Literature and the Anorexic Body* (Cambridge: Cambridge University Press, 2002), 15.

17. Silver, 44.

18. Victoria Coulson, *Henry James, Women and Realism* (Cambridge: Cambridge University Press, 2007), 192.

19. James, *Daisy Miller*, 206.

20. *Complete Letters*, 213.

21. Gordon, *Private Life of Henry James*, 242.

22. Silver, *Victorian Literature*, 5.

23. Silver, 15.

24. Gordon, *Private Life of Henry James*, 242; Anne Boyd Rioux, *Constance Fenimore Woolson: Portrait of a Lady Novelist* (New York: Norton, 2016), 259–60.

25. Leon Edel, ed., *The Letters of Henry James* (Cambridge, Mass.: Harvard University Press, 1980), 3:463.

26. Sharon L. Dean, *Constance Fenimore Woolson: Homeward Bound* (Knoxville: University of Tennessee Press, 1995), 172.

27. Dean, 173.

28. *Complete Letters*, 215.

29. *Complete Letters*, 294.

30. *Complete Letters*, 508.

31. *Complete Letters*, 250.

32. Coulson, *Henry James, Women and Realism*, 193.

33. *Complete Letters*, 316, emphasis added.

Letter from Vesuvius

Heather Hartley

April 7, 2021
Napoli

Dear Constance,

I've been meaning to write for some time now. Early spring has arrived in Napoli and *la ginestra* is out, the wild broom, a spray of yellow shooting out from long strong stems, a color so vibrant in this early April after a long gray winter, a color that somehow contains the heated flush of the high-rising heat of August in the late heart of summer when it's forty degrees in the shade, when there's nowhere to hide from this blazing, when you can do nothing but embrace it. It's been said that wild broom is the flower of Vesuvius, that when nothing else can survive in the volcano's clay and ash and dirt, here are bright blooms that survive and thrive like little earthbound star bursts.

Poet Giacomo Leopardi's gorgeous and candid and striking 1836 canto XXXIV of "La Ginestra" ("Wild Broom; or, The Flower of the Desert," canto XXXIV) begins,

Qui su l'arida schiena
del formidabil monte
sterminator Vesevo,
la qual null'altro allegra arbor nè fiore,
tuoi cespi solitari intorno spargi,
odorata ginestra,
contenta dei deserti . . .[1]

> Here on the arid spine
> of the formidable mountain,
> destroyer Vesuvius,
> brightened by no other tree or flower,
> you scatter round your lonely bushes,
> fragrant broom,
> content in the desert . . .

Do you ever feel like that, a wild bloom in the desert? You writing deep into the night (I'm thinking now of your fifteen years in Europe, 1879 to 1894, when you would write thirteen hours or sometimes more at a stretch, literally writing all night, sometimes standing up to work, with pain in your arms or hands or neck or all three)—with the deserted dark of a city around you—or another city or yet another one—while the window in your bedroom observes you like a big black eye, welcoming you to its edge, beckoning with its ledge, you writing persistently, at times feverishly but above all steadily, your capacity for work prodigious, to your niece Kate Mather you wrote, in speaking of your 1894 final novel *Horace Chase*, "I don't suppose any of you realize the amount of time and thought I give to each page of my novels; every character, every *word* of speech, and of description is thought of, literally, for years before it is written out for the final time. I do it over and over; and read it aloud to myself; and lie awake and think of it all night. It takes such entire possession of me that when, at last, a book is done, I am pretty nearly done myself."[2]

And from those windows in your bedroom, you breathe in the crisp or frigid air—be careful not to take cold, the cold that you fear (me too, I don't do well with the cold; I'm writing to you in a big wool sweater), the cold that keeps you from working, that gets deep in your bones and that was possibly your last word on earth, *freddo*—the same windows that in the day reveal stunning views—whether Rome or Bellosguardo in Florence or Sorrento or London or Lake Leman or elsewhere.

I read somewhere that you love heights—and in your short stories that take place abroad, especially in Italy, you give us exquisite views, often from heights. In "Dorothy" you write, "For fair indeed is the outlook from that supremely blessed plateau [of Bellosguardo], whether towards the north, south, east, or west, with perhaps an especial loveliness towards the west, where the Arno winds down to the sea."[3]

I wonder if your love of heights, and the perspective that can be gained from such a point of view, helped to give you fierce strength and focused direction to write stories that plumb the depths of character's most secret yearnings and hidden fears written with a sort of inherent vertigo where the deeper you dive into the swirling dark, the more that can be seen, revealed, in those vistas that are intimate, human, visceral, internal, vast. I think of your short story "'Miss Grief'" when the male narrator says, "A woman who possessed the divine spark of genius, which I was by no means sure (in spite of my success) had been granted to me—. . . I felt as if I ought to go down on my knees before her, and entreat her to take her proper place of supremacy at once."[4]

With the views summoning you—both internal and external—and with your insatiable, inquisitive nature to see and experience new places, to see old places anew   that kind of wanderlust is the touchstone of your life

If I may be so bold, you and I share this wanderlust. We've both lived in Italy, you in Florence and Rome principally, me in Napoli for the past four years. Before Napoli, I was in Paris for over fifteen years. We've both spent decades of our adult lives abroad. As is said by the narrator in "A Florentine Experiment," "Countries attract us in different ways. We are comfortable in England, musical in Germany, amused in Paris (Paris is a country), and idyllic in Switzerland; but when it comes to the affection, Italy holds the heart—we keep going back to her."[5]

And wanderlust, this desire of travel can haunt you. Sometimes it follows you, other times it leads you, then again sometimes it dogs you. And it rewards you. It's addictive and visceral and unpredictable. It's hungry. It demands time and energy and money. In 1863, seven years before your literary career began and well before you first traveled to Europe, you wrote to a close friend in reference to her travels in Europe and the Middle East, "I wish I could be in 'exile' too, if I could visit the most beautiful and famous places the world can show!"[6] You knew a sort of exile in your own way, in your search for a home and in your search for home.[7] You never stopped looking for home—elusive, alluring, ineluctable, out of reach. You never stopped looking for home even when you said you'd found it.

Alone in Sorrento, in the summer of 1882, you wrote to Henry James, who would inscribe a volume of Percy Bysshe Shelley's poetry in 1887, "Constance Woolson / from her friend and *confrère* Henry,"[8] "To be ill alone in a foreign land is a dreary experience. And it seemed to me as I lay feverish & coughing, that I must go home; go home, get my precious books, & little household gods together, a dog or two, & never stir again."[9]

How a singular letter of introduction to Henry James who came to be known as the Master for his prodigious literary talents and notable accomplishments and impressive reputation and maybe a little bit his *manière d'être*—but then I can ask you, you know him so well, does that description ring true to you?—the letter of introduction from his cousin Henrietta Pell-Clarke—was life changing for you. Arriving in Europe in 1879 for the first time, letter in hand, you and your sister Clara had this: a window open on the international literary world—that dizzying vista.[10] And the bright presence and central importance of letters—as well as their aching, abyss-hulking ash dark absence—is a leitmotif in your life.

It's true that I'm writing to you out of order, taking bits of your short stories, your personal history and placing them here or there, choosing snippets of one letter of yours to a friend, tipping in something that was said by someone else—it's true that I'm cutting and pasting your life together in this letter, but I know that you know that not everything can follow a straight, chronological, logical order all of the time. As you told Arabella Carter Washburn, when beginning to write a new story, "Now I must look into chaos."[11] So, if I may, let us look into the chaos together and let us begin *in media res*.

I've been thinking of views, from your windows, from your gardens in Rome when James came to visit you in 1881, a year after you'd met for the first time in Florence, when you exclaimed about your first meeting, "He has been perfectly charming to me for the last three weeks."[12] This Roman rooftop garden was dotted with lemon trees, Rome the city that you once called your "true home."[13] Sometimes you went there to write—a dizzying perspective from the heights—and I'm reminded of how your beguiling character Dorothy and her young friends in your short story "Dorothy" like to lean over the parapet at the Villa Dorio on the hilltop of Bellosguardo—a name you hold dear to your heart!—and Dorothy, courting danger, dazzled by it and at the same time careless, that recklessness that only youth knows, Dorothy, "whose supple figure conveyed the idea that she could fly—almost"[14]— that there is something that soars in your work, that takes risks, that explores with sensitivity and deftness and care the intricacies and conundrums and workings of the psychology and comportment of your characters. Many writers and readers and critics see this in your novels and short stories and in the myriad of accolades and praise to you over time—impossible to list them all here because it would take pages and pages and I'm sure I'd miss some, get something wrong. I include one citation about your 1880 short story "Rodman the Keeper" from the *Boston Literary World*: "the artist's power—the virile force, that artistic completeness . . . which makes her place secure as one of the most vigorous woman writers of the country."[15] Power, virility, force, vigor—your work is muscular and lithe, like a prima ballerina assoluta with her skill and capacity for control and consummate artistry—and her faculty and heart-hope for flight—at times dancing the allegro with swift pe-

tit assemblés and stretching jetés, other times the adagio, in slow, fluid movements—the page a *pas de deux* between reader and writer.

And I imagine you sitting at your desk as you read this, your desk with
the volume of Shelley from James, various novel and short story proofs, a little spray of flowers, maybe hyacinths, lacy white and light pink with their fra-
grance like honeycomb and the sea at twilight and I think of your short story
"The Street of the Hyacinth," which takes place in Rome and of the protagonist, painter Miss Ettie F. Macks and her steadfast earnestness and determination upon confronting the mondain, successful writer Raymond Noel, whom
she sees and desires as a mentor. She says to him, "I made up my mind to come
over [to Europe] at any cost, if it was a possible thing to bring it about. It
wasn't easy, but—here we are. In the lives of all—almost all—artists, I have
noticed—haven't you?—that there comes a time when they have to live on
hope and their own pluck more than upon anything tangible that the present
has to offer. They have to take that risk. Well, I have taken it; I took it when we
left America. And now I will tell you what it is I want from *you*."[16]

I read recently that hyacinths symbolize sincerity and peace and beauty and
commitment and power and pride and sometimes jealousy and that it is the
flower of the illuminate sun god Apollo. I'm not sure about hyacinths meaning all of these things all at the same time—you would know better loving wilderness as you do and studying botany so much, being so knowledgeable about
flora and fauna—but if it's true about sincerity and commitment and power and
pride, then Miss Ettie F. Macks with her fortitude and gray eyes with "a clear
directness in her glance"[17] lives on the right street, the Street of the Hyacinth.
What comes through is her independence, her open sincerity, her resilience—
her power.

By the hyacinths on your desk is a thick stack of letters—from your dear
sister Clara, Henry James, your cherished friend Francis Boott, Arabella Carter, your nephew Samuel Mather, your friend Edmund Clarence Stedman, to
whom you wrote, after some criticism was given about your 1875 story "Castle Nowhere": "For I wo'nt [*sic*] write it [the novel] at all unless I write it as I
please."[18]

This determination and resolve about your work are a constant in your life.
You're writing about your first novel, *Anne*, that was first serialized in *Harper's Monthly* beginning in December 1880 and was very well received and popular, so much so that in the spring 1882, when you were in Sorrento—not so far
from where I am writing to you now, with that same singular quality of southern Italian light, a light full of whelk-shell pink warmth—I imagine you savored
the view—the cerulean gem that is the Bay of Naples, the soft brown dou-

ble domes of the Vesuvius in the distance brushed with a swath of yellow wild bloom—and I think of the letter that your publishers Harper & Brothers sent to you that winter along with a check by which they doubled your pay and included a contract to publish *Anne* in book form.

You wrote to Henry James about this—we don't have his response to you, the letter destroyed, along with so many letters fallen into the abyss, that burning and intense absence of lost correspondence in your life and in James's—but we have a letter that you wrote to him after this containing an apology a part of which reads: "If I feel anything in the world with earnestness it is the beauty of your writings, & any little thing I may say about my own comes from entirely another stratum; & is said because I live so alone, as regards to my writing, that sometimes when writing to you, or speaking to you—out it comes before I know it."[19]

Anne, in serialization, had the potential to reach 100,000 readers in *Harper's Monthly* and, in book form, sold a formidable 57,000 copies. James's *The Portrait of a Lady* had a readership of approximately 12,000 in *Atlantic Monthly* installments; the novel would go on to sell more than any of his previous or future books, for a total of 6,000 copies in book form. *Anne* outsold *The Portrait of a Lady*.[20]

I'm not too good with math but I mention these numbers because they reveal a sort of emotional algebra,[21] to borrow and re-vision the phrase from writer and diarist Anais Nin, in which enthusiasm for and interest in and some kind of personal, affective connection of a reader to a book is translated into numbers. And among readers of *Anne* are the reviewers, and along with many other American and British periodicals, the *Californian* newspaper praised *Anne*, noting, "We observe from the reviews that Miss Woolson's novel has brought to the front again the undying hope and expectation of the Great American Novel."[22]

Throughout your career, you received a lot of press and along with that came a certain amount of renown, of fame. You markedly preferred prominence in the press, in words, over any preeminence of images or portraits of yourself. (And from what I understand you were none too fond of fancy dress. There's a rare photo of you in formal dress and a long, dark coat with a fur collar, in a hat and black leather gloves. Your mother and sister were behind it in a concerted effort on their part for you to not look too "literary" but rather fine and fashionable as the times saw fit for a woman.)[23]

And there's a well-known photograph of you—the portrait that was published with Henry James's essay "Miss Woolson," appearing in *Harper's Weekly* in the February 12, 1887, issue—where you've turned away from the camera, in profile, part of your face hidden. To both Henry James and John Hay in 1883 you wrote, "I do not at all think that because a woman happens to write a little, her face, or her personality in any way, becomes the property of the public."[24] From what I understand, this was your position throughout your life.

You're a very private person and reserved in society even though your niece Clare Rathbone Benedict wrote, "My aunt had a passionate and dramatic nature, and a high temper . . . but she was extremely gracious and a wonderful friend. . . . I don't think that cousin Henry [James] had those characteristics— he had intellect, humour and an extraordinarily fine perception of other people's feelings and ideas."[25]

In spite of all of yours and James's travels and journeys and distances, in one sense, you didn't leave one another. You even lived together (in separate apartments) for six weeks in Florence in Villa Brichieri in spring 1887. He cared for you when you were sick as you did for him. He worried about your overworking—he was not alone, many people worried—and back in 1888 he wrote to Dr. Baldwin, "I take for granted she is overworking—but her powers to keep that up have long mystified me. . . . Everything beyond three hours a day (with continuity) in the sort of work she does is a nail in her coffin—but she appears to desire that her coffin shall have many! Please don't repeat this to her, I have bored her half to death with my warnings."[26] You were not always in the same cities, but your friendship was binding and deep, at times fraught with complications and possible jealousies and worry and hinted-at, slant-spoken competition and complex, conflicted sentiments; nonetheless there was a rare quality to your friendship.

This companionship was constant and this care continued on when you went to Venice, a city you visited numerous times—the city a beacon in some ways—the last city you would live in. On an earlier trip in 1889 with your niece Kate, you wrote to your friend Stedman, "To have put a few years of Venice into one's life, will be to have wrestled so much from darkness."[27] And you returned to Venice again in 1893, alone this time—coming back to the deep, vertiginous nightfall of a city of water, you crossing the lagoon in a gondola—"the perfection of earthly motion is a *gondola*"[28]—crossing the Grand Canal like crossing the River Styx, wrestling with the obscurity—the inner darkness that haunted you and the winter shadows of the city itself. James wrote to Ariana Curtis in 1893, "I shall do my best to prove to Miss Woolson that Venice is better than Cooperstown. I am very glad to hear that she has at last a roof of her own. The having it, I am sure, will do much to anchor her."[29] And you found the Casa Semitecolo at the mouth of the Grand Canal.

It can sometimes be easy to write about the end—an inevitable anchoring and knowing that it is the end—the provocative and incantatory and absolute end. The end that can also be a departure point, in some sense a beginning. Venice in 1894 marks the end of your life. You were just fifty-three years old when you died. You were a year older than I am now. Young. It was winter and there was fog and cold and the air was dank. Imagine the water: freezing. The *freddo* that you feared. Years earlier, you'd wondered "whether the end of the riddle of my existence may not be, after all, to live here, & die here [in Venice]."[30]

On January 24, 1894, you rang for Suor Alfonsa from your bedroom and asked for a light—some sort of light in the midnight darkness—and a cup of milk from a particular pink china cup. You'd not been well for weeks. You didn't let anyone know. You'd never liked to be a bother, to feel yourself an imposition. Throughout your life, you desired and cherished and cultivated your independence. I admire how much you fought for your freedom, for literary and fiscal and spiritual independence.

But in Venice this time, you didn't feel strong enough to take on the work of a new novel, nor the exertion of finding yet another home.

Alone in your bedroom on the third floor that night of January 24th, I imagine your window is a big black eye watching you. Was it welcoming you over its edge, or did you just want to take in the night air? Did you hover there near the window in a hyphen of time—standing tall, downward fall—tormented by what to do? Return to bed for your milk, return to the draughts of laudanum some solace from the pain, return to the fevered night, or. . . .

In your last notebook entry, talking about your trip to the lagoon on Christmas Eve, you wrote, "I should like to turn into a peak when I die, to be a beautiful purple mountain, which would please the tired sad eyes of thousands of human beings for ages."[31] From such heights, the depths. The shadowy water of the lagoon moved swiftly under your windows. The silent street below. You fell three floors to your death. The deep water of the Grand Canal carries secrets that only the water knows.

From your apartment you had a commanding view onto the Grand Canal. From such heights, the depths. In 1883, in Winnie Howells's autograph book you wrote, "[Venice] is my 'Xanadu.'—But not for always; Xanadu never lasts, you know!"[32] And it's perhaps this ephemeral quality of a city slowly sinking into the sea that is part of its lasting—and at the same time momentary—allure.

It's true that I've mixed up beginnings and endings in my letter to you, written things out of linear order. But in Venice you walk down one street with the intention of going one place and you end up entirely somewhere else. Endings and beginning get mixed up, blurred. Like your friendship with James—of some things we can only guess—susurrus, resonance, echo—like the water of the lagoon. Venice is the city of masks, of getting lost, of guessing.

And guessing persists about the apocryphal and spectacular and haunting demise of your dresses. Imagine James in buttoned up coat and top hat—April cold and damp and windy—sitting alone in a gondola deep in the lagoon as dusk comes on and as the gondolier rows, surrounded by your dark dresses, your "principal mourner"[33] gutted, reeling from your death three months earlier, here to help your sister Clara sort through your papers and notes and manuscripts—and your dresses. To Grace Carter, James wrote two days after your death, "I write you in the midst of much bewilderment & uncertainty I am so utterly in the dark about everything. . . . I had not even heard a word of her being ill."[34]

James grasps a dress with tenderness, crinoline blowing in the wind and it gusts up in his face, and gently pulling it away, he presses his fingertips to the cuirass bodice of the dress that gives under his touch, these accouterments, this armor, this ardor James has for you, that you have for him, both fettered and unfettered, both declared and silenced, and his fingers get caught in the stays of the dress and fumbling to untie the ribbons he makes to throw the dress over, all the while little hooks on the dress tug at his scarf, tear the threads of his woolen coat and disentangling himself, distraught and bereft, he throws the dress over, then one after another, tulle and lace and silk spreading out in the swell, slick-black nymphaea dark-blooming in the churning lagoon, the dresses encircle the gondola and bleed black like ink spilt on paper, and desperate and adamant, he tries to press the dresses down with his hands, the gondolier proffers his pole, James refuses, the dresses stain his fingers, his palms, soak the sleeves of his coat, the indelible ink of your friendship washed in water, not washed away—that which is permanent in that which passes away.

It's true that I've lingered in Venice in this letter—not from any particular dalliance with the city—although such a provocative city can call forth coquetry—but because it is a key city in your life, not just in your death. In Lord Byron's "Childe Harold's Pilgrimage," canto IV, stanza XVIII, he writes about Venice:

> Although I found her thus, we did not part,
> Perchance even dearer in her day of woe
> Than when she was a boast, a marvel, and a show. (lines 7–9)[35]

In your life, Venice is both "woe" and "show"—these dichotomies—and by extension, Venice with its deep lagoon and three hundred bridges represents both separation and connection, these dichotomies.

Letters also represent both separation and connection. They are dialogues, and you and James had a decades-long tête-à-tête, one that served as a bridge to your sentimental and intellectual and literary lives. Emily Dickinson wrote, "A Letter always feels to me like immortality because it is the mind alone without corporeal friend,"[36] and at the same time I would say that the physicality of the letter—the paper and envelope itself—constitutes an object to be reckoned with, a sort of corporeal remembrance. A remembrance that you both wanted destroyed. You made a pact to burn your letters to each other—bonfire of cotton rag singed, India ink spilt, the blackened ash of your correspondence—the spellbinding blaze that consumes. Your letters from Venice the last to survive.

It's getting late here and the sun is going down. It's turning chilly again. *Freddo*. I've wrapped myself in a big scarf and have turned up the heat. A friend writes, "How long you think all this will last? How to proceed?" and in the next line, "Need more chocolate."

I imagine dusk as it descends on Vesuvius tonight, the color of champagne and dark crystals. I imagine the yellow wild broom in nightfall, glowing like miniature lit lanterns on the slopes of Vesuvius. Goethe wrote—and I'm paraphrasing, taking out of context, cutting and pasting because sometimes that seems to be the only way to proceed—how wonderful it would be if there were more Vesuviuses. For me, I think one "destroyer Vesuvius" is enough in this world.

I read that wild broom is a perennial, that it keeps coming back regardless of the terrain—dry or sandy or damp—resilient and tenacious and ubiquitous—that it was medicinal in the past, that it has no thorns. That its branches make brooms—to brush clear a pathway, to sweep away the dirt of the world, to sweep it away for good.

I wonder if the yellow wild broom will survive this umbrage-dark ruin of a world beyond the window above my desk, beyond Napoli and beyond Italy, I wonder if the yellow wild broom will bloom for us—resolutely, fully, permanently. I turn to you, dear Constance.

In thoughts,

Heather

With special thanks to Anne Boyd Rioux for her excellent and detailed biography, *Constance Fenimore Woolson: Portrait of a Lady Novelist*.

NOTES

1. Giacomo Leopardi, "La Ginestra," Poesia di Giacomo Leopardi, lines 1–7, https://www.poesiedautore.it/giacomo-leopardi/la-ginestra; English translation: Steven J. Willet, "Wild Broom; or, The Flower of the Desert," *Arion: A Journal of Humanities and the Classics* 23, no. 1 (Spring–Summer 2015), https://doi.org/10.2307/arion.23.1.0023.

2. Sharon L. Dean, ed., *The Complete Letters of Constance Fenimore Woolson* (Gainesville: University Press of Florida, 2012), 517.

3. Constance Fenimore Woolson, *Collected Stories*, ed. Anne Boyd Rioux (New York: Library of America, 2020), 463.

4. Woolson, 645.

5. Woolson, 573.

6. Woolson, "To Flora Payne Whitney" [1863/64?], in Dean, *Complete Letters*, 2.

7. Sharon Dean, *Constance Fenimore Woolson: Homeward Bound* (Knoxville: University of Tennessee Press, 1995).

8. Dean, 218.

9. Woolson, "To Henry James," August 30, 1882, in Dean, *Complete Letters*, 207.

10. Dean, *Constance Fenimore Woolson: Homeward Bound*, 82.

11. "Constance Fenimore Woolson: Her Early Cleveland Days, Her Home There and Her Friends," *New York Herald*, November 10, 1889, 11, quoted in Anne Boyd Rioux, *Constance Fenimore Woolson: Portrait of a Lady Novelist* (New York: Norton, 2016), 109.

12. Woolson, "To Mary Crowell," Spring 1880, in Dean, *Complete Letters*, 134.

13. Woolson, "To Edmund Clarence Stedman," August 4, 1882, in Dean, *Complete Letters*, 204.

14. Woolson, *Collected Stories*, 465.

15. Rioux, *Constance Fenimore Woolson: Portrait*, 141.

16. Woolson, *Collected Stories*, 423.

17. Woolson, 424.

18. Woolson, "To Edmund Clarence Stedman," December 12, 1876, in Dean, *Complete Letters*, 83.

19. Rioux, *Constance Fenimore Woolson: Portrait*, 152. See also Woolson, "To Henry James," August 30, 1882, in Dean, *Complete Letters*, 211.

20. Rioux, *Constance Fenimore Woolson: Portrait*, 152.

21. Anna G, "June, 1946: Emotional Algebra," *The Anais Nin Dialogues*, September 10, 2012, http://theanaisnindialogues.blogspot.com/2012/09/june-1946-emotional-algebra.html.

22. Rioux, *Constance Fenimore Woolson: Portrait*, 154.

23. Rioux, 97.

24. Woolson, "To John Hay," April 24, [1883], in Dean, *Complete Letters*, 233; Woolson, "To Henry James," May 7, [1883], in Dean, *Complete Letters*, 248.

25. Rioux, *Constance Fenimore Woolson: Portrait*, 217.

26. Rioux, 228–29.

27. Woolson, "To Edmund Clarence Stedman," August 10, 1889, in Dean, *Complete Letters*, 377.

28. Woolson, "To Katharine Livingston Mather," June 21, 1880, in Dean, *Complete Letters*, 142.

29. Leon Edel, *Henry James: The Middle Years, 1882–1895* (Philadelphia: Lippincott, 1962), 348.

30. Woolson, "To Henry James," May 7, 1883, in Dean, *Complete Letters*, 246.

31. Rioux, *Constance Fenimore Woolson: Portrait*, 297.

32. Rioux, 167. See also Woolson, "To Winifred Howells," May 11, 1883, in Dean, *Complete Letters*, 253.

33. Rioux, *Constance Fenimore Woolson: Portrait*, 309.

34. Rioux, 309.

35. Lord Byron, "Childe Harold's Pilgrimage," canto IV, stanza XVIII, https://moodle2.units.it/pluginfile.php/136570/mod_resource/content/1/Byron%20Childe%20Harold%20canto%20IV.pdf.

36. "Letters from Dickinson to Higginson," letter from June 1869, Dickinson Electronic Archives, http://archive.emilydickinson.org/correspondence/higginson/l330.html.

Lost in Translation, from Woolson's *For the Major* to Grego's *Per il Maggiore*

Edoarda Grego

"I am James Joyce. I understand that you are to translate *Ulysses*, and I have come from Paris to tell you not to alter a single word." This is what the author of *Ulysses* said in 1936 to a translator in Copenhagen when he heard about the possibility of a Danish translation of his novel. According to his biographer, Richard Ellmann, Joyce arrived with no warning on the doorstep of Mrs. Koster Hensen's home because publisher Martins Forlag hoped she would undertake this major responsibility.[1] Unfortunately, Hensen was already involved in other projects, and a Danish version of *Ulysses* was not produced until after Joyce died in 1941. Since then, however, his outburst has often been repeated in commentary on translation. "Not to alter a single word!" said theorist and translator Di Jin in 2014. "Joyce, who was gifted with the mastery of a number of foreign languages, was undoubtedly well aware that words *must* be altered in translation."[2] He would have known he was asking for the impossible, especially as he hoped for a growing audience around the world.

Translations have been done for ages, particularly in Europe, where there are so many languages, readers and speakers cannot know them all. While scientific, commercial, and practical texts can hardly suffer from a mechanical translator like AltaVista or any other form of artificial intelligence, literary translations inevitably rely on sophisticated connections between language and culture, words and their connotations, and word choices as creative selections. When I began translating *For the Major* into Italian, the guidance of many theoretical minds offered me ways to recognize and resolve complicated dilemmas. With the help of Walter Benjamin, for example, I have privileged style, rhythm, and "climate," which emphasizes how much language is a part of a place and its culture. Like Umberto Eco, I have respected a word's connotative layers, particularly when translating a line of poetry or, in *For the Major*, a church hymn. From Laura Bocci, I have discovered the value of thinking about word choice after casting the author as a text's "father" and the translator as a maternal presence, a model that is useful in *For the Major* as a Reconstruction story that is strongly gendered. Here, I am offering translation as an experiment much like Woolson's own lifelong experiment in translating an incomprehensible postwar South into a language that has given Woolson's novella a larger international audience.

What exactly does it mean "to translate"? *Webster's Third New International Dictionary* focuses on the effort "to turn something into one's own or another language," while the *Cambridge International Dictionary of English* notes even more blandly the effort "to change [words] into a different language."[3] The *Oxford English Dictionary* states something more helpful: "to convert or render (a word, a work, an author, a language, etc.) into another language; to express or convey the meaning of (a word or text) using equivalent words in a different language."[4] The latter seems to hit the point because those "equivalent words" are not always easy to find. As Peter Newmark, one of the most important scholars in the field, writes in speaking about literary texts, "[T]ranslation is a craft consisting in the attempt to replace a message and/or statement in one language by the same message and/or statement in another"; all literary translations, however, require "a compromise, a balancing."[5] It is in the spirit of compromise that I had to ask many times for help. In desperation, I emailed members of the Woolson Society when I found it much harder to complete *Per il Maggiore* than to translate Woolson's later Italian stories such as "The Street of the Hyacinth" ("Via del Giacinto") and "The Front Yard" ("Il giardino davanti casa"). Compared to the Italian context/environment of these short fictions, the context/environment of *For the Major* was truly foreign.

In deciding what to do, I was committed to Walter Benjamin's three imperatives for a translator—style, rhythm, and climate—including the corollary, "Do not use too many words." Benjamin locates the classic example of the expertly produced plain language translation in Martin Luther's interlinear rendering of the Bible. "The task of the translator," Benjamin writes, "consists in finding the particular intention toward the target language which produces in that language the echo of the original."[6] Easier said than done! Luther's method was to maintain a word count by selecting words of the same register and quality as those in the original text and also to respect understatement. With luck and a good ear, a little miracle delivers style and rhythm even when translating the language of the nineteenth century.

But the most difficult challenge is the "climate." Coming to *For the Major* in twenty-first-century Italy, I had to imagine a very different kind of world—in time, history, usage, and customs—a place in the North Carolina mountains where people, news, and books traveled incredibly slowly, where few engines were available to help with domestic work. Even the natural surroundings were difficult to sketch because almost everything has changed since the hard years immediately following the American Civil War. I was fortunate to take a trip to Asheville, the source for Woolson's "Far Edgerley," the scene of her book. But as an Italian from Trieste, I found it difficult to picture the Farms as the home of the Carrolls, whose every belonging existed in a place that has now vanished. How could the language I wanted to find as translator reflect a place and a house that were gone?

My solution was to read and reread Woolson's small volume for a sense of total immersion, then to "compromise" as Newmark directed or to take Chih Hsien Hsieh's advice: "Translation itself is . . . an endless process of negotiation."[7] The Farms became "Fattorie" Carroll, "Good Queen Bertha's Honey-Broth" became "Il Pane al miele della buona regina Berta," and Woolson's junior warden at the nearby Episcopal Church became the "vice-coadiutore," while Madam Carroll remained "Madam Carroll," which is too beautiful an expression to be altered in Signora Carroll. I think that choice produces a particular nineteenth-century flavor. To translate from one language and its idiosyncrasies to another, from one country and its usages to another, from one time and its customs to another in a different climate means both unavoidable risks and beneficial accidents.

In my continuing task, I was heartened by Umberto Eco's book on translation, *Dire quasi la stessa cosa*—that is, "tell almost the same thing."[8] So much of Hsieh's "negotiation" hangs on that "almost." As Eco observes in the English-language version, *Experiences in Translation*, "Interpreting means making a bet on the sense of the text," going on to state, "Of course, the whole history of a culture assists the translator in making relatively safe bets, in the same way as the whole theory of probability assists the gambler at the roulette table."[9] That is most noticeably the case with poetry: the translator must decide, in primis, whether to follow poetical structure (strophe, stanza, lines, rhythm, rhymes) perhaps at the expense of content, or to maintain the content as nearly as possible with a prose version. I chose a hybrid option, a negotiation that partially satisfies both form and content.

For instance, a scene at the Major's bedside includes a hymn stanza: four seven-syllable lines with two alternate rhymes ("appear" and "near"), an iambic meter by way of rhythm, with three main accents or stresses that are very near the rhythm of spoken English:

The dáy is pást and góne,
The évening shádes appéar;
O máy we áll remémber well
The níght of déath draws néar.[10]

I found it was impossible to maintain the length of the lines: first, because English as a language has many monosyllabic words; and second, because Italian has many long words. Translating that simple, dignified hymn risked creating unsuitably expansive lines.

Yet that is what I negotiated: expanding seven-syllable lines to eleven syllables whose rhythm is almost (the famous Eco's "almost"!) the same, that is, iambic, with three main accents or stresses. The hymn in Italian remains slow and calm, giving the idea of a serene wait for a happier second life. In addition, the two rhymes have been maintained in the same second and fourth lines:

Il giórno trascórso se n'è andáto;
Le ómbre della séra sono sórte;
È béne che noi tútti ricordiámo
Che già s'appréssa la nótte della mórte.[11]

My hybrid solution retains the balance between form and content by using style and rhythm to capture a long ago "climate" at the Major's deathbed.

When creating such solutions, I was reassured by the work of Laura Bocci, a translator of classic German literature who has a special regard for psychoanalysis. In her memoiristic *Di seconda mano: Né un saggio, né un racconto sul tradurre letteratura* (At secondhand: Neither an essay nor a story about translating literature), Bocci expresses a very fascinating idea: if fatherhood is generally ascribed to the author, the translator has a maternal function: to give birth to what was fertilized by another. As Bocci observes, "Se all'autore, a prescindere dal sesso, si attribuisce in genere la 'paternità' del testo, e con essa il ruolo produttivo per eccellenza, il traduttore svolge invece una funzione 'riproduttiva,' e dunque femminile per definizione" (If the author, regardless of sex, is generally attributed the "paternity" of the text, and with it the productive role par excellence, the translator instead carries out a "reproductive" function, and therefore feminine by definition).[12] After the author's strong, brave act of creation, the translator extends creative care that is loving, patient, and sleepless, even in the face of a blank computer screen and an unresponsive editor. In further comments, Bocci elaborates by describing the original text and its translation "come due amanti clandestini che tentino una fuga d'amore già in partenza fallita, e per questo più eroica, più coraggiosa" (like two clandestine lovers attempting an elopement that has already failed from the start, and is therefore more heroic, more courageous). As Bocci describes it, theirs is a near marriage to which the translator brings a "dote" (dowry) and "si adatterà, cambierà, si trasformerà" (she will adapt, change, transform herself) until "lui," the brave text, "pur resistendo, non potrà non cambiare con la traduzione" (while resisting, cannot help but change with the translation).[13] Although this may seem to some like an awkward paradigm for translating a female author like Woolson, my own creative care led me to a remarkable discovery: a kindred spirit in Madam Carroll and even in her stepdaughter Sara.

What an unusual portrait of Reconstruction they suggest! Where reviewers during the 1880s noticed the authority of Major Carroll and the pretended "youth" of his second wife, Kathryn McKee, in her contribution to this volume, focuses on Woolson's two women, whose strength reveals the fragility of the novella's men. The Carrolls' son Scar is feeble, Madam Carroll's son Julian suddenly dies, and Major Carroll begins to fade almost from the moment he is introduced. Their failed Reconstruction (which might have been radical, vengeful, and resistant) is quickly replaced in For the Major by Bocci's chief "feminine" virtue and a translator's principal tool: empathy. Invoking Edith Stein's dissertation in 1916, Bocci later writes, "Empatia è . . . la capacità di abitare contemporaneamente due mondi diversi, come per un dono dell'ubiquità che piova dal cielo" (Empathy is . . . the ability to inhabit two different worlds at the same time, as if by a gift of ubiquity that rains from the sky).[14] Inhabiting "two different worlds at the same time" perfectly describes the position of an astute translator. Madam Carroll is both aging and youthful; Sara is both northern in her schooling and southern in her birth. Together, they plot the version of a reconstructing nation that President Abraham Lincoln proposed in 1865, a "just and lasting peace" requiring "charity" instead of "malice."[15] At the Farms, Woolson's locus of Reconstruction, I found myself as her patient translator nurturing a newborn text for a European audience.

In conclusion, I must add that "negotiating" is not easy, and I have been prepared to accept some failures. As the well-known translator Gregory Rabassa said, echoing Joyce, "There are those who, like Nabokov, view translation as a criminal act that can only be judged as to whether it is a felony or just a misdemeanor and there are so many critics who do enjoy walking the perp."[16] My own gratification has come in the court of public opinion, where an accomplished translation is accepted by a publisher and bought by readers, as Per il Maggiore has been.

NOTES

1. Richard Ellmann, *James Joyce* (1959; Oxford: Oxford University Press, 1983), 692.

2. Di Jin, *Literary Translation: Quest for Artistic Integrity* (New York: Routledge, 2014), 25.

3. Merriam-Webster, *Webster's Third New International Dictionary*, s.v. "translate," https://www.merriam-webster.com/dictionary/translate; *Cambridge International Dictionary of English*, ed. Paul Procter (Cambridge: Cambridge University Press, 1995).

4. *Oxford English Dictionary*, s.v. "translate, v.," OED Online, https://www.oed.com.

5. Peter Newmark, *Approaches to Translation* (Oxford: Pergamon, 1981), 7, 168.

6. Walter Benjamin, "The Task of the Translator," in *Selected Writings*, vol. 1: *1913–1926*, ed. Marcus Bullock and Michael W. Jennings (Cambridge, Mass.: Belknap, 2002), 258.

7. Chih Hsien Hsieh, "Write into the Future by Recounting the Past: The Mandarin Translations of James Joyce's *Ulysses*," in *The European Avant-Garde: Text and Image*, ed. Selena Daly and Monica Insinga (Newcastle upon Tyne: Cambridge Scholars, 2012), 69.

8. Umberto Eco, *Dire quasi la stessa cosa: Esperienze di traduzione* (Milan: Bompiani, 2003).

9. Umberto Eco, *Experiences in Translation*, trans. Alastair McEwen (Toronto: University of Toronto Press, 2008), 16, 17.

10. Constance Fenimore Woolson, *For the Major* (New York: Harper & Brothers, 1883), 140.

11. *Per il Maggiore*, ed. and trans. Edoarda Grego (Palermo: Sellerio, 2012). The difficulty in translating poetry reminds me of the extraordinary case of Dorothea Tieck, daughter of the famous Ludwig, who translated Cervantes's *Don Quixote* (1799–1801). She alone among many renowned translators was able to create in German a verse-and-rhyme version of Shakespeare's 154 sonnets. For three years, she labored anonymously while her father told everybody the translator was a "young friend" working under his expert and benevolent supervision. Dorothea was one of the many female shadow translators of that period and afterward.

12. Laura Bocci, *Di seconda mano*: *Né un saggio, né un racconto sul tradurre letteratura* (Milan: Rizzoli, 2004), 31.

13. Laura Bocci, "Sulla traduzione letteraria," https://www.laurabocci.it/sulla-traduzione-letteraria-2/.

14. Bocci, "Sulla traduzione letteraria." Stein was a Jewish phenomenologist who studied with Edmund Husserl, converted to Catholicism, and became a Carmelite nun before dying at Auschwitz in 1942. She was later beatified as Saint Teresa Benedicta of the Cross.

15. The final text of President Lincoln's Second Inaugural Address reads, "With malice toward none, with charity for all, with firmness in the right, as God gives us to see the right, let us strive on to finish the work we are in, to bind up the nation's wounds." See "A Nation's Grief," *Harper's Weekly*, April 29, 1865, 258.

16. Gregory Rabassa, *If This Be Treason: Translation and Its Dyscontents. A Memoir* (New York: New Directions, 2005), 8.

CONTRIBUTORS

Kristin M. Comment is an independent scholar and retired secondary educator who currently teaches at Framingham State University in Massachusetts. Her essays on Constance Fenimore Woolson, Emily Dickinson, Rose Terry Cooke, and Charles Brockden Brown have appeared in *Constance Fenimore Woolson's Nineteenth Century: Essays, Legacy*, and *Early American Literature*. She holds a PhD from the University of Maryland, College Park, and master's degrees from the State University of New York at Stony Brook and Framingham State University. In recent years, she has served on the Massachusetts Commission on LGBTQ Youth and coauthored a model LGBTQ curriculum unit on *The Great Gatsby* and Willa Cather's "Paul's Case" for the Massachusetts Department of Elementary and Secondary Education.

Kathleen Diffley is Professor Emerita of English at the University of Iowa, Director of the Civil War Caucus, and a former president of the Woolson Society. She is the author of *The Fateful Lightning: Civil War Stories and the Magazine Marketplace, 1861–1876* (2021) and *Where My Heart Is Turning Ever: Civil War Stories and Constitutional Reform, 1861–1876* (1992, 2020). She has also edited *To Live and Die: Collected Stories of the Civil War* (2002) as well as *Witness to Reconstruction: Constance Fenimore Woolson and the Postbellum South, 1873–1894* (2011), which illuminates the neglected world of Reconstruction's southern backwaters.

Caroline Gebhard was a founding member of the Woolson Society in 1995, after publishing her first essay on Woolson in 1992. She has contributed to the prizewinning *Alabama Women: Their Lives and Times* (2017) and coedited a special issue of *Legacy* on Alice Dunbar-Nelson (2016). She has also coedited *Post-Bellum, Pre-Harlem: African American Literature and Culture, 1877–1919* (2006) and is coediting *African American Literature in Transition, 1880–1900* (forthcoming), again with Barbara McCaskill. She has helped lead humanities projects, including the NEH-funded *Literary Legacies of Macon County and Tuskegee Institute* (2019–21). Her resulting coauthored chapter will appear in the *Routledge Companion to Public Humanities Scholarship* (forthcoming). In 2024, Tuskegee University named her Professor Emerita of English.

Edoarda Grego, an accomplished teacher and translator, earned her degree in American literature at Italy's University of Trieste after completing a thesis on Constance Fenimore Woolson. She has published four translations of Woolson's fiction with Sellario Editore in Palermo, Italy: *Per Il Maggiore (For the Major)* in 2015, *Vigilia di Natale* ("A Christmas Party") in 2009, *Il giardino davanti casa* ("The Front Yard") in 2007, and *Via del Giacinto* ("The Street of the Hyacinth") in 2002.

Heather Hartley is the author of two volumes of poetry, *Adult Swim* (2016) and *Knock Knock* (2010). She was the longtime Paris editor at *Tin House* magazine. Her short fiction, essays, and poems have appeared in or on *PBS Newshour*, the *Guardian*, *Slice*, and other venues. She has presented writers at Shakespeare and Company Bookshop in Paris and has taught creative writing at the American University of Paris and the University of Texas at El Paso MFA online program. She teaches at the University of Kent Paris School of Arts and Culture.

Sharon Kennedy-Nolle, a former president of the Woolson Society, has published work on Woolson in several venues and has written, more generally, on the literature and culture of the Civil War and Reconstruction. Her book, *Writing Reconstruction: Race, Gender, and Citizenship in the Postwar South*, was the 2015 selection for the Gender and American Culture Series of the University of North Carolina Press. Chosen as the 2020 Chapbook Editor's Pick by Variant Literature Press, *Black Wick: Selected Elegies* was published in 2021. She lives and teaches in New York, where she was appointed the Poet Laureate of Sullivan County for 2022–24. She was awarded a Poet Laureate Fellowship for 2023–24 from the Academy of American Poets.

John Wharton Lowe retired as the Barbara Methvin Distinguished Professor of English and Latin American and Caribbean Studies at the University of Georgia. He was the author or editor of ten books, including *Calypso Magnolia: The Crosscurrents of Caribbean and Southern Literature* (2016), which won the prestigious C. Hugh Holman Award. Most recently, he edited *Black Hibiscus: African Americans and the Florida Imaginary* (2023) and, before his death, completed the authorized biography of Ernest J. Gaines. He was also editing two Library of America volumes that gathered together all of Gaines's novels and short stories.

Etta M. Madden is Professor of English (Emerita) at Missouri State University. Her books include *Engaging Italy: American Women's Utopian Visions and Transnational Networks* (2022) and *Eating in Eden: Food and American Utopias* (2006). A William J. Fulbright award prompted her research on Woolson and U.S. authors in Italy, work that was advanced by fellowships from the New York Public Library and the Library Company of Philadelphia as well as participation in an NEH seminar at the American Academy in Rome.

Kathryn B. McKee is McMullan Professor of Southern Studies and Professor of English at the University of Mississippi, where she also directs the Center for the Study of

Southern Culture. She is the author of *Reading Reconstruction: Sherwood Bonner and the Literature of the Post–Civil War South* (2019) and coeditor, with Deborah Barker, of *American Cinema and the Southern Imaginary* (2011). Her particular areas of interest include nineteenth-century U.S. literature, postbellum southern literature, film studies, humor studies, and writings in and of the Global South.

Lisa Nais is a senior lecturer at the University of Salzburg. She holds a doctorate from the University of Aberdeen, and her research interests include magazine culture, literary networks, and neglected women writers of the fin de siècle. She has published on Henry James, Constance Fletcher, and Edith Wharton.

Anne Boyd Rioux is the author of *Constance Fenimore Woolson: Portrait of a Lady Novelist* (2016), which was reviewed on the cover of the *New York Times Book Review* and chosen by the *Chicago Tribune* as one of the ten best books of the year. She has also edited two collections of Woolson's stories (2018, 2020). Additionally, she wrote *Meg, Jo, Beth, Amy: The Story of Little Women and Why It Still Matters* (2018) and edited the Penguin Classics edition of *Little Women*. She has received four NEH awards, two for public scholarship.

Susan L. Roberson is retired Regents Professor of English at Texas A&M University–Kingsville. She is the author of *Antebellum American Women Writers and the Road: American Mobilities* (2011) and editor of three collections: *Women across Time: Mujeres a Través del Tiempo: Sixteen Influential South Texas Women* (2022), *Defining Travel: Diverse Visions* (2002), and *Women, America, and Movement: Narratives of Relocation* (1998), as well as numerous essays on American travel writing. *Geographies of Travel: Images of America in the Long Nineteenth Century*, a study of American travel writing about the United States, is forthcoming.

Aaron J. Rovan is on staff at the Ohio Humanities Council and holds a PhD in English from West Virginia University. His doctoral dissertation, "Sacramental Ethnicity: Women's Culture and Vernacular Religion in Twentieth-Century America" (2022), engages with the development of white ethnic identity in the United States as articulated through women's vernacular religious traditions. His work has appeared in the scholarly journals *Women's Studies* and *Mosaic*, as well as in *Folklife* magazine, published by the Smithsonian's Center for Folklife and Culture Heritage, and Ohio Humanities' annual publication *Lumen*.

Sidonia Serafini is an Assistant Professor of English at Georgia College & State University. Her teaching and research interests include early African American literature and print culture, multiethnic American women's writing, and archival and periodical studies. With Barbara McCaskill she has coedited *The Magnificent Reverend Peter Thomas Stanford, Transatlantic Reformer and Race Man* (2020), and her essays have appeared in *Southern Quarterly*, *Women's Studies*, and the *Journal of Transatlantic Studies*, with essays forthcoming in *American Periodicals* and *American Literature*. She also serves as Co-Director of *Black Activism: A Transatlantic Legacy*, a website that examines the imprint of Black activism in the United States and the United Kingdom, past and present.

Katherine Barrett Swett, a writer who has taught for many years at the Brearley School in Manhattan, received her PhD from Columbia University. She has published both criticism and poems about Woolson. Most recently, *Voice Message* (2020), her collection of poetry, won the Donald Justice Prize.

Cheryl B. Torsney, a former president of the Woolson Society, has been researching Woolson's work since 1984. The author of *Constance Fenimore Woolson: The Grief of Artistry* (1989) and editor of *Critical Essays on Constance Fenimore Woolson* (1992), she has also written a wide range of articles about all things Woolson, including her love of dogs, ferns, and the outdoors. She has served multiple institutions as a senior academic affairs administrator and Professor of English.

Karen Tracey, Associate Professor of English at the University of Northern Iowa, is the author of *Plots and Proposals: American Women's Fiction, 1850–1890* (2000) and articles on Confederate literature, nineteenth-century short fiction, and the novels of E. D. E. N. Southworth. Her current project centers on literary representations of Modern Spiritualism.

Lisa West is Professor of English at Drake University in Des Moines, Iowa, where she teaches courses in American literature before 1900, environmental writing, and the novel. A native Clevelander raised in the shadows of a burning Cuyahoga River and downwind of the polluted Lake Erie, she finds her hometown less alienating when understood in relation to Woolson's excursions in the region, from Zoar to the Great Lakes. She has published on Woolson's literary relatives James Fenimore Cooper and Susan Fenimore Cooper, as well as earlier American writers such as Susanna Rowson, Charles Brockden Brown, Lydia Maria Child, and Catharine Maria Sedgwick.

INDEX